# PISA and PIRLS
## The Effects of Culture and School Environment

**Other World Scientific Titles by the Author**

*PISA Ranking: Issues and Effects in Singapore, East Asia and the World*
ISBN: 978-981-3200-72-2

*World University Rankings: Statistical Issues and Possible Remedies*
ISBN: 978-981-3200-79-1

*Tests and Exams in Singapore Schools: What School Leaders, Teachers and Parents Need to Know*
ISBN: 978-981-3227-05-7
ISBN: 978-981-3227-06-4 (pbk)

*Creativity Fostering Teacher Behavior: Measurement and Research*
ISBN: 978-981-3234-15-4

# PISA and PIRLS
## The Effects of Culture and School Environment

Kaycheng SOH

NEW JERSEY · LONDON · SINGAPORE · BEIJING · SHANGHAI · HONG KONG · TAIPEI · CHENNAI · TOKYO

*Published by*

World Scientific Publishing Co. Pte. Ltd.
5 Toh Tuck Link, Singapore 596224
*USA office:* 27 Warren Street, Suite 401-402, Hackensack, NJ 07601
*UK office:* 57 Shelton Street, Covent Garden, London WC2H 9HE

**Library of Congress Cataloging-in-Publication Data**
Names: Soh, Kay Cheng, author.
Title: PISA and PIRLS : the effects of culture and school environment / Kaycheng Soh.
Description: New Jersey : World Scientific, 2019. | Includes bibliographical references.
Identifiers: LCCN 2018041494 | ISBN 9789813276536
Subjects: LCSH: Programme for International Student Assessment. | Academic achievement--
 Social aspects. | School environment--Social aspects.
Classification: LCC LB3051 .S619 2019 | DDC 371.26--dc23
LC record available at https://lccn.loc.gov/2018041494

**British Library Cataloguing-in-Publication Data**
A catalogue record for this book is available from the British Library.

Copyright © 2019 by World Scientific Publishing Co. Pte. Ltd.

*All rights reserved. This book, or parts thereof, may not be reproduced in any form or by any means, electronic or mechanical, including photocopying, recording or any information storage and retrieval system now known or to be invented, without written permission from the publisher.*

For photocopying of material in this volume, please pay a copying fee through the Copyright Clearance Center, Inc., 222 Rosewood Drive, Danvers, MA 01923, USA. In this case permission to photocopy is not required from the publisher.

For any available supplementary material, please visit
https://www.worldscientific.com/worldscibooks/10.1142/11163#t=suppl

Desk Editor: Shreya Gopi

Typeset by Stallion Press
Email: enquiries@stallionpress.com

Printed in Singapore

# Contents

*About the Author*     ix

*Prologue*     xi

**Part I    Cultural and Social Environment**     1

**Chapter 1    The Influence of Culture on Academic Achievement: Illustration Using PISA 2009 Data**     3

Education is closely related to culture and dependent on governance style. Through correlation analysis, this study explores the influences of culture and democracy on PISA performance among 38 countries for which data are available.

**Chapter 2    Social Environments for Learning in Finland and Singapore: Perceptions of Students and Principals in PISA 2009**     21

Finland and Singapore are two countries with top performance in PISA 2009 but with very different social environments. This study looks into the influence of teacher–student relations, disciplinary climate, and teacher stimulation in the two countries on achievement.

**Part II    Principals' Roles and Views**     45

**Chapter 3    Principals as Instructional Leaders? A Lesson from the PIRLS 2011**     47

Principals play many roles in the school, one of which is the role of an instructional leader. Though factor analysis, it was found that principals' activities formed two negatively correlated dimensions, namely, providing instructional leadership and handling student problems. The relations of the roles with achievement performance was explored.

**Chapter 4** **Principals' Leadership and Views on Teachers and Students in PISA 2012: Comparisons between OECD Members and Partners** — 59

How principals see teachers and students can be expected to influence student achievement. This study compares the perceptions of OECD Members and OECD Partners and relates the differences to student achievement.

**Part III** **Reading, Science, and Mathematics** — 77

**Chapter 5** **PIRLS 2011 Reading and the Effects of Home, School, and Classroom Factors: Confirming and Contradicting Findings** — 79

Through factor analyses of PIRLS data, one home factor, three school factors, and two classroom factors were identified. The 45 countries participated in PIRLS 2011 were classified as high or low in Reading achievement by way of K-means cluster analysis using some of the factor constituents as criteria.

**Chapter 6** **Reading Achievement, Materials, Times, and Purposes in PISA 2010: Comparing OECD Members and Partners** — 97

The contributions of reading materials, time for reading, and purpose of reading to Reading achievement in PISA were evaluated through correlation and regression analyses. Comparisons were made between OECD Members and OECD Partners.

**Chapter 7   Reading Competencies as Predictors of Science Achievement: Lessons from PISA 2009 Data**     117

Through correlation and regression analyses, how and to what extent Reading sub-skills contribute to PISA Science achievement were explored.

**Chapter 8   Reading Competencies as Predictors of Mathematics Achievement: Lessons from PISA 2009**     133

Through correlation and regression analyses, how and to what extent Reading sub-skills contributed to PISA Mathematics achievement were explored.

**Chapter 9   Collaborative Problem Solving in PISA 2015: Highlights and Reflections**     149

This chapter highlights the findings of Collaborative Problem Solving, which was a new inclusion in PISA 2015, and discusses some of the implications and problems.

**Chapter 10   PISA's New Venture in Creative Thinking: Some Conceptual and Methodological Concerns**     161

PISA will venture into the learning and teaching of creative thinking in the coming 2021 survey. This chapter discusses the conceptualization and instrumentation for surveying creative thinking from historical and international perspectives.

**Part IV   Trustworthiness of International Comparisons**     175

**Chapter 11   Readability of PISA Reading Tasks as a Predictor of Reading Performance**     177

Using released sample items, the readability of PISA Reading test was evaluated by applying several readability indices. Comparisons were then made between the indices and the class level intended for PISA test.

**Chapter 12 Ecological Fallacy in Predicting Reading Achievement: The Case of PIRLS**     191

Contrary to expectations, negative correlations were found for country means for PIRLS Reading with student engagement, instructional strategies, and instructional resources. Ecological fallacy was suggested as the reason for the paradox.

**Chapter 13 Mathematics Achievement and Interest *Negatively* Correlated!**     209

PISA used four items to measure students' mathematics interest. Factor analysis show the four items to form one factor. Contrary to expectations, negative correlations was found between mathematics achievement and interest. The paradox is explained in terms of ecological fallacy.

**Chapter 14 Does Ranking Tell the Truth in International Academic Comparisons? An Example from PISA 2012 and 2015**     221

In international comparative studies, an improvement in ranking is taken to mean an improvement in achievement. Using the data of PISA 2012 and 2015, it is shown that while there are countries with consistent positive or negative gains, there is also a sizable group of countries with inconsistent, opposite signs for score and ranking.

*Epilogue*     233

# About the Author

**Dr SOH Kaycheng** is currently Research Consultant at the Singapore Centre for Chinese Language, Nanyang Technological University. He holds the degrees of Doctor of Philosophy (Education) of the National University of Singapore and Master of Education (Educational Psychology) of the University of Manchester. He was conferred the honour of Senior Fellowship and Eminent Scholar by the Singapore Centre for Chinese Language in recognition of his research contributions to Chinese Language pedagogy.

Positions Dr Soh held include Senior Fellow and Head of Centre for Applied Research in Education, National Institute of Education, and Head of Testing and Guidance, Institute of Education. He also served consecutively as Deputy Director (Languages), Assistant Director (Curriculum), Ministry of Education, and Principal, Nanyang Academy of Fine Arts.

Dr Soh has published very widely on topics such as world university rankings, international achievement rankings, creativity, and language learning in learned journals. His books include *Creativity Fostering Teacher Behavior: Measurement and Research* (2018), *Tests and Exams in Singapore Schools: What School Leaders, Teachers and Parents Need to Know* (2017), *PISA Ranking: Issues and Effects in Singapore, East Asia and the World* (2017), *World University Rankings: Statistical Issues and Possible Remedies* (2017), *Teaching Chinese Language in Singapore: Retrospect and Challenges* (2016), *Social and Educational Rankings: Problems and Prospects* (2013), *Analyzing Data & Interpreting Outcomes: Statistical Toolbox for Teacher–Researchers* (2009), *Workshop on Action Research: Transforming Teachers to Action Researchers* (2008), *Chinese Language without Tears: Tips for English-Speaking Parents* (1999) and *On Assessment: Ten Talks for Educational Practitioners* (1978).

# Prologue

This volume is, in a sense, a sequel to *PISA Ranking: Issues and Effects in Singapore, East Asia, and the World* (Soh, 2017; World Scientific). This new monograph focuses on primary and secondary students' Reading performance *in Programme of International Students Assessment* (PISA) and *Progress in Reading and Literacy of Students* (PIRLS). Reading here is used as a proxy of students' general academic performance as it has very high correlations with Mathematics and Science.

Part I sets the scene and provides a broad backdrop to the other chapters, bringing together cultural and social factors which are conceptualized as contributing conditions for student achievement. An attempt was made to relate Gere Hofstede's *Cultural Dimensions* and the Economist Intelligence Unit's *Democracy Index* to student achievement. Finland and Singapore were contrasted to study the influence of social environment on academic performance.

Part II highlights the roles and impact of school principals on academic achievement. The two chapters cover the principals' instructional leaderships and their views on the teachers and students in the context of school administration and its effects.

Part III has two articles on the effects of environmental and school conditions which have influences on Reading performance. OECD Members and OECD Partners were compared on the various conditions. Additionally, Reading was studied for its predictive power of Mathematics and Science in PISA. PISA is also looking into collaborative problem-solving and creativity. The two relevant chapters here discuss some conceptual and instrumentation issues.

Part IV deals with the trustworthiness of international comparative studies, using PISA and PIRLS data to illustrate. The first article concerns itself with readability of PISA tests, followed by two articles on the paradoxical finding of negative correlations where positive ones are expected; the paradox is resolved with reference to ecological fallacy. The last chapter discusses the issue of interpreting inter-year difference as indicating improvement.

The fourteen articles in this volume are secondary analyses of PISA and PIRLS data. It is readily appreciated that for large-scale studies like these involving many countries and tens of thousands of students, there is by necessity a time lag between data collection and reporting, and understandably an even larger time lag between original studies and secondary studies. This raises the issue of the current validity of the data and therefore that of the findings of secondary analysis. Fortunately, normally, education systems do not change very quickly unless drastic measures are introduced. This being the case, it stands to reason that the findings of the re-analyses reported here are still valid — to be taken, perhaps, with a little pinch of salt to allow for some probable effect of time.

Large-scale comparative studies like PISA and PIRLS (and TIMSS as well) function like national censuses, albeit at an international level, and provide very rich data for further in-depth analyses that surface hidden relations and differences which are relevant to education systems. I therefore hope that such secondary analyses will enhance our understanding of the original reports, by highlighting the inherent sensitivity and limitations of the original tests.

Soh Kaycheng

# Part I
# Cultural and Social Environment

## Chapter 1

# The Influence of Culture on Academic Achievement: Illustration Using PISA 2009 Data

The OECD's *Programme for International Student Achievement* (PISA; Organization for Economic Co-operation and Development, n.d.) ranks 65 nations (and *economies*) on the academic achievement of 15-year-old students in Reading, Mathematics, and Science. These nations can be expected to differ widely in culture, although cultural differences do not feature as a potential factor in student performance. As schools are established by nations differing in culture and thereafter function in their respective cultural contexts, the importance of a possible cultural influence on the operation of schools and, in turn, on student learning cannot be over-emphasized.

## Education and Economics

In the educational context, student achievement is analogous to productivity in economics. Here, a nation's culture serves as a filter through which certain practices are accepted, encouraged, and implemented while others are abhorred, avoided, and discouraged. This implies that culture can have an influence on student achievement through encouraging certain instructional approaches and discouraging others (e.g., Rubenstein, 2006). For instance, rote memorization, especially of culturally treasured classics, is traditionally encouraged and practiced among East Asian nations while rote learning is viewed with suspicion and even condemnation among

Western nations. For another example, personal experience shows that East Asian students see lecturers or workshop leaders as the know-all experts who are expected to impart knowledge (and who are, therefore, not to be overtly questioned), whereas Western students enjoy the opportunity of expressing their views (which may be right or wrong) and expect to be asked for their opinions. In short, a didactic approach to teaching, in contrast to a more participative one, is preferred by East Asian students. Such different practices and expectations, being influenced by cultural differences, can be expected to lead to differences in achievement, both quantitatively (how much is learned) and qualitatively (how and what is learned).

Boykin *et al.* (2005) demonstrates how culture was associated with the perception of achievement. They studied the culture-based perception of academic achievement of 138 Fifth-grade students (66 African Americans and 72 European Americans) with low-income backgrounds. The study intended to determine whether the students' perception of achievement was mediated by culture. Analysis revealed a main effect for the cultural learning orientation. Communal high achievement was endorsed more than individual or competitive high achievement. There was, however, an interaction effect between cultural group and cultural learning orientation. African American students endorsed high-achieving peers via communalism, with a clear-cut rejection of individualism and competition. On the other hand, European American students' endorsement pattern was not so distinct. The authors concluded that African American students typically might not reject high-achieving peers *per se* but rejected the cultural factors that so often were yoked to achievement in traditional schooling contexts.

Although the culture–productivity connection has been extensively studied in economics, it does not seem to have been actively pursued in education. However, a few such studies will be summarized to drive home the message that academic achievement (as a form of educational productivity) can be beneficially seen with a cultural perspective.

In the educational context, Navarrete, Betancourt, and Flynn (2007) posited that culture (i.e., values, beliefs, and norms) has a direct effect on academic achievement and also an indirect effect on behavior via the psychological process of attribution, i.e., student perception of the causes of their achievement or the lack of it. Fatalism is an attribute characterized as subjugation to nature and the belief that there is little one can do to alter fate. Latinos have been found to have higher levels of fatalism compared to Anglos and this belief has been shown to influence medical treatment adherence and cancer screening behaviors among Anglo and Latino populations. The authors suspected that fatalism may be influencing achievement in Latinos. They hypothesized that fatalistic cultural value and family SES would influence achievement directly and/or through their effects on attributions for academic success or failure among Anglo and Latino high school students. They studied 93 Anglo and 56 Latino high school students. A LISREL analysis shows (1) family SES has a significant direct path to achievement, and (2) fatalism has a negative indirect path to achievement via stability of causes for failure. The model has a Goodness of Fit Index of 0.95, indicating a high degree of validity. This implies that culture does have an influence on achievement.

While the studies summarized above typify the quantitative approach to studying the relation between culture and educational productivity, Trumbull and Rothstein-Fisch (2011) adopted an ethnographic, qualitative approach for their study. The authors studied seven Spanish/English bilingual elementary teachers with an average of 12.7 years of teaching experience. The study focused on the Individualistic–Collective perspective and data was collected by using problem-solving scenarios in a pretest–posttest design. The authors concluded that *"If high academic achievement for all students is a goal, then achievement motivation theory must move beyond a cultural universalist stance to the recognition that cultural values influence students' social and academic goals"* (44). Based on the informants' responses, they concluded that *"in the context of the achievement gap that separates dominant culture students from their non-dominant culture peers it behooves achievement motivation researchers to persevere with efforts to deepen our understanding of what motivates students"* (47). This, again, underlines the influence culture has on the motivation to learn, which in turn influences achievement or educational productivity.

Notwithstanding the limitation of the above-cited studies, it is readily appreciated that more needs be done to study the cultural influence on educational productivity for better insight into how schools have been unheedingly affected by their surrounding cultural milieu and what can be done to enhance their performance in terms of student achievement. In this regard, the PISA data (world-wide in that it covers a large number of nations on earth) can prove useful as it enables such a study at the widest possible scope hitherto available.

## Culture and Productivity

Hofstede's (1984) study of Cultural Dimensions has spawned much research into the relation between culture and productivity, especially in the economic realm. Hofstede (2001) initially surveyed IBM employees to study differences in corporate culture. In his study, Hofstede examined the attitudes and work values of more than 116,000 employees of IBM in more than 40 countries. The data was factor-analyzed and resulted in four Cultural Dimensions:

- *Power Distance*: This indexes the inequality in power between superiors and subordinates within an organization. Organizations with higher Power Distance tend to have longer chains of command with more rigid procedures for communication (especially upward communication).
- *Individualism*: This is the opposite of collectivism. Organization high on Individualism tends to value the individuals' self-actualization and development.
- *Masculinity*: This defines the role of gender in an organization. In high masculinity organizations, high-level posts and better-paying jobs are taken mostly, though not exclusively, by male staff members; there is obvious lack of gender equitability.
- *Uncertainty Avoidance*: This has to do with the organization's tolerance for ambiguity and its concern to maintain written rules and rituals.

Later in 1990, Hofstede added a fifth Cultural Dimension, *Confucian Work Dynamic*, which is characterized by traditional Chinese culture with the concern for orderliness, thrift, persistence, and sense of shame. It is also referred to as *Long-term Orientation* and, as the name implies, has an orientation towards the future, as seen in values like thrift and persistence. This is well reflected in the Chinese proverb "*Bitter now, sweet later*" and the Western concept of delayed gratification. Thus, although the fifth Cultural Dimension is purported to have been derived from Confucianism, it perhaps is similar to the Protestant or Puritan Ethic, minus the religious connotation. This dimension was added after finding that East Asian countries such as China, Japan, and Korea acted quite differently from other countries due to the influence of Confucianism. However, the validity of this fifth Cultural Dimension was questioned on philosophical and methodological grounds by Fang (2003). According to Neill (2012), there is a sixth dimension in the Hofstede model, the dimension of *Indulgence versus Restraint* (IVR). Indulgence is the degree to which a society allows the free gratification of human drives related to enjoying life and having fun. On the other hand, Restraint stands for suppression of gratification of needs, which are regulated by strict social norms.

Hofstede's first four Cultural Dimensions have since been widely used in cross-cultural research, especially in connection with studies of economic development. In the realm of economic development, Mathers and Williamson (2011) suggested that formal institutions need to map onto the informal or cultural rules if they are to function and sustain. In other words, informal (cultural) and formal institutions complement one another to support economic growth. Following this logic, Mathers and Williamson (2011) claimed that the success or failure of formal economic institutions depends on pre-existing informal or cultural rules. This suggests that culture has the ability to influence productivity of economic freedom by a filtering process through which the constraints must pass.

To verify the validity of such a contention, Mathers and Williamson (2011) studied the interaction effect of culture, economic freedom, and economic growth. They created a set of panel data of growth rates of 141 countries, using the database of the Fraser Institute's Economic Freedom of the World Index. In their conceptualization, culture was defined as customary beliefs and values transmitted by social groups fairly unchanged from one generation to the next. For measuring culture, they used data from the World Values Surveys to capture the level of trust, respect, self-determination, and obedience. Justifying the choice of these cultural characteristics, the authors argue thus,

> These traits serve as rules governing interaction between individuals, including market production and entrepreneurship. Trust, respect, and individual self-determination are thought to stimulate social and

economic interaction, whereas obedience is thought to limit economic interaction and development by decreasing risk-taking, a trait essential to entrepreneurship (11).

Their analysis shows that both economic freedom and culture had positive impacts on economic growth independently as *main effects*. In addition, they also found an *interaction effect* of economic freedom and culture on economic growth. The findings indicate that the two independent variables of culture and economic freedom need to be considered in conjunction and not separately when economic growth is of interest. However, it is not clear whether economic freedom (a form of democracy?) is an intervening or moderating variable for the correlation between cultural and economic measures. This obviously needs be clarified by further research.

There are many studies showing a relation between culture and the economic well-being of countries. For example, using Hofstede's Cultural Dimensions, Cox, Friedman, and Tribunella (2011) studied the relation between culture and economic productivity. Productivity was measured as national gross domestic product per capita (GDPC) and data on the GDPC of 217 nations was gleaned from the Nation Master database. The authors found Power Distance had a substantial *negative* correlation of $r = -0.65$ with GDPC, while Individualism had a positive correlation of $r = 0.70$ with economic outcome. The correlations of Masculinity and Uncertainty Avoidance with GDPC were not statistically significant, with $r = 0.01$ and $r = -0.11$, respectively. In other words, countries which stress superior–subordinate inequality and have less respect for individuals tend to have also poorer economic performance, and vice versa. The findings thus attest that culture has an influence on economic productivity.

Gorodnichenko and Roland (January 2011) studied the relation between economic productivity and culture of about 80 nations by regressing output per capita on Cultural Dimensions. In the multiple regression analysis, they obtained a beta-weight of −0.49 for Power distance, 0.65 for Individualism, 0.06 for Masculinity, and 0.17 for Uncertainty Avoidance. These show that an emphasis on superior–subordinate inequality is detrimental to economic development while an emphasis on Individualism is beneficial. The findings corroborate with those of Cox *et al.* (2011) cited above.

## Stability of Cultural Dimensions

Before focusing on the cultural influence on educational productivity, it is necessary to take a closer look at Cultural Dimensions, which assume the role of independent variables here in this study, because more than 30 years have passed since Hofstede's (1984) original study. The time-gap between then and now gives rise to the question of validity of the Cultural Dimensions over time.

Not long ago, Fernandez *et al.* (1997) re-examined the rankings of nations in terms of Hofstede's (1984) original Cultural Dimensions, 25 years after their first appearance. The sample consisted of 7201 respondents from nine countries in four continents who were employed business professionals and advanced business students. Overall, the findings suggest that there have been significant shifts in value classifications in some countries since Hofstede's earlier study. Fernandez *et al.* reached their conclusions on the changes in mean values for the nine countries.

However, the present writer believes that the focus should be on the within-country correlations for each of the four Cultural Dimensions between two points of time. In other words, comparing the relative profiles of countries should be of greater relevance. For this purpose, correlations for seven countries common to the two studies were calculated and they are 0.33 for Power Distance, 0.42 for Individualism, −0.02 for Masculinity, and −0.33 for Uncertainty Avoidance. It may thus be concluded that, in spite of changes in mean values, the seven countries studied by Fernandez *et al.* show a certain degree of stability in their cultural profiles over a quarter of a century. Besides, it needs be highlighted that the changes in mean values might be attributed to the difference in the two sets of respondents — employees in general for Hofstede's original study but professionals and advanced business students for Fernandez *et al.*'s.

More recently, Wu (2006) studied Taiwanese and American administrative personnel in two universities. The participants of the two universities were matched on functional equivalence. To represent the administrative system of universities, both *academic units* and *administrative units* were surveyed in these two universities. For one university, 147 (response rate 81.7%) participants returned their survey questionnaires. The results show that the cultural values in both universities are different from those found by Hofstede (1984) for the two countries some 30 years back. It was therefore concluded that cultural values have changed over time. This change was attributed to changing political, societal, and economic environments which have since taken hold in the two countries. It was also argued that changes in Power Distance would, for instance, cause changes in expected leadership styles.

As with Fernandez et al.'s (1997) study summarized above, Wu's (2006) conclusion was based on between-time-within-country comparisons. However, the present writer is of the view that between-countries-with-time comparisons make better sense in evaluating whether there are changes. Wu's data shows Taiwan to be higher on Power Distance and lower on Individualism (Table 1). These are consistent with the earlier findings of Hofstede (1984), indicating no change in cultural characteristics in the two countries. It is of note that these two Cultural Dimensions have been found to be more predictive of productivity by other researchers (see summarized studies earlier). However, for Uncertainty Avoidance, Taiwan has come very close to America in Wu's data, while there was an obvious difference in Hofstede's data. There is a reversal in Masculinity in that Taiwan has become more masculine than America. It is also of note that the respondents of Wu's study worked in higher education whereas Hofstede's respondents were employees of multinational electronic companies. The institutional difference might have contributed to the differences observed between the two studies.

Putting the findings of Fernandez et al. (1997) and Wu (2006) together, there is evidence, though limited in scope, showing that in spite of changes in absolute score values, the relative profiles for Hofstede's

Table 1. Comparisons of Taiwan and America on Cultural Dimensions.

|  | Wu (2006) | | Hofstede (1984) | |
| --- | --- | --- | --- | --- |
|  | Taiwan | America | Taiwan | America |
| Power Distance | 3.02 | 2.55 | 58 | 40 |
| Individualism | 2.09 | 2.80 | 17 | 91 |
| Uncertainty Avoidance | 5.47 | 5.57 | 69 | 46 |
| Masculinity | 3.58 | 1.90 | 45 | 62 |

*Note*: Individualism was reversed from Wu's Collectivism.

first four Cultural Dimensions remain stable. In short, countries that emphasized Power Distance and Individualism in the past continue to do so decades later.

Most recently, Khastar *et al.* (2011) proposed to re-think the levels of analysis in cross-cultural comparisons of management styles in an attempt to redefine the theoretical and methodological approaches of organizational research.

## Data and Their Sources

For this study, the data of cultural factors were gleaned from three separate sources: Cultural Dimensions (Hofstede, 1984), Democracy Index (EIU, 2012), and PISA 2009 (OECD, 2010 and n.d.). When merged, there were 28 OECD Members and 10 OECD Partners appearing in all three lists making up a total of 38 nations for which the relevant data were extracted. The three types of data are described briefly below.

### *Cultural dimensions*

Hofstede's (1984) Cultural Dimensions presents four Cultural Dimensions for 64 nations. The four Cultural Dimensions are Power Distance, Individualism, Masculinity, and Uncertainty Avoidance. The dimension names are self-explanatory and no further elaboration is needed. For parsimony, the four sets of scores were factor analyzed using the principal components analysis with Promax rotation based on the inter-correlations among the dimensions (Table 2). This resulted in two oblique factors

Table 2. Factor Structure of Cultural Dimensions.

|  | Power–Collectivity | Masculinity–Certainty | Communality |
|---|---|---|---|
| Power Distance | 0.900 | — | 0.812 |
| Individualism | −0.596 | — | 0.817 |
| Masculinity | — | 0.896 | 0.827 |
| Uncertainty Avoidance | 0.503 | 0.576 | 0.517 |
| Total variance explained | 47.4% | 27.0% | — |
| Correlation |  | 0.132 | — |

*Note*: "—" denotes factor loadings less than 0.300.

which have a rather weak correlation of r = 0.13. Thus, with only 1.7% shared variance, the two factors can be reasonably taken to be independent. Factor scores were generated for subsequent analysis. (See Methodological Note 1.)

Put together, the two factors explained 74% of the total variance. The first factor explains 47% total variance and is loaded positively by Power Distance but negatively by Individualism. This characterizes a culture which pays great premium to a distinct power structure where superior–subordinate relations and rules are highly emphasized. It is accompanied with value for Collectivity as indicated by the negative loading of Individualism. Hence, this factor is named Power–Collectivity. The second factor explains 27% total variance and is loaded mainly by Masculinity and accompanied by Uncertainty Avoidance. This characterized a macho culture which stresses sureness and success. It is hence named Masculinity–Certainty. Factor scores were generated for subsequent analysis.

## *Democracy index*

This is the Economist Intelligence Unit's (2012) *Democracy Index 2011* which ranks 167 nations and classifies them into Full democracies, Flawed democracies, Hybrid democracies, and Authoritarian regimes according to their scores. The Overall score on which the nations are ranked is made up of scores for five indicators: Electoral process and pluralism, Functioning of government, Political participation, Political culture, and Civil liberties. The Index provides a snapshot of the state of democracy worldwide, covering almost the entire population of the vast majority of the world's independent states. This data was used as a validating measure of Cultural Dimensions and would not be entered into the achievement prediction formula.

## *PISA achievements*

These include the national means for Reading, Mathematics, and Science of the PISA 2009 (OECD, 2010). Although PISA measures the achievements in three subjects of 15-year-olds from 65 participating nations, the focus is on Reading. The correlations of the three subjects are unusually high, with the correlation coefficient reaching 0.95 and beyond. PISA stresses that these three measures are process-oriented, to assess the students on their *"abilities to cope with future challenges"* (referred to as *"literacy"*) rather than the traditional product-oriented tests, which assess acquired content knowledge. (See Methodological Note 2.) Factor analysis yielded one factor explaining 98% total variance with very high factor loadings: Reading 0.99, Mathematics 0.98, and Science 0.99. Factor scores were generated as a general indicator of academic achievement without differentiating subjects and used in subsequent analyses.

## How Do the Measures Correlate?

The premise of this study is that culture and achievement are related and that culture, to some extent, predicts achievement. These were verified by first conducting a correlation analysis and then a multiple regression analysis.

As expected, Achievement and Power–Collectivity have a moderate *negative* correlation of −0.42 (Table 3). This indicates that there is an overlap of 18% shared variance between the two measures. More specifically, nations which emphasize power structure, superior–subordinate relations, and restrictive rules tend to have nearly 20% poorer achievement. It is also interesting that Masculinity–Certainty does not correlate with Achievement.

The sizable negative correlation of −0.64 between Power–Collectivity and Democracy Index is an evidence of the validity of the former

Table 3. Correlations for All Nations (N = 38).

|  | Achievement | Power–Collectivity | Masculinity–Certainty | Democracy Index |
| --- | --- | --- | --- | --- |
| Achievement | 1.00 | **−0.42** | −0.06 | 0.12 |
| Power–Collectivity |  | 1.00 | 0.12 | **−0.64** |
| Masculinity–Certainty |  |  | 1.00 | −0.20 |
| Democracy Index |  |  |  | 1.00 |

*Note*: Coefficients in bold are statistically significant (p < 0.05).

measure, since it shows that nations which emphasize power structure, superior–subordinate relations, and restrictive rules tend can be expected to be *less* democratic politically.

## How Different Are OECD Members and OECD Partners?

With the above findings, a pertinent question is how different OECD Members and OECD Partners are in the three measures. Results of the comparisons are shown in Table 4. As shown therein, when compared with OECD Partners, OECD Members scored higher on Achievement with a medium-to-large effect size of Glass's $\Delta = 1.33$ (see Methodological Note 1). At the same time, the OECD Members scored much *lower* on Power–Collectivity, with a very large effect size Glass's $\Delta = -1.31$ but higher on Masculinity–Certainty with a medium Glass's $\Delta = 0.34$. In short, the OECD Members had higher PISA achievement accompanied by higher democracy (as indicated by the lower Power–Collectivity). (See Methodological Note 3.)

The differences led to the question whether the cultural and political variables operated in the same manner in the two sets of nations; in other words, whether the Simpson's paradox found for academic excellence at the university level (Soh, 2012) is also found here at the high school level. To answer this question, separate calculations of the correlations were run for OECD Members and OECD Partners (Table 5).

It is of note that Power–Collectivity has negative correlations with Achievement, although the coefficient for OECD Partners misses the 0.05 level of significance. Nevertheless, while the correlation between

Table 4. Mean Comparisons Between OECD Members and OECD Partners.

|  | OECD (N = 28) Mean | SD | Partners (N = 10) Mean | SD | Mean difference | Effect size |
|---|---|---|---|---|---|---|
| Achievement | 55.1 | 5.1 | 48.3 | 14.2 | 6.8 | 1.33 |
| Power–Collectivity | 46.5 | 9.3 | 58.7 | 4.9 | −12.2 | −1.31 |
| Masculinity–Certainty | 50.8 | 11.2 | 47.0 | 5.4 | 3.8 | 0.34 |

**Table 5.** Correlations for OECD (N = 28) and Partner (N = 10) Nations.

|  | Achievement | Power–Collectivity | Masculinity–Certainty | Democracy Index |
|---|---|---|---|---|
| Achievement | 1.00 | **−0.41** | −0.10 | **0.58** |
| Power–Collectivity | −0.36 | 1.00 | 0.27 | **−0.65** |
| Masculinity–Certainty | −0.36 | −0.02 | 1.00 | **−0.56** |
| Democracy Index | **−0.64** | 0.09 | 0.14 | 1.00 |

*Notes*: (1) Coefficients above the principal diagonal are for OECD Members and those below for OECD Partners. (2) Coefficients in bold are statistically significant ($p < 0.05$).

Democracy Index and Achievement is moderately positive for OECD Members, it is sizably *negative* for OECD Partners. This Simpson's paradox encourages caution in the interpretation of the relations between achievement and cultural-political characteristics.

## How Is Achievement Predicted?

With the findings above, it is informative to find out how cultural and political characteristics predict achievement in the 38 countries. This was done by running a hierarchical multiple regression with Achievement as the criterion. Two resultant models are shown in Table 6. (See Methodological Note 4.)

Membership of OECD was entered as the first predictor. This resulted in $R = 0.393$ with an Adjusted R-square of 0.131, indicating that the membership predicted 13% of the criterion variance. This suggests that a nation is 13% better in Achievement if it is an OECD Member.

When cultural measures were entered as the second block of predictors, the multiple regression coefficient increased to $R = 0.486$ with an Adjusted $R = 0.170$. This indicates an increase of 4% Achievement predicted. However, only one cultural predictor (Power–Collectivity) has a significant beta-weight. Note also that the coefficient is *negative*, indicating that a nation which emphasizes Power Distance will score 4% lower in Achievement when compared with another that does not have this emphasis.

**Table 6.** Hierarchical Regression of Achievement on Cultural-Political Measures.

|  | Stage 1 | Stage 2 |
|---|---|---|
| R | 0.393 | 0.486 |
| Adjusted R-squares | 0.131 | 0.170 |
| Standardized regression coefficients | | |
| OECD | **0.393** | 0.225 |
| Power–Collectivity | — | **−0.312** |
| Masculinity–Certainty | — | −0.077 |

*Note*: Coefficients in bold are statistically significant ($p < 0.05$).

**Table 7.** Hierarchical Regression of Achievement on Cultural-Political Measures.

|  | Model 1 | Model 2 |
|---|---|---|
| R | 0.372 | 0.528 |
| Adjusted R-squares | 0.114 | 0.213 |
| Standardized regression coefficients | | |
| OECD | **0.372** | 0.132 |
| Power–Collectivity | — | **−0.417** |
| Masculinity–Certainty | — | −0.108 |

*Note*: Coefficients in bold are statistically significant ($p < 0.05$).

As Japan and Korea are two East Asian nations which are OECD members with high Achievement, they were excluded from the next run of the regression analysis. The results maintain the above model with some modifications (Table 7). In the new model, OECD membership predicts 11% of Achievement (i.e., 1% less than the earlier model does), but the cultural measures predict 10% more of Achievement variance and become even stronger predictors. Again, only Power–Collectivity was able to predict Achievement.

## So What If That Is?

This study is an attempt to see academic achievement in a cultural-political context, using data from PISA 2009 to illustrate. Basically, the tenet that nations' achievement is associated with their cultural and political characteristics is supported. Academic achievement at the school level is influenced by many factors, and the cultural-political condition has here been shown to account for a sizable variation among nations.

Nonetheless, a caveat is needed here. The three sets of data collated for this study were collected at different times and for different research purposes: Cultural Dimensions (Hofstede, 1984), Democracy Index (EIU, 2012), and PISA 2009 (OECD, 2010). These differences might invalidate the conclusion reached in this analysis. However, in spite of this limitation, the study has at least demonstrated the possibility of such an interaction, and further investigation using contemporary data sets would verify the findings of this analysis.

## Methodological Notes

1. Factor analysis is a family of statistical techniques used to uncovered the hidden structure of a set of correlations and present them in a more cohesive and simplified manner that facilitates a more parsimonious interpretation of the data. The specific technique used in this study is the principal components analysis with Promax rotation. In contrast with the more commonly used Varimax rotation, Promax allows the resultant factors to correlate instead of treating them as independent (orthogonal). However, the resultant correlation between factors is small and the result should be highly similar had Varimax been used. Factor scores have a mean of zero and a standard deviation of unity. This is not convenient for reporting and interpretation. The four sets of factor scores were therefore scaled to have a mean of 50 and a standard deviation of 10. This transformation does not affect the relative strengths of the nations on the scales.
2. Factor analysis of PISA Reading, Mathematics, and Science means (treated as scores) yielded only one factor and hence rotation was not performed.

3. The conventional method of comparison is the t-test, an inferential statistic. However, one condition of the use of the t-test is that the sample (nations) is randomly selected. Since the nations participated in PISA do not form a random sample, the t-test cannot be validly used. In its place, comparisons were made in terms of standardized mean difference (SMD) or effect sizes, which were then interpreted with reference to the criteria recommended by Cohen (1988): 0.0 to 0.2, trivial or negligible effect; 0.2 to 0.5, small effect; 0.5 to 0.8, medium effect; and 0.8 or greater, large effect. The effect size was calculated as Glass's $\Delta$ = (Mean difference)/(OECD Members standard deviation).
4. Hierarchical regression analysis allows predictors to be entered as blocks in sequence. Thus, the first block predicts as much criterion variance as it can capture and subsequent blocks predict variance that is left over. This enables the blocks to maintain their relative precedence.

## References

Boykin, A. W., Albury, A., Tyler, K. M., Hurley, E. A., Bailey C. T., and Miller, O. A. (2005). Culture-based perceptions of academic achievement among low-income elementary students. *Cultural Diversity and Ethnic Minority Psychology*, **11**(4), 339–350.

Cox, P. L., Friedman, B.A., and Tribunella, Y. (2011). Relationships among cultural dimensions, national gross domestic, and environmental sustainability. *Journal of Applied Business and Economics*, **12**(6), 46–56.

Fang, T. (December 2003). A critique of Hofstede's fifth national culture dimension. *International Journal of Cross Cultural Management*, **3**(3), 347–368.

Fernandez, D. R., Carlson, D. S., Stepina, L. P., and Nicholson, J. D. (1997). Hofstede's country classification 25 years later. *The Journal of Social Psychology*, **137**(1), 43–54.

Gorodnichenko, Y. and Roland, G. (January 2011). Which dimensions of culture matter for long run growth? Available at http://eml.berkeley.edu/~ygorodni/GorodnichenkoRoland_AEAPP.pdf

Hofstede, G. (1984). *Culture's Consequences: International Differences in Work-Related Values*. Newbury Park, CA: Sage.

Hofstede, G. (2001). *Culture's Consequences: Comparing Values, Behaviors, Institutions, and Organizations across Nations*. Thousand Oaks, CA: Sage

Khastar, H., Kalhorian, R., Khalouei, G. and Maleki, M. (2011). Levels of analysis and Hofstede's cultural differences: The place of ethnic culture in organizations. *International Conference on Financial Management and Economics*, IPEDR Volume 11, 320–323. IACSIT Press, Singapore.

Mathers, R. L. and Williamson, C. R. (May 2011). Cultural context: Explaining the productivity of capitalism. *Kyklos*, **64**(2), 231–252.

Navarrete, B., Betancourt, H., and Flynn, P. (2007). *Culture and Achievement Motivation in Latino and Anglo American High School Students in USA*. Paper presented at the 31st Interamerican Congress of Psychology, Mexico City, July 2007.

Neill, C. (June 7, 2012). Geert Hofstede: The Six Dimensions of National Culture. *The Rhetorical Journey*. Available at http://www.conorneill.com/2012/06/geert-hofstede-6-dimensions-of-national.html

OECD (2010). *Pisa 2009 Results: What Students Know and Can Do — Student Performance in Reading, Mathematics and Science (Volume 1)*. Available at http://dx.doi.org/10.1787/9789264091450.en

OECD (n.d.) *PISA 2009 Assessment Framework — Key Competencies in Reading, Mathematics and Science*. Available at http://www.oecd.org/pisa/pisaproducts/pisa2009assessmentframework-keycompetenciesinreading-mathematicsandscience.htm

Rubenstein, I. Z. (2006). Educational Expectations: How They Differ Around the World: Implications for Teaching ESL College Students. *Community College Journal of Research and Practice*, **30**, 433–441.

Trumbull, E. and Rothstein-Fisch, C. (2011). The intersection of culture and achievement motivation. *The School Community Journal*, **21**(2), 25–54.

Wu, M-Y. (2006). Hofstede's cultural dimensions 30 years later: A study of Taiwan and the United States. *Intercultural Communication Studies*, **15**(1), 33–42.

Economist Intelligence Unit (2012). *Democracy Index 2011: Democracy under Stress*. The Economist.

# Appendix

Table A1. OECD and Partners Countries.

| OECD | Partners |
|---|---|
| Australia | Argentina |
| Austria | Brazil |
| Belgium | Chinese Taipei |
| Chile | Hong Kong China |
| Czech Republic | Indonesia |
| Denmark | Panama |
| Finland | Shanghai China |
| France | Singapore |
| Germany | Thailand |
| Greece | Uruguay |
| Hungary | |
| Ireland | |
| Israel | |
| Italy | |
| Japan | |
| Korea | |
| Mexico | |
| Netherlands | |
| New Zealand | |
| Norway | |
| Poland | |
| Portugal | |
| Spain | |
| Sweden | |
| Switzerland | |
| Turkey | |
| United Kingdom | |
| United States | |

## Chapter 2

# Social Environments for Learning in Finland and Singapore: Perceptions of Students and Principals in PISA 2009

International studies of student performance such as TIMSS (*Trends in Mathematics and Science Study*), PIRLS (*Programme in International Reading and Literacy Study*) of the International Association for the Evaluation of Educational Achievement (TIMSS & PIRLS International Study Centre, n.d.) and PISA (*Programme for International Student Achievement*) of the Organization for Economic Co-operation and Development are supposed to provide useful information for the evaluation and development of education systems. These studies try to do this by comparing participating countries on achievements in core subjects such as Reading, Mathematics, and Science, and relate these results to background conditions or factors believed to be responsible for achievement or the lack of it. However, in the highly competitive world of today, this noble intention seems to have been overlooked or even side-stepped as countries keenly compare their own rankings with those of other countries. This attitude of one-up-man-ship cannot escape attention as it glaringly shows up in postings on the Internet.

Moreover, such competitiveness is encouraged by the way international studies report their results. Instead of presenting the results as tabulated information for diagnostic and planning use, league tables (like those for competitive sports) are compiled not in alphabetical order of countries but in a form tacitly implying that some countries are more worthy than others. For example, the Executive Summary of the PISA 2009 specifically highlights high-ranking countries:

> ***Korea and Finland are the highest performing OECD countries, with mean scores of 539 and 536 points, respectively...*** Top-performing countries or economies in reading literacy include Hong Kong–China (with a mean score of 533), Singapore (526), Canada (524), New Zealand (521), Japan (520) and Australia (515) (OECD, 2011a; original emphasis).

Note the wording such as *"highest performing"* and *"top-performing"*, coupled with the country means in parentheses. These are presentation devices which have a sensationalizing effect, pitching one country against another, thus reinforcing the competitiveness.

At the country level, the competitive tone of national responses cannot be denied. From Finland,

> Young Finns were again among the best performers in the assessment of reading, mathematical and scientific literacy in PISA 2009...In the main focus area, reading literacy, the mean performance of Finnish students was ranked third, after Korea and the non-OECD participant Shanghai. In mathematical literacy, the performance of young Finns was second best among the OECD countries and sixth among all participating countries and economies. Finland was outperformed by Shanghai, Singapore, Hong Kong, Korea and Taiwan. In scientific literacy, Finland came second after Shanghai. (Embassy of Finland, 2010)

And from Singapore,

> Singapore students have fared very well in an international study conducted under the auspices of the Organisation for Economic Cooperation and Development (OECD). Out of 65 countries and economies that took part in the Programme for International Student Assessment (PISA) 2009, Singapore students ranked fifth in Reading, second in Mathematics and fourth in Science. Singapore also had the second highest proportion (12.3%) of students who are top performers[1] in all three domains. (Ministry of Education, Singapore, 2012)

As evidenced in the quotes above, countries are obviously exclusively interested in how much better they are when compared with other countries. They do not seem to be interested in factors or conditions which might have led to the outstanding performance of their students.

Comparison need not necessarily lead to competition. As educational measurement is relative and not absolute, it is only by comparison with other countries that a country finds out how her students have been learning. International studies such as TIMSS, PIRLS, and PISA purport to have developed common yardsticks supposedly transcending national and cultural influences, and thereby provide the desired information. This, however, is still a contentious assumption — but a discussion on this issue is beyond the scope of the present study.

Once comparisons have been made, there are two routes open to the participating countries. First is the competitive route by which a country is labelled as doing better or poorer than the others. This is the route preferred by the agencies (e.g., IEA and OECD) when they publish league tables, capitalizing on minute and spurious differences, often in the decimals, to make their rankings. The educational value of so doing is doubtful but the game goes on nevertheless, since competition is the order of the day. In contrast, the second route is to use the comparison not as a competition but as a necessary first step to be followed by an intra-country study of factors and conditions that contribute to the achievement. This is a diagnostic approach that has more practical and educational value, helping a country to identify her strengths and weaknesses so that future planning can really be based on the evidence.

The second route is believed to be of practical and educational value because, understandably, student achievement (or the lack of it) is influenced by a host of factors and conditions: characteristics of an education system which may and may not be within the control of schools. Understanding how such factors and conditions operate to influence achievement is at the core of educational planning. It is here where international studies are most valuable and useful. Although international studies do provide information of this nature through their background surveys, these seem to have been unfortunately rendered to second place when competitive rankings loom large, as reflected in national responses as cited earlier.

Armed with this context, the present study seeks to answer the following three questions:

1. Do Finland and Singapore really differ in Reading performance?
2. Have students in Finland and Singapore different social environments for learning?
3. Is there a relationship between Reading performance and social environment for learning?

## Do Finland and Singapore Really Differ in Reading Performance?

Although Finland and Singapore have both been hailed as outstanding performers in PISA 2009, it has also been highlighted that Finland (ranked third with a Reading mean of 536) out-scores Singapore (which has a Reading mean of 526). The difference of 10 scale points in Reading creates the difference in ranking.

However, the difference in score (and therefore ranking) may be apparent but spurious; that is to say, Finland's 536 looks numerically different from Singapore's 526, but that difference could well be due to measurement error attributable to chance occurrence. If this is true, the two countries, then, should logically be taken to be equivalent in score and hence have the same ranking.

PISA 2009 assessed the 15-year-olds of participating nations in Reading, Mathematics, and Science, which are core subjects of the school curriculum. The tests for these three subjects were developed and then translated into the language of instruction of participating nations. PISA asserted that these tests were process- and future-oriented (OECD, 2010b) rather than the traditional product- and past-oriented tests that assess acquired knowledge. It is of note that this assertion remains a contentious issue (e.g., Mortimore, 2009; Sjoberg, 2007).

These three subjects correlate with very high coefficients: $r = 0.95$ between Reading and Mathematics, $r = 0.98$ between Reading and Science, and $r = 0.98$ between Mathematics and Science. Such extremely high correlations are unusual for educational assessment; however, they imply that whatever is found for Reading could very well be applicable to Mathematics and Science.

Table 1. Comparisons between Finland and Singapore on Reading.

|  | OECD Mean | OECD SD | Finland (n = 5,810) Mean | Finland SD | Singapore (n = 5,283) Mean | Singapore SD | Effect size |
|---|---|---|---|---|---|---|---|
| Reading | 493 | 93 | 536 | 175.3 | 526 | 80.0 | 0.06 |
| Access | 495 | 101 | 532 | 205.8 | 526 | 101.8 | 0.03 |
| Integrate | 493 | 94 | 538 | 175.3 | 525 | 87.2 | 0.07 |
| Reflect | 494 | 97 | 536 | 167.7 | 529 | 80.0 | 0.04 |
| Cont. text | 494 | 95 | 535 | 175.3 | 522 | 80.0 | 0.07 |
| Non-cont. text | 493 | 95 | 535 | 182.9 | 539 | 80.0 | −0.02 |

*Source*: OECD (2010a).

In PISA 2009, scores for each of the subject tests were scaled to have a mean of 500 and a standard deviation of 100. Theoretically, the scores span at least from 200 to 800, thus allowing for three standard deviations on either side of the mean. In other words, the range of scores is at least 600. Doing this, presumably, was to enable fine discrimination between countries based on the differences in country means, which were then used to rank the countries on a long scale, with the tacit assumption that the longer the scale, the more sensitive or discriminating it is.

Table 1 shows for Reading and its subtests the means and standard deviations for OECD, Finland, and Singapore (see Methodological Note 1). It is obvious that both these countries scored far above the OECD averages in all six measures. Although the difference of 10 was used to separately rank the two countries as being third and fifth, respectively, it is worth noting that the effect size (i.e., standardized mean difference, SMD) is a trivial 0.06 and is best ignored (see Methodological Note 2). Another way of looking at the 10-point difference is that it is one-tenth of a standard deviation of 100. Yet another way of looking at the difference is that Finland and Singapore are separated by 1.7 points on the 600-point Reading scale.

At the sub-skill level, Finland scored higher on Access, Integrate, Reflect, and Continuous Text. On the other hand, Singapore scored higher on Non-continuous Text. Again, all the effect sizes are too small to be of interest. The absolute values of the SMDs vary from 0.03 to 0.07, all trivial in magnitude by the criteria suggested by Cohen (1988).

In sum, notwithstanding the seeming differences in country means, Finland and Singapore should be taken as equivalent in performance on the Reading scale and its subscales, and should be assigned the same ranking. Darrel Huff (1954), the author of *How to Lie with Statistics,* once said: a difference is a difference if only it makes a difference. It is doubtful that the inter-country differences make a difference in a substantive and practical sense.

This finding has an implication beyond these two countries. Educational measures are fallible and not perfectly reliable; this is a fact which needs be given due consideration. PISA does not take into account measurement error when ranking the participating countries. It does not report the score reliability.

If it is assumed (generously) that the Reading scores have a Cronbach's alpha coefficient (which is a commonly used indicator of score reliability) of $\alpha = 0.9$ (which is very high and not always attained in educational measures), the standard error of measurement (SEM) can be estimated with the appropriate formula (see Methodological Note 3). This yields a SEM = 32. And, with 95% confidence, a score may take on any value bounded by the score ± 2SEM (i.e., score ± 64 in the case of Reading). Since Shanghai–China has the highest score of 556, there is no score above it. The score that is 64 points lower than Shanghai–China's 556 is 492. Thus, all scores from 492 to 556 should be considered equivalent, when measurement error is given due consideration. By this token, the top 26 countries in PISA 2009 (i.e., from Shanghai–China down to the United Kingdom and Hungary) should be given the same ranking and grouped together, to be taken as performing on par with one another in spite of the seemingly different scores.

Nonetheless, the mean scores for the 65 participating countries in fact span from 314 (Kyrgyzstan) to 556 (Shanghai–China), with a range of 342 and not 600. This yields a standard deviation of 51 and not 100 as intended. The corresponding SEM is therefore only 16 and, by the same token, the 2SEM is 32 (not 64). This means any scores falling within the bounds of 524 to 556 should be taken as equivalent, with due consideration for measurement error. Thus, the top six countries which should be considered as performing on par (in the same group) are Shanghai–China (556), Korea (539), Finland (536), Hong Kong–China (533), Singapore (526), and Canada (524).

As suggested in an earlier article (Soh, 2013a), transforming test scores to a scale with a specific mean and standard deviation is purposive to match a pre-determined specification. And this choice is arbitrary. The 500 ± 100 scale of PISA Reading may be unnecessarily long with 600 points for 65 countries. Had this been 50 ± 10 like the T-scale commonly used in standardized educational testing, the difference between Finland and Singapore would be reduced to 1.0 score point or 0.2 point on a 60-point scale. Then, the spurious precision problem is obvious.

The high fallibility of educational measures (as is the case with the PISA tests) does not allow international studies to be taken as if they were using nano-metrics that go into the $10^{th}$ decimal place, although playing up differences in the second and even the third decimal values is a common practice. Doing this gives a deceptive sense of importance. To illustrate, had the PISA scores been (arbitrarily, and legitimately at that) scaled to have a mean of 5000 and a standard deviation of 1000, Finland would have scored 5360 and Singapore 5260 with a difference of 100. This grossly exaggerated 100-point difference (distorted as a magnifying glass distorts) seems so impressive, creating the impression that Finland indisputably out-performed Singapore. But it can be demonstrated that the SMD will remain the same and unchanged from a trivial 0.06, not to mention that the standard error of measurement will simply now be 320 point on that very long scale, still bracketing the six top-scoring countries as equivalents. In short, it is not the apparent numeric differences that counts; their meaningfulness has to be evaluated in terms of score reliability assessed by way of effect size or measurement error.

In the context of this study, Finland and Singapore are equivalent in Reading and the difference between the two countries has been uncritically taken at face value and sensationalized with no regard for effect size and measurement error. As a matter of fact, capitalizing on small differences (spurious precision) to rank countries is only one of the seven conceptual and methodological woes in social and educational rankings (Soh, 2013b).

## Have Students in Finland and Singapore Different Social Environments for Learning?

Background surveys of international studies typically gather information on provisions and perceptions. For instance, PISA 2009 reports on the selection and grouping of students, governance of schools, accountability and assessment, resources, and learning environment, and relates these background factors to reading achievement. Of special interest to the present study is the social environment, which covers teacher–student relations, disciplinary climate, and teacher stimulation. These are referred to as *social environment* because they involve continuous interactions among teachers and students in the classroom to influence student learning and consequently reading achievement.

### *Teacher–student relations*

The first aspect of the social environment for learning is teacher–student relations. There is a plethora of discussion on the importance and benefits of good teacher–student relations. For instance, most recently, Rimm-Kaufman (2013) has this to say:

> Improving students' relationships with teachers has important, positive and long-lasting implications for students' academic and social development...If a student feels a personal connection to a teacher, experiences frequent communication with a teacher, and receives more guidance and praise than criticism from the teacher, then the student is likely to become more trustful of that teacher, show more engagement in the academic content presented, display better classroom behavior, and achieve at higher levels academically.

In fact, interest in teacher–student relations has a long history. As early as some 70 years ago, Bush (1942) conducted such a study involving 250 Grade 9–14 students located in the western part of the United States. Teacher–student relations tend to be seen as a one-way relationship with the teacher in the dominant position, but Schlechty and Atwood (1977) emphasized the reciprocal nature of student–teacher relations thus:

> Teacher–students relations, like all human relationships in groups, are reciprocal. This fact, however, has somehow escaped many educational researchers and practitioners. Few seem to recognize, for example, that when one says that a teacher "lost control" of the class, it is but the reverse side of the proposition that some students or student gained

control...While dominance and subordinates may indeed be inherent in the role of teacher and student respectively, it seems an oversimplification to consider that the students is entirely passive. (285)

That may have been true in the past, but things have obviously changed in more recent times. In *Pisa 2009 at a Glance* (OECD, 2011), it was reported that in 20 out of 38 countries, the proportion of students who reported that teachers listened to them rose significantly between 2000 and 2009, and, over the same period of time, more students reported that they were treated fairly by teachers and got extra help from teachers when they needed it. Moreover, teacher–students relations improved most in countries where they had been weakest, such as Germany, Korea, and Japan. As an aside, it is interesting that teacher–student relations seem to have been influenced by the culture of each country. However, the PISA report concludes,

> Positive student–teacher relationships are crucial for establishing a classroom environment that is conducive to learning. Research finds that students, particularly socio-economically disadvantaged students, learn more and have fewer disciplinary problems when they feel that their teachers take them seriously. (94)

In the context of PISA 2009, good teacher–student relations are operationalized by the following conditions:

- Students getting along with teachers
- Teachers showing interest in students' wellbeing
- Teachers listening to what students have to say
- Students in need receiving extra help from teachers
- Teachers treating students fairly

As shown in Table 2, Finland tended to have lower percentages than the OECD averages for factors related to teacher–student relations, whereas Singapore tended to have percentages above the OECD averages.

For the six statements about teacher–student relations, Singapore has higher percentages, indicating that students in Singapore enjoyed better

Table 2. Teacher–Student Relations Effect Size.

| | OECD | Finland (n = 5,810) | Singapore (n = 5,283) | Effect size |
|---|---|---|---|---|
| I get along well with most of my teachers. | 85 | 67 | 91 | 0.55 |
| Most of my teachers are interested in my wellbeing. | 66 | 49 | 61 | 0.23 |
| Most of my teachers really listen to what I have to say. | 67 | 62 | 74 | 0.24 |
| If I need extra help, I will receive it from my teachers. | 79 | 64 | 88 | 0.53 |
| Most of my teachers treat me fairly. | 79 | 60 | 87 | 0.58 |
| Overall | 75 | 60 | 80 | 0.43 |

*Source*: OECD (2010b).

relations with their teachers (Table 2). For three of the five statements (i.e., "*getting along with teachers*", "*receiving extra help from teachers*", and "*being treated fairly by teachers*"), the effect sizes are medium in magnitude. For the other two (i.e., "*teachers being interested the students' wellbeing*" and "*teachers listening to students*"), the effect sizes are small (See Methodological Note 4). Overall, Singapore has 20% more students endorsing the statements of positive teacher–student relations with an effect size of 0.43, which is small but close to medium in magnitude.

## *Disciplinary climate*

A phenomenon related to teacher–student relations is the disciplinary climate in the classroom. When students generally observe ground rules in the classroom, the disciplinary climate is positive and this is believed to be conducive for learning. It is a truism that in a conducive environment students focus on and engage in the learning task. In such a classroom, the teacher directs her attention and energy to purposive instruction without being distracted or having to hold up teaching just to handle misbehaving students.

The importance of disciplinary climate is explicated in *Pisa 2009 at a Glance* (OECD, 2011: 96) thus,

Classrooms and schools with more disciplinary problems are less conducive to learning, since teachers have to spend more time creating an orderly environment before instruction can begin. Interruptions in the classroom disrupt students' concentration on, and their engagement in, their lessons.

It is reported therein that, in general, across OECD countries, the disciplinary climate during lessons improved between 2000 and 2009. Chile, Greece, and Italy were mentioned as the countries which have benefitted most from the improvement; on the other hand, Australia, the Czech Republic, and Ireland have more classroom disruptions. No reasons were offered for the changes.

Disciplinary climate has usually been seen as a dichotomous situation on a high-low scale. However, Cohen and Thomas (1984) concluded that it was more complex than this, and their factor analysis of data from 52 Australian secondary schools showed four qualitatively different categories: controlled, conflictual, libertarian, and autonomous. More recently, Ma and Willms (2004) re-analyzed data from the National Education Longitudinal Study of nearly 25,000 Eighth Grade students from more than a thousand public and private schools across the United States. When the 27 variables were submitted for a factor analysis, seven factors resulted. Incidentally, as the authors did not discuss the inter-factor correlations, it is assumed that the factors are orthogonal resulting for Varimax rotation. The seven factors together explain nearly 60% of the total variance (variance of each factor in parentheses) as labelled below:

1. Discipline concern (24.1%)
2. Teacher–student relations (10.5%)
3. Class disruption (6.5%)
4. Tardiness and absenteeism (5.4%)
5. Counselling about discipline (5.0%)
6. Discipline experience (4.1%)
7. Strict rules (3.8%)

It is of interest that the first and major factor is loaded by variables which have to do with cutting class, physical conflicts among students, theft, vandalism, alcohol, drugs, weapons, and physical and verbal abuse by teachers. The second factor (Teacher–student relations) which explains a sizable proportion of the variance is characterized by variables dealing with getting along with teacher, fair discipline, teachers' interest in students, teachers' praise for student effort, feeling of teachers' *put-down*, and teachers listening to students. The third factor (Class disruption) is influenced by variables having to do with other students disrupting class, not feeling safe in school, disruptive students getting in the way of learning, and misbehaving students getting away with it. These three factors together explain 41% of the total variance (or 68% of common variance) and can be reasonably taken to be the major disciplinary climate conditions.

PISA 2009 operationalizes disciplinary climate with the following conditions (but phrased *negatively*):

- Students listening to what the teacher say
- Noise and disorder in the classroom
- Students taking a long time to quieten down
- Students working well
- Students starting working for lessons to begin

Table 3 shows the percentages of students endorsing "*never or hardly*" or "*in some lessons*" for the *negatively* worded statements. Thus, higher

Table 3. Disciplinary Climate.

|  | OECD | Finland (n = 5,810) | Singapore (n = 5,283) | Effect size |
|---|---|---|---|---|
| Students don't listen to what the teacher says. | 71 | 60 | 78 | 0.37 |
| There is noise and disorder. | 68 | 52 | 81 | 0.58 |
| The teacher has to wait a long time for the students to quieten down. | 72 | 63 | 80 | 0.36 |
| Students cannot work well. | 81 | 80 | 84 | 0.10 |
| Students don't start working for a long time after the lessons begins. | 75 | 68 | 78 | 0.21 |
| Overall | 73 | 65 | 80 | 0.32 |

*Source*: OECD (2010b).

percentages indicate a better disciplinary climate or a more conducive classroom atmosphere for learning. For these, Finland tended to have percentages lower than the OECD averages whereas Singapore tended to have percentages above the OECD averages.

For the five statements, the higher percentages for Singapore have effect sizes varying from .10 to .58, with a medium effect size for *"There is noise and disorder"*, indicating that Singapore classrooms tended to be quieter and more orderly. There are three small effect sizes for *"Students don't listen to what the teacher says"*, *"The teacher has to wait a long time from the students to quieten down"*, and *"Students don't start working for a long time after the lessons begins"*. These double-negative responses indicate that students in Singapore enjoy a somewhat more disciplinary climate conducive to learning than their counterparts in Finland. The difference in *"Students cannot work well"* has a small effect size which may be negligible, showing that the two countries differ only marginally in this regard. Singapore's overall percentage is 15% higher than that of Finland and the effect size is a small one of 0.32.

## *Teacher stimulation*

In the classroom context, teacher stimulation takes the form of motivating students and engaging them during lessons. As is true of many aspects of research on teaching and learning, teacher stimulation has a long history. Research interest in student engagement as a reflection (the other side of the coin) of teacher stimulation started in the 1980s with the concept narrowly defined in terms of time-on-task and later broadened to include students' willingness to actively participate in classroom and school activities. The concept is further expanded to students' use of cognitive, meta-cognitive, and self-regulatory strategies to monitor and guide their own learning (Chapman, 2003).

The critical role the teacher plays in stimulating student learning is succinctly propounded by the Center for Comprehensive School Reform and Improvement (2010):

> Teachers are key players in fostering student engagement. **They work directly with the students and typically are the most influential in a**

**student's educational experience.** Creating a culture of achievement in their classroom, developing interactive and relevant lessons and activities, and being encouraging and supportive to students are all ways in which teachers can foster student engagement in the classroom (para. 4; emphasis added).

It is the direct interaction teachers have with their students that makes the teachers most influential on students' achievement, perhaps second only to the influence of the family. And there is ample evidence showing the positive effect of student engagement on achievement. For example, Reyes, Brackett, Rivers, White, and Salovey (2012) analyzed data from about 1,400 Fifth and Sixth Graders through classroom observations, student reports, and report card grades.

The authors concluded that *"positive relationship between classroom emotional climate and grades was **mediated by engagement**, while controlling for teacher characteristics and observations of both the organizational and instructional climates of the classrooms. Effects were robust across grade level and student gender"* (700; emphasis added). It is important to note the conclusion about the mediating effect of engagement, as this suggests that the effects of other conditions would otherwise be minimal. Another example showing the beneficial effect of student engagement is the study by Guo, Connor, Tompkins, and Morrison (2011). The study involved about 1400 Third Grade students who were taking part in a longitudinal research project (the NICHD Study of Early Child Care and Youth Development). When home condition and First Grade reading scores were controlled, higher levels of student engagement (reflecting teacher stimulation) were associated with higher reading achievement.

The two examples above are related to the relation between engagement/stimulation and achievement among elementary students. In a meta-analysis commissioned by the New Zealand Ministry of Education, Gibbs, and Poskitt (2010) concluded that for Year 4–7 students, there is a qualitative difference between highly engaged students and marginally or poorly engaged students in many social and personal characteristics: connection to school, teachers, and peers; sense of agency; effort; commitment to learning, intrinsic motivation; confidence; achievement orientation; and self-regulation. By synthesizing findings of previous research studies, the authors pointed up seven important factors: relations with teachers and other students; relational learning; disposition to be a learner; motivation and interest in learning; personal agency/cognitive autonomy; self-efficacy; and goal orientation. While some of the factors are more personal, other are social in nature. With reference to the first two factors, the authors suggested to teachers that they need be stimulating or motivating by nurturing trusting relations through caring about the students, knowing them well, and being fair to them. They further suggested ways by which students can be maximally engaged in the learning process.

Teachers have been looking for ways and means to stimulate student learning. These range from the traditional questioning during lessons, to peer tutoring, to the use of digital gadgets such as iPads (Gillen, 2013) and cell phones (Neilsen, 2012). In the context of PISA 2009, with its focus on reading, teacher stimulation is operationalized traditionally as teachers stimulating student thinking and engagement, thus,

- Teachers asking students to explain the meaning of text
- Teachers asking questions to challenge students for better understanding of text
- Teachers giving time for students to think
- Teachers recommending books or authors
- Teachers encouraging students to express opinions
- Teachers helping to relate reading and lived experience
- Teachers showing the links between text and students' knowledge

The percentages are for students who endorsed "*never or hardly*" or "*in some lessons*", although the statements are positively worded. In this case, a *higher* percentage indicates a *less* stimulating or motivating instructional strategy.

As shown in Table 4, Singapore has higher percentages for six of the seven statements, indicating that their students are getting more motivation than their counterparts in Finland. In other words, teachers in Singapore are more likely than their counterparts in Finland to engage their students by asking questions which stimulate them to think and to explain as a way of promoting comprehension as well as relating reading

**Table 4.** Teacher Stimulation.

| | OECD | Finland (n = 5,810) | Singapore (n = 5,283) | Effect size |
|---|---|---|---|---|
| The teacher asks students to explain the meaning of a text. | 52 | 35 | 51 | 0.31 |
| The teacher asks questions that challenge students to get a better understanding of a text. | 59 | 35 | 57 | 0.42 |
| The teacher gives students enough time to think about their answers. | 60 | 63 | 68 | 0.10 |
| The teacher recommends a book or author to read. | 36 | 38 | 22 | −0.33 |
| The teacher encourages students to express their opinions about a text. | 55 | 47 | 49 | 0.04 |
| The teacher helps students relate the stories they read to their lives. | 33 | 17 | 36 | 0.41 |
| The teacher shows students how the information in texts builds on what they already know. | 43 | 24 | 45 | 0.42 |
| Overall | 43 | 24 | 47 | 0.20 |

*Source*: OECD (2010b).

to past experiences. Most of the effect sizes are small and those for "*giving student time to think*" and for "*encouraging student to express their opinions*" are negligible. Interestingly, teachers in Finland were more likely to recommend books or authors to the students, although the effect size is small. The overall percentage of Singapore is 23% higher than that of Finland, with a small effect size of 0.20.

### Is there a relationship between Reading performance and social environment for learning?

As reported earlier, the difference in Reading between Finland and Singapore is reasonably attributable to measurement error and the effect size is a trivial one. These justify the conclusion that the two countries in fact performed on par in Reading, notwithstanding an apparent difference of 10 points on a 600-point scale. The same goes to the comparisons between the countries on the Reading subtests. In short, there is no difference between Finland and Singapore, contrary to what many are made to believe. At the same time, for the three aspects of social environment, students in Singapore enjoyed better teacher–student relations, a more conducive disciplinary climate, and, to a lesser extent, higher teacher stimulation.

Since there is no difference in Reading performance between the two countries, there is no variance in Reading, and therefore no co-variance between Reading and social environment, notwithstanding the differences in the later measures. In short, as far as the two countries are concerned, the answer to the third question is neutral: there is no relationship (correlation) between Reading performance and social environment for learning.

## Discussion and Conclusion

The findings that Finland and Singapore should be considered as equivalent in Reading may cause some degree of unease as test results tend to be taken literally without due consideration of measurement error. Ignoring measurement error is further encouraged by the way test results have been reported; for instance, reporting score reliability is *not* done in most international studies. The doubtful assumption with which test results are taken to be accurate and exact (i.e., without measurement error) is further accentuated by the competitive way countries try to one-up each other and the way reports highlight even trivial differences.

However, the fallibility of educational scores is a real and serious technical problem, and up till today no educational tests can claim to be totally free from measurement error, for the simple reason that testing is sampling of behaviour and sampling, by its very nature, involves sampling error which shows up as part of the scores obtained by using any tests. Under such circumstances, caution is advised in the use of test scores; we must acknowledge and account for measurement error when interpreting test results. We also need to guard against spurious precision and avoid reading too much meaning into small differences which could well be the result of measurement error or which lack substantive significance.

The finding that students in Singapore report that they enjoyed better relations with their teachers, a more conducive classroom atmosphere, and were more actively motivated by their teachers also needs to be read with caution. Recall that the data is based on surveys of student perceptions. As is true of all surveys, there is the possibility of acquiescence (i.e., the tendency to agree), motivated faking, and cultural bias (i.e., the same statements having different meanings in different cultures). No doubt, care has been amply taken in international studies to control for such influences, but it is doubtful that this noise can be totally eliminated. These kinds of biases do not appear in reliability formula but they are there all the same. Again, due caution is necessary when reading the survey results.

Granting that, the differences between Finland and Singapore in social environment for learning, as perceived by the students, could well reflect their different ethoses in education.

Given the necessary caution against the two types of measurement errors, the lack of a positive correlation between Reading performance and social environment for learning warrants an explanation, as this finding of no-relation does not align with many studies, some of which are cited above. Huang (2013, paras. 7 and 9), a UNESCO EPR intern who has work experience in both Finland and Singapore contrasts them thus:

> The Singaporean system has traditionally been renowned for its heavy student homework and examinations… Could it be that the heavier the academic workload, the less room for individual development? …The Finnish education system, by comparison, maintains a generally positive public image of being offered in a happy and peaceful learning environment, with strong focus on individual development and without significant pressure to 'compete' in traditional area.

In this vein, Webster (2012, paras. 8–10) characterized the two education systems as follows:

> For a number of years Finland's education system was heralded as the savior of our own faltering institution. Here is a country which takes a relaxed and positive approach to education, where students spend fewer hours at school than almost any other country in the world, there are fewer exams, grades are almost entirely non-existent, there are no league

tables and education is free from the age of 7 right through to the completion of university...Singapore is a far more straight-forward system involving intense and rigorous teaching methods in strict environments where testing is frequent and extremely high stakes...Singapore represents so much of what teachers pushing for change and revolution wish to turn their backs on and yet you cannot deny that what they do works.

Thus, the findings suggest that teachers in Singapore are more concerned with ensuring student learning through hand-holding and explicit direction, whereas teachers in Finland are more attuned to letting their students have the freedom to explore and develop on their own without closely monitoring the process of learning.

The PISA tests were first developed in English and French as source languages (OECD, 2012: 36) and then translated into the media of instruction of the participating countries. In this case, students in Finland took the test in Finnish (which is also the students' first language or mother tongue) whereas students in Singapore took it in English since this is the medium of instruction. A relevant fact that is always overlooked is that there is a sizable proportion of students whose dominant home language is *not* English, although administratively this is referred to as the First Language in Singapore's education system. Specifically, based on a press release (Ministry of Education, Singapore, 2004), it is estimated that English was the dominant home language of 60% of 15-year-olds ethnic Chinese students (who were the majority of the student population) while the remaining 40% had Chinese or one of the several Chinese dialects as their dominant home language. Two interesting points arise from this. Firstly, it is very impressive that students in Singapore could score so well in PISA 2009 in a language which is in fact a second or even foreign language (in the strictly linguistic sense of the term). Secondly, the students' varied language backgrounds could have prompted the teachers in Singapore to adopt a more direct instructional approach as reflected by the students' perceptions reported above.

Another explanation for *a lack of relation* between achievement (Reading) and social environment for learning might be ecological fallacy.

In the literature, the common findings of a positive correlation between achievement and a conducive learning environment have come from *individual studies* using students as the unit of analysis. In contrast, international studies (like PISA) are *ecological studies* reporting and comparing country means, although the data were collected at the individual level. Findings of these two types of studies may or may not coincide; and when the findings of one type are generalized to the other, ecological fallacy is committed. Note the subtle difference in the two statements below:

- Students who learn in a conducive environment tend to achieve higher test scores.
- Countries where students learn in a conducive environment tend to achieve higher test scores.

The two statements seem to be reporting the same research outcome, but they are not; one is on *students* and the other is about *countries*. Although a country's performance has to be obtained from her students, as is invariably done in international studies, the correlation at the individual (student) level does not always coincide with the correlation at the aggregated or ecological (country) level. Such a subtle conceptual difference has been neglected in educational research and its consequences are yet to be uncovered.

However, the ecological fallacy issue has been raised in medical research (e.g., Oakes, 2009; Schwartz, 1994) and is receiving increasing attention. Perhaps educational research, especially international studies, should start catching up, lest it confuses and frustrates the consumers of research (mainly educators, administrators, and policymakers who more often than not are not sufficiently versed in statistical procedures and concepts) by carefully differentiating individual and ecological studies at the point of reporting.

## Methodological Notes

1. For social environment, the data re-analyzed for the present study was gleaned from the relevant tables in the PISA 2009 report (2012; Teacher–student relation, Figure IV.4.1: 89, Disciplinary climate, Figure IV.4.2: 91, and Teacher stimulation, Figure IV.4.3: 93). The data was collected from 15-year-old students, 5810 in Finland and 5283 in Singapore.

2. Standardized mean difference (SMD) is an effect size indicator calculated with the formula below:

SMD (Glass's $\Delta$) = (Finland mean — Singapore mean)/Finland SD

where the means were replaced by the percentages, where appropriate. The obtained SMD were then evaluated for its magnitude and interpreted in accordance with Cohen's (1988) criteria:

| | |
|---|---|
| 0.0 to 0.2 | Trivial or negligible effect |
| 0.2 to 0.5 | Small effect |
| 0.5 to 0.8 | Medium effect |
| 0.8 or above | Large effect |

3. Standard error of measurement (SEM) indicates the extent to which a score can vary within a range and is estimated with the formula below:

$$SEM = SD\sqrt{(1-r)}$$

where SD is the standard deviation of a set of scores and r is the reliability coefficient for the scores. In this case, r is the Cronbach's alpha coefficient, $\alpha$. By convention, a minimum $\alpha = 0.7$ is acceptable for research purposes but $\alpha = 0.9$ is required for using the scores for making decisions about the individuals (in this case, the countries).

4. For each statement, the percentages for Finland and Singapore were compared by way of difference in percentage, evaluated by SMD. This required the calculation of the pooled standard deviation of percentages which was then used as the denominator to divide the inter-country difference. The pooled standard deviation of percentages was estimated with the formula below:

$$SD = \sqrt{(PQ/N)}$$

where P is the pooled frequency for agreement, Q the pooled frequency for disagreement, and N the pooled total of students.

# References

Bush, R. N. (1942). A study of student–teacher relationships. *Journal of Educational Research*, **35**(9), 645–656.

Chapman, E. (2003). Assessing student engagement rates. ERIC Digest, ED482269. ERIC Clearinghouse on Assessment and Evaluation. Available at http://www.ericdigests.org/2005-2/engagement.html

Cohen, B. and Thomas, E. B. (1984). The disciplinary climate of schools. *Journal of Educational Administration*, **22**(2), 113–134.

Cohen, J. (1988). *Statistical Power Analysis for the Social Sciences, Second Edition*. Hillsdale: Erlbaum.

Embassy of Finland, Washington (December 7, 2010). *Finnish Students High Performers in PISA*. Available at http://www.finland.org/Public/default.aspx?contentid=207507&nodeid=35833&culture=en-US

Guo, Y., Connor, C. M., Tompkins, V., and Morrison, F. (2011). Classroom quality and student engagement: contribution to third-grade reading skills. *Frontiers in Psychology*, **2**(157), 1–10. doi: 10.3389/fpsyg.2011.00157

Gibbs, R. and Poskitt, J. (2010). *Student Engagement in the Middle Years of Schooling (Years 7 — 10): A Literature Review*. Report to Ministry of Education. Available at http://www.educationcounts.govt.nz/publications/schooling/student-engagement-in-the-middle-years-of-schooling-years-7-10-a-literature-review/part-a-an-exploration-of-the-student-engagement-literature

Gillen, J. (July 18, 2013). *Study shows iPads increase student engagement and achievement*. Examiner.com. Available at http://www.examiner.com/article/study-shows-ipads-increase-student-engagement-and-achievement

Huang, K. C. (January 30, 2013). *PISA-perfect? Comparing Education in Finland and Singapore*. Education, UNESCO Bangkok Office. Available at http://www.unescobkk.org/education/news/article/pisa-perfect-comparing-education-in-finland-and-singapore/

Ma, X. and Willms, D. (2004). School disciplinary climate: characteristics and effects on Eight Grade achievement. *Alberta Journal of Educational Research*, **50**(2), 169–188.

Ministry of Education, Singapore (December 7, 2010*). International OECD Study Affirms the High Quality of Singapore's Education System*. Press Releases. Available at http://www.moe.gov.sg/media/press/2010/12/programme-for-international-student-assessment-2009.php

Ministry of Education, Singapore (2004). *Refinements to Mother Tongue Language Policy*. Press Release EDUN N 25-02-004. Available at http://www.moe.gov.sg/media/press/2004/pr20040109.htm

Mortimore, P. (2009). *Alternative Models for Analysing and Representing Countries' performance in PISA*. Brussels: Education International Research Institute.

Neilsen, L. (May 6, 2012). *Using cell phone to support student engagement and achievement in speaking and listening*. The Innovative Educator. Available at http://theinnovativeeducator.blogspot.sg/2012/05/using-cell-phones-to-support-student.html

Oakes, J. M. (2009). Commentary: individual, ecological and multilevel fallacy. *International Journal of Epidemiology*, **38**(2), 361–368.

OECD (2012), *PISA 2009 Technical Report*, PISA, OECD Publishing. Available at http://dx.doi.org/10.1787/9789264167872-en

OECD (2010a), *PISA 2009 Results: What Students Know and Can Do — Student Performance in Reading, Mathematics and Science (Volume I)*. Available at http://dx.doi.org/10.1787/9789264091450-en

OECD (2010b). *PISA 2009 Results: What Makes a School Successful? — Resources, Policies and Practices (Volume IV)*. Available at http://dx.doi.org/10.1787/9789264091559-en

OECD (2011). *PISA 2009 at a Glance*. OECD Publishing. Available at http://www.oecd.org/pisa/pisaproducts/pisa2009/46660259.pdf

Reyes, M. R., Brackett, M. A., Rivers, S. E., White, M., and Salovey, P. (2012). Classroom emotional climate, student engagement, and academic achievement. *Journal of Educational Psychology,* **104**(3), 700–712.

Rimm-Kaufman, S. (2013). *Improving Students' Relationships with Teachers to Provide Essential Supports for Learning*. American Psychological Association. Available at http://www.apa.org/education/k12/relationships.aspx#high-quality

Schlechty, P. C. and Atwood, H. E. (1977). The student–teacher relationship. *Theory into Practice*, **16**(4), 285–289.

Sjoberg, S. (2007). PISA and "Real life challenges": Mission impossible? Contribution to Hopman (Ed.): *PISA according to PISA* revised version. Available at http://folk.uio.no/sveinsj/Sjoberg-PISA-book-2007.pdf

Soh, K. (2013a). Finland and Singapore in PISA 2009: similarities and differences in achievement and school management. *Compare: A Journal of Comparative and International Education*. Published online. Available at http://dx.doi.org/10.1080/03057925.2013.787286

Soh, K. (2013b). *Social and Educational Ranking: Problems and Prospects.* New York: Untested Ideas Research Center.
Schwartz, S. (1994). The fallacy of the ecological fallacy: the potential misse of a concept and the consequences. *American Journal of Public Health*, **84**(5), 819–824.
Webster, A. (2012). How PISA Rankings Could Make or Break A Country's Education System. *Edudemic*. Available at http://www.edudemic.com/2012/08/the-importance-of-pisa-rankings-for-countries/

# Part II
# Principals' Roles and Views

# Chapter 3

# Principals as Instructional Leaders? A Lesson from the PIRLS 2011

The concept of *principal as instructional leader* is reminiscent of the one-room-one-teacher little red house of the early history of gathering a small group of children to learn together — an invention for an economy which did not foresee its growth and impact in years to come. When the little red house grew larger both in terms of enrolment and space, the *school* as we know it today emerged. The growth necessitated some form of organization and, usually though not always, the most capable among the teachers was designated the *principal teacher* or the *principal*. For the British, this is the *head teacher* or *head master*. The job titles mean the same thing, referring to the one who led a group of teachers, small in number though it may be as compared with the army of teachers in a present-day mega school.

Today, *instructional leader* is always an item in the job specifications of the principal. As the one-teacher-one-room congregations gave way to larger schools staffed by multiple teachers, the need arose for a principal teacher to manage them. Today, schools are no longer run by teachers, and the principal has evolved into a manager and personnel officer (Maddox, 2013). In a very real sense, principals belong to the management while teachers are workers (and teachers indeed have been referred to as *educational workers* in some countries). Nowadays, the jobs performed by teachers and by principals are so differentiated and specialized that even a principal interested in academic matters has little time and expertise to devote to instructional leadership.

That this is so has been emphatically acknowledged by Hoerr (2007–2008) who was a teacher, then principal, and now a superintendent.

According Hoerr, the many additional duties over and above classroom instruction are not the main obstacle to the principal's instructional leadership. In his candid view, in the past, a principal could be the resident instructional expert who offered advice to everyone but this is not true now — teachers today know much more about how students learn than the principal does. Moreover, today's teachers do not necessarily look to the principal for answers to professional or instructional problems as they have other resources that help them.

This gives rise to a question of whether the principals as school leaders influence student learning and, if they still do, by what mechanisms or via what routes. This is the focus of the present study.

## Principal Leadership and Student Achievement

It is a truism that student achievement is the core business of the school. And the conventional wisdom is that the principal as the leader of school has an impact on student achievement through setting school policy, procuring resources, and guiding teachers. In this regard, a pertinent question is whether the principal does indeed impact student achievement. And, if indeed he does, via what processes. Possible answers to such questions can be found in some recent studies.

After an extensive meta-analysis of earlier studies, Leithwood, Anderson, Mascall, and Strauss (2006) proposed a model linking student achievement and principal leadership through four mediating paths, thus:

1. *Rational Path*: This path is rooted in the school staff's knowledge of and skill in curriculum, teaching, and learning. The school leader requires technical knowledge about schooling, problem solving capacities, and relevant leadership practices.
2. *Emotional Path*: This path is closely related to the Rational Path and directs cognition, including perception, attention, access, and judgment that help a productive response to the environment.
3. *Organizational Path*: This path deals with structures, culture, policies, and standard operation procedures in managing a school which, collectively, make up the working conditions of teachers and influence their emotion and collective memory as members of an organization.

4. *Family Path*: This path encompasses the student's family life, including work habits in the family, academic guidance and support by the parents, stimulation to think, provision of health and nutritional conditions, and physical settings.

Leithwood *et al.* (2006) stressed that the principal as a school leader should attend to all four paths at the same time with consideration for their influence. Moreover, it is of note that the authors cited studies showing that the Family Path predicts as much as 50 per cent of student achievement and that the school's effort did account for student achievement but only 20 per cent, leaving 30 per cent unaccounted for.

More recently, Robinson (2010) studied the impact of principals' instructional leadership on student achievement and proposed a model of leadership capabilities. The three interrelated capabilities studied are (1) the use of deep leadership content knowledge, (2) the ability to solve complex school-based problems, and (3) the development of trust with staff, parents, and students. The author further suggested that developing leadership frameworks, standards, and curricula that develop their skilful integration are more important than the fine-grain specification of each capability. In other words, broad principles reflecting the frame of mind of school leadership are more critical than specific skills.

Based on a meta-analysis, Robinson (2010) conceptualized the principal's instructional leadership as involving the planning, evaluation, coordination, and improvement of teaching and learning — in sum, learning-oriented leadership. Based on another meta-analysis, Robinson (2010) identified four dimensions of leadership: (1) leading through promoting and participating in teacher learning and development; (2) establishing goals and expectations; (3) planning, coordinating, and evaluating teaching and curriculum; and (4) strategic resourcing and ensuring an orderly and supportive environment. In comparison with Leithwood *et al.* (2006), Robinson (2010) focused only on conditions within the school boundary (i.e., the Rational and the Organization Paths) and did not take into consideration a possible family influence.

Another recent study of the effect of principals' leadership on student learning is Chen (2010). The Leadership Practices Inventory was completed by principals to determine their leadership practices. State-wide assessment data for three school years (2004–2006) were also secured from the Academic Excellence Indicator System Report. Based on the findings, Chen (2010) concluded that principals' collaborative working style with teacher leaders seems to have a positive impact on student achievement and, conversely, the failure to enlist teacher leaders in a common vision might have a negative effect on student learning. Moreover, the perceptions of teacher leaders reflected a need for the principal to take challenges and seek challenging opportunities to change and grow. Recognizing teacher leaders' contributions and celebrating team accomplishments is likely to have a positive and indirect impact on a school's academic performance. Furthermore, schools that had higher leadership scores tended to have better achievement scores, and distributed leadership is most likely to contribute to school improvement and to build school capacity for improvement. Such findings emphasize the need for the principal to be participative, appreciative, and proactive — in short, close to the ground rather than directing from the office.

Even more recently, Turnbull, Whit, and Arcaira (2012) reported a two-year project investigating the effect of principals' instructional leadership on student achievement. More than 70 principals of elementary, middle, and high schools in Kentucky, Illinois, and Iowa participated. In the project, the principals gained knowledge of actual classroom teaching by spending time in the classroom. They relieved part of their managerial responsibilities to school administration managers. In contrast, the principals in the comparison condition spent all their time on school administration. The study showed mixed results: (1) There was no statistically significant relationship between the principals' time use and student achievement; (2) schools in which principals had a change in time use did not outpace the comparison schools in student achievement. There was one exception: in one cohort, for four schools whose principals had a change in time-use, students scored significantly higher than their counterparts in the comparison schools at the end of one year; however, the effect was no longer true after the second year. In short, the principals' *direct* involvement in classroom instruction did not affect student achievement. This suggests that the principals' impact on student achievement is more likely *indirect*, mediated through their influence on school policies, curriculum, teacher guidance, and provision of needed resources. The finding also implies that managing schools and teaching students requires different knowledge and skills such that efficient principals may or may not be efficacious teachers.

Recently, Branch, Rivkin, and Hanushek (Winter, 2013) adopted a value-added approach to evaluate the impact on student achievement of principals' leadership. The author analyzed observational data for the years 1995–2001 of school principals (N = 7,420). They also secured annual observational data of principals (N = 28,147) from the archives. Their regression analysis shows that one standard deviation above the mean on principal effectiveness was associated with seven additional months of learning of student achievement. Moreover, the impact was even more notable for schools with high poverty rates of students. This implies that strong principal leadership is especially important to revitalize schools with a high proportion of students from disadvantaged homes. However, the study does not describe how principal effectiveness was measured. The definition appeared to be tautological: effective principals were defined as those whose schools had high student achievement. It would be more convincing had principal leadership been measured independently without recourse to student achievement.

In all fairness, Branch *et al.*, (cited in Winter, 2013) did acknowledge that the fundamental challenge of measuring the impact of school leaders was to separate their contributions from many other factors that might have contributed to student achievement. They also recognized that principals can influence student achievement through many channels and that the precise mechanisms vary across districts, with the regulatory and institutional structures defining their authority as school leaders.

The studies summarized above were carried out in their respective national contexts. An international perspective was adopted by Soh (2013), comparing two highly acclaimed achieving countries, namely Finland and Singapore. In PISA 2009, both these countries scored very high on Reading, with a small difference attributable to measurement error or spurious precision. They, however, somewhat differ in school management style. Principals of schools in Finland were more actively involved in the selection of teachers but principals of Singapore schools were more involved in assessment policies, course content, course offering, and other matters at the classroom level related to teachers and teaching. It appears that Finish principals function more as managers while their Singaporean counterparts are more hands-on. The conclusion is that different leadership styles of principals can lead to the same level of student achievement — *All roads lead to Rome*? National policies and cultural characteristics were invoked as explanatory factors of the observed differences in the principals' leadership styles.

According to Cuban (2013), principals play multiple managerial, instructional, and political roles in and out of schools, and the instructional leader role has been spotlighted as a must for them. As the theory and rhetoric go, it is a role crucial to improving teacher performance and, in turn, student academic achievement. Yet studies are clear that principals spending time in classrooms do not necessarily lead to better teaching or student achievement. There is hardly any positive association between principals walking in and out of classrooms and conferring with teaches. The reality of daily principal actions conflicts with the theory. When a correlation is found between principals' influence on teachers and student, it occurs where principals create and sustain an academic ethos in the school, organize instruction across the school, and align school lessons to district standards and standardized test items.

The summaries above may be limited in scope. They, however, suggest that the questions on the principal's impact on student achievement is complex and that factors mediating between the principal's leadership and student achievement need be given due consideration.

## Principal Leadership Activities in PIRLS 2011

### *Data*

In the PIRLS 2011 Report (Mullis, Martin, Foy, and Drucker, 2012), Chapter 6, Exhibit 6.3 *Principals Spend Time on Leadership Activities* (p. 168) displays, for the 45 participating countries, leadership activities as reported by the principals. Like PISA, the PIRLS data affords another opportunity to study the relationship between student achievement and principal leadership at an international level. The data takes the form of "Percent of students whose principals spend *a lot of time*" on the listed activities. The percentages are taken as a proxy measure of the importance placed by the principals in managing their schools.

## Priorities of leadership activities

The priorities principals placed on the leadership activities are shown in terms of descriptive statistics for the nine activities in Table 1.

As can be seen from Table 1, *"keeping an orderly atmosphere"* is the most important to the principals. This is followed by *"promoting the school's vision"*, *"developing the curriculum"*, and *"monitoring students' progress"*. Next in importance are *"monitoring teachers' teaching"* and *"addressing disruptive behaviour"*. Finally, the principals participated in activities for *"own professional growth"* and advised teachers *"on questions or problems"*.

It is also noteworthy that there are vast differences between countries in leadership activities, as shown by the ranges (i.e., differences between the maximum and minimum). As shown in Table 1, for six of the nine leadership activities, the ranges are around 75 percent and even the remaining three activities have differences around 65 per cent. In other words, the countries are quite heterogeneous in their priorities for the nine leadership activities undertaken by the principals.

Table 1. Principals' Leadership Activities.

| Activity | Mean | SD | Max | Min | Range |
|---|---|---|---|---|---|
| Keeping an orderly atmosphere in the school | 67.1 | 17.6 | 98 | 24 | 74 |
| Promoting the school's educational vision or goals | 58.7 | 16.1 | 86 | 23 | 63 |
| Developing the school's curricular and educational goals | 59.1 | 20.4 | 90 | 13 | 77 |
| Monitoring students' learning progress to ensure that the school's educational goals are reached | 55.6 | 21.7 | 86 | 10 | 76 |
| Monitoring teachers' implementation of the school's educational goals in their teaching | 48.2 | 22.0 | 82 | 6 | 76 |
| Addressing disruptive student behavior | 44.2 | 18.3 | 82 | 9 | 73 |
| Initiating educational projects or improvements | 40.9 | 13.6 | 78 | 16 | 62 |
| Participating in professional development activities specifically for school principals | 37.5 | 18.9 | 81 | 5 | 76 |
| Advising teachers who have questions or problems with their teaching | 35.1 | 16.6 | 74 | 7 | 67 |

54  PISA and PIRLS: The Effects of Culture and School Environment

Table 2. Factor Structure of Leadership Activities.

| | F1<br>Instructional Leadership | F2<br>Student Problems |
|---|---|---|
| Curriculum | **0.909** | 0.087 |
| Vision | **0.868** | 0.272 |
| Initiating projects | **0.809** | 0.274 |
| Student learning | **0.808** | 0.366 |
| Teacher teaching | **0.783** | 0.460 |
| Professional development | 0.555 | **0.668** |
| Advising teachers | 0.457 | **0.730** |
| Orderly atmosphere | 0.229 | **0.864** |
| Disruptive behavior | 0.118 | **0.899** |
| Total variance | 45.4% | 33.7% |
| Correlation | −0.60 | |

*Notes*: Factor-defining variables are in bold.

## *Factor structure of leadership activities*

Factor analysis was run to organize the nine specific activities into broader dimensions of principal leadership. For this, two correlated factors were obtained (Table 2). The first factor is made up of activities related to curriculum, vision, projects, learning, and teaching. These activities mainly pertain to instructional leaderships and the factor explains 45 per cent of the differences between countries. The second factor is made up of activities which have to do mainly with student behavior and school atmosphere. This factor explains 34 per cent of the inter-country differences.

It is of note that the two factors have a sizable *negative* correlation of $r = -0.60$, indicating an overlap of 36 percent. In other words, demonstrating instructional leadership and attending to student problems compete for the principals' time and effort. When principals spend time and effort on one aspect of school management, the other aspect suffers.

## *Correlations among reading and factors*

The main concern of the present study is the extent to which principals' leadership impact student achievement, using Reading as an indicator.

Table 3. Correlations Among Reading and Factors (N = 45).

|  | Reading | Instructional Leadership | Student Problems |
|---|---|---|---|
| Reading | 1.00 | 0.22 | **−0.52** |
| Instructional Leadership |  | 1.00 | **−0.60** |
| Student Problems |  |  | 1.00 |

*Note*: Coefficients in bold are statistically significant ($p < 0.05$).

As shown in Table 3, the correlation between the PIRLS Reading means and the factor scores for Instructional Leadership is a non-significant $r = 0.22$, suggesting that the principals' leadership activities related to classroom instruction (the first factor) has very little impact on student achievement.

On the other hand, there is a statistically significant negative correlation of $r = -0.52$ between activities related to student problems (the second factor) and Reading. This negative correlation calls for careful interpretation as to the direction of influence, as correlation is bi-directional. It could be interpreted to mean countries scoring lower in Reading have more student problems. It is as valid an interpretation that countries with more student problems scored lower in Reading. Since PIRLS is a survey and not a true experiment, the direction of influence is equivocal and the data available here is unable to definitively support either interpretation. Most probably, the two variables interactively form a vicious circle where poor reading leads to poor student behavior which in turn lead to poor reading. Whatever it is, the correlation indicates a share variance of 27 percent between the two variables; in other words, poor student behavior, if seen as a cause, may cost up to near 30 per cent of student achievement.

## Discussion and Conclusion

The aim of this study is to find out whether principals' leadership activities influence student achievement in Reading by using the PIRLS 2011 data, with countries as the unit of analysis in contrast with most studies which use students. An implication of this approach is that the findings are valid for the countries but may and may not be so for individual students, in view of possible ecological fallacy. The findings are summarized and discussed below.

In the forefront of the principal's mind is to ensure an orderly atmosphere in their school. This is understandable as conventional wisdom has it that a conducive environment is a necessary condition for effective learning, although by itself it is insufficient, and effective instruction at the classroom level is also needed. Beyond this concern, principals have been actively involved in promoting the school's vision, developing the curriculum, and monitoring students' progress, and rightly so. In doing this, they set the stage as directors for the drama called *schooling* to be played out as expected by their education systems. In a sense, this is the main function the principals as school managers have to perform to enable actors (i.e., teachers and students) to play their roles.

The finding that the principals' active involvement in instructional matters has little to contribute to student achievement may look disappointing and contrary to expectation or rhetoric, but it is consistent with the results of projects which involved principals in actual teaching in the classroom (e.g., Turnbull et al., 2012). However, this should not be mistaken as showing that principals' leadership activities make no contribution to student achievement. On the contrary, the findings that there is a sufficiently strong *negative* correlation between student achievement and disruptive behavior points to the way principals make their contribution.

Although principals may not value-add directly to student achievement through classroom instruction and other classroom-based activities (e.g., observing lessons), they can contribute to student achievement by way of effective management at the school level, especially by handling student behavior so that efficient teaching and learning can take place. By so doing, the vicious circle between student achievement and disruptive behavior can be broken and turned into a virtuous circle by which good behavior leads to better learning which in its turn reinforces good behavior.

Obviously, the principal and the teachers have different roles to play in different arenas; the former as a manager at the school level (analogous to the director of a drama), and the latter as instructors at the classroom level (actors in a play). When the director and the actors play out their respective roles with a mutual understanding of each other's functions, the drama called *schooling* can be exciting and beneficial to everyone concerned.

Effective-schools research shows that successful schools are invariably led by a principal who is recognized as an instructional leader. However, Terry (1996) synthesizes and clarifies the recent perspectives on the principal's instructional leadership, using data including professional educational journals, trade books on leadership, and anthologies of articles written by professional educators. It is suggested that there is a need for restructuring the principal's role so that the principal focuses on administrative functions and delegates instructional and curricular responsibilities to a curriculum director who works with lead teachers. The findings of the present study using international data resonates with this and implies that the role of principals as instructional leaders is different from the teacher's role as instructor in the classroom; the two roles are complementary.

## References

Branch, G. B., Rivkin, S. G., and Hanushek, E. A. (2013). School leaders matter: measuring the impact of effective principals. *Education Next*, **13**(1). Available at http://educationnext.org/school-leaders-matter/

Chen, Y.-H. (2010). *Principals' Distributed Leadership Behaviors and Their Impact on Student Achievement in Selected Elementary Schools in Texas.* Accessed November 4, 2011. Available at http://repository.tamu.edu/handle/1969.1/ETD-TAMU-1477

Cuban, L. (2013). *Inside the Black Box of Classroom Practice: Change without Reform in American Education.* Harvard Education Press.

Hoerr, T. R. (2007–2008). The principal connect/what is instructional leaderships? *Educational Leadership*, **65**(4), 84–85.

Leithwood, K., Anderson, S. E., and Strauss, B. (2010). School leaders' influences on student learning: the four paths. In T. Bush, L. Bell, and D. Middlewood, Eds. *The Principles of Educational Leadership and Management.* London: Sage.

Madddox, M. (18 June 2013). *Instructional leadership not for principals.* BellaOnline: The Voice of Women. Available at http://www.bellaonline.com/articles/art36597.asp

Mullis, I. V. S., Martin, M. O., Foy, P., and Drucker, K. T. (2012). *PIRLS 2011 International Results in Reading.* TIMSS & PIRLS International Study Centre, Lynch School of Education, Boston College.

Robinson, V. M. (2010). From instructional leadership to leadership capabilities: Empirical findings and methodological challenges. *Leadership and Policy in Schools*, **9**(1), 1–26.

Soh, Kaycheng (2013). Finland and Singapore in PISA 2009: similarities and differences in achievement and school management. *Compare: A Journal of Comparative and International Education.* DOI: 10.1080/03057925.2013.787286

Terry, P. M. (1996). *The Principal and Instructional Leadership.* Paper presented at the Annual Meeting of the National Council of Professors in Educational Administration (Corpus Christi, Texas, August 1996).

Turnbull, B. J., Whit, R. N., and Arcaira, E. R. (2012). *Achievement Trends in Schools with School Administration Managers.* Washington, DC: Policy Studies Associates.

# Chapter 4

# Principals' Leadership and Views on Teachers and Students in PISA 2012: Comparisons between OECD Members and Partners

Of all school personnel, the principal is entrusted to lead the school in translating national education policy into classroom practices through selecting and monitoring teacher performance, managing finance to procure needed facilities and materials, and, above all, monitoring student behavior and achievements. This being the case, it is a truism that how the principal perceives and deals with the teachers and students can be expected to impact on student achievement as one of the ultimate goals of educating. In short, principal leadership may be seen as the cause and student performance the effect.

In an early study, Hallinger, Bickman, and Davis (May 1996) explored the nature and extent of the school principal's effects on reading achievement in a sample of 87 U.S. elementary schools, testing a multidimensional model using principal and teacher questionnaires and student test scores. They examined relations between selected school context variables, principal instructional leadership, instructional climate, and student reading achievement. No direct effects of principal instructional leadership on student achievement was found. However, they found evidence supporting the belief that a principal can have an indirect effect on school effectiveness and this was attained through actions that shape the school's learning climate.

Later, Suskavcevic and Blake (2004) opined that pervasive and sustained student learning is more likely to occur in schools with strong instructional leadership. In their study, they involved a national representative data set to examine the association between U.S.A. middle school principals' leadership styles and student achievement on the TIMSS 1999 Mathematics and Science achievements. They found statistically significant correlations among principals' leadership style and student performance on the TIMSS results and stronger correlations between the two variables.

Leithwood, Louis, Anderson, and Wahlstrom (2004) conducted a comprehensive review and summarized a broad range of empirical research and related literature. They found that principal leadership is second only to teaching among school-related factors in its impact on student learning. They cited authors as saying that the impact of principal leadership tends to be greatest in schools where the learning needs of students are most acute. High-quality leaders achieved this impact by setting directions through charting a clear course that everyone understands, establishing high expectations, and using data to track progress and performance. The effective principals also developed people through providing teachers and others in the system with the necessary support and training to succeed. Moreover, the principals made the organization work by ensuring that the entire range of conditions and incentives in districts and schools fully supports teaching and learning.

Moffitt (2007) asserted that effective principal leadership is imperative in contributing to student achievement and that they should mold the culture of the school to create an environment conducive to learning. He cited studies highlighting the evidence of school leadership behavior contributing to student achievement. His study involved 63 elementary teachers and six principals and conducted focus group interview and surveys. The results supported the literature and indicated that principal leadership was critical to student achievement in elementary school students.

Later, Sebastian and Allensworth (2012) examined the influence of high-school principal leadership on classroom instruction and student achievement, with consideration for key organizational factors such as professional capacity, parent–community ties, and the school's learning climate. They employed multilevel structural equation modeling to examine the relationships among principal leadership, school organizational structures, classroom instruction, and student grades and test gains. Findings show that within schools, variation in classroom instruction is associated with principal leadership through multiple pathways, the strongest of which is the quality of professional development and coherence of programs. Between schools, differences in instruction and student achievement are associated with principal leadership only via the learning climate. These findings suggest that in high schools, establishing a safe, college-focused climate may be the most important leadership function for promoting student achievement.

More recently, Shortridge's (2015) research was based on the premise that specific leadership behavior has been found to impact students' academic outcomes. The author intended to examine the impact of middle school principals' leadership styles on students' academic achievement. Particularly, the study compared the principals' leadership styles of principals of middle schools that have met or not met their school achievement indicators. Transformational, transactional, and laissez-faire leadership styles were investigated and analyzed within the context of student achievement outcomes. It was found that achievement status accounted for 22.4% of the variability in leadership style taken together, but most for transformational leadership (7.6 percent), followed by transactional leadership (5.7 percent), but none for laissez-faire leadership.

There is a plethora of studies on the relation between principal leadership and student achievement in the literature. The studies summarized above are admittedly more selective than comprehensive for the purpose of providing a backdrop to this study. As the studies show, while it is certain that principal leadership does have a positive impact on student achievement, the influence does not seem to be a direct outcome but an indirect one via some intervening factors, especially of the teachers and school culture. Moreover, it is necessary to point out that studies such as those cited are within-country or localized investigations mainly with the student as the unit of analysis. Therefore, whether the same relation between principal leadership and student achievement will be found between-country when the country is the unit of analysis remains a question.

With this in mind, and capitalizing on the data available in international comparative academic surveys such as PISA, the present study sought to compare more advanced countries (OECD Members) and less advanced countries (OECD Partners) on principal leadership and principals' views on teachers and students, and relate these to student achievement.

## Data

The data re-analyzed in the present study were gleaned from the relevant tables of PISA 2012 reports (OECD, 2013 and 2014).

### *Gross domestic product*

There are 65 countries (referred to as *economies* in PISA reports) that participated in PISA 2012. Of these, there are 34 OECD Members and the remaining 31 are OECD Partners. Generally, the OECD Members as a group are more developed in socio-economics and education than are the OECD Partners as a group. More specifically, the Gross Domestic Product (adjusted for purchase power parity) average of OECD Members is USD33,732 (from Turkey's USD15,195 to Luxembourg's USD84,672) and that of OECD Partner is USD21,247 (from Vietnam's USD4,095 to Qatar's USD77,265). Thus, on average, OECD Members are 59 percent richer than OECD Partners.

### *Investment in education*

Although the GDP figures do not show the amount invested in education, it stands to reason that countries which are better off economically will tend to spend more on education. For example, in terms of cumulative expenditure per student between six and 15 years, the OECD Members average is USD83,382 (from Turkey's USD19,821 to Luxembourg's USD197,598) compared with OECD Partners average USD33,760 (from Vietnam USD6,969 to Cyprus's USD109,575). That is, on average, OECD Members spend 60 percent more to educate the students than do OECD Partners. This works out to be 7 percent more per year.

Although the difference in investment in education between the two sets of countries cannot be directly translated into the quality of education thus "purchased", it is reasonable to assume that part of the difference in student achievement is attributable to differential financial investment in education, which results in differential provisions such as teacher quality, learning materials, and facilities, etc., etc. PISA does track such educational provisions through its surveys on principals, teachers, and students (OECD, 2014) and related the survey results to those of performance in the assessed subjects of Mathematics, which is the focus of PISA 2012.

## Achievements

### Mean comparison

Before an attempt to relate principal leadership and achievement, it is necessary to have an overview of achievements in the three subjects of Mathematics, Reading, and Science in the OECD Members and OECD Partners countries. As shown in Table 1, on all three measures of achievements, the OECD Members outperformed OECD Partners and the effect sizes are all large (Glass's $\Delta > 0.8$). In terms of tests scores, the differences are close to half a standard deviation of the PISA scales, which were scaled to have means of 500 and standard deviations of 100.

Notably, the OECD Members' means are close to the scaled means (500) while the OECD Partners' are lower by about 50 scale points, that is, half a standard deviation. It is also of note that the standard deviations of the OECD Members are much smaller (half or less) than those of the

Table 1. Comparisons on Mathematics, Reading, and Science.

|  | Members (N = 34) Mean | SD | Partner (N = 31) Mean | SD | Mean Difference | Effect Size |
|---|---|---|---|---|---|---|
| Mathematics | 494 | 29.4 | 451 | 67.7 | 43 | 0.89 |
| Reading | 496 | 24.0 | 449 | 53.8 | 47 | 1.21 |
| Science | 501 | 28.7 | 454 | 58.2 | 47 | 1.08 |

Table 2. Correlations among Mathematics, Reading, and Science.

|  | All (N = 65) | | | Members (N = 34) | | | Partner (N = 31) | | |
| --- | --- | --- | --- | --- | --- | --- | --- | --- | --- |
|  | Math | Reading | Science | Math | Reading | Science | Math | Reading | Science |
| Mathematics | 1.00 | 0.96 | 0.97 | 1.00 | 0.90 | 0.93 | 1.00 | 0.45 | 0.43 |
| Reading |  | 1.00 | 0.98 |  | 1.00 | 0.93 |  | 1.00 | 0.98 |
| Science |  |  | 1.00 |  |  | 1.00 |  |  | 1.00 |

*Note*: All correlation coefficients are significant ($p < 0.05$), two-tailed, for appropriate degrees of freedom.

OECD Members, indicating that while the OECD Members are more homogeneous, the OECD Partners are more heterogeneous.

## *Correlations*

As Table 2 shows, for all 65 countries that participated in PISA 2012, the three subjects have extremely high correlations — in fact, near perfect correlations, with r's varying from .96 to .98. When Members and Partners are separated, the three subjects are still very highly correlated for the OECD Members (varying from .90 to .93), but not for Partners; specifically, Mathematics has only moderate correlations with Reading ($r = 0.45$) and Science ($r = 0.43$), but Reading and Science remain very highly correlated ($r = 0.98$).

The different patterns of correlations suggest that the Mathematics curriculum and instruction may be more coordinated and integrated with Reading and Science in OECD Member countries, but are more discrete and diversified in OECD Partner countries. However, Reading and Science remain highly correlated, perhaps because of the dependence of Science on Reading in both sets of countries.

## Effect of Principal Leadership on Student Achievement

### *Principal leadership of OECD Members*

Table 3 shows the results of comparisons on principal leadership between OECD Members and OECD Partners. As shown, for OECD Members, between lower and upper secondary education and also between general

**Table 3.** Principal Leadership.

|  | Members (N = 34) Mean | SD | Partner (N = 31) Mean | SD | Mean Diff. | Effect Size |
|---|---|---|---|---|---|---|
| In lower secondary education | 0.00 | 0.47 | 0.55 | 0.61 | −0.55 | −0.90 |
| In upper secondary education | 0.02 | 0.50 | 0.63 | 0.35 | −0.61 | −1.74 |
| Mean difference | −0.02 | | −0.08 | | — | — |
| Effect size | −0.04 | | −0.13 | | — | — |
| In general program | −0.04 | 0.51 | 0.58 | 0.60 | −0.61 | −1.20 |
| In vocational program | −0.06 | 0.51 | 0.44 | 0.29 | −0.50 | −1.72 |
| Mean difference | 0.02 | | 0.14 | | — | — |
| Effect size | 0.04 | | 0.23 | | — | — |
| In public schools | −0.04 | 0.49 | 0.55 | 0.62 | −0.59 | −1.05 |
| In private schools | 0.11 | 0.56 | 0.94 | 0.57 | −0.83 | −1.46 |
| Mean difference | −0.15 | | −0.39 | | — | — |
| Effect size | −0.31 | | −0.63 | | — | — |

*Source*: OECD (2011), Table IV.4.8
*Note*: Effect sizes were calculated as the differences divided by the OECD Members' standard deviations.

and vocational programs, the differences in principal leaderships are small (Glass's $\Delta = -0.4$, and 0.4). The difference between public and private schools is also small in effect (Glass's $\Delta = -0.31$) and in favor of the latter. Thus, principal leadership was uniform for all kinds of education provided in OECD Member countries.

## *Principal leadership of OECD Partners*

As for OECD Partners, the difference between lower and upper secondary education has a negligible effect (Glass's $\Delta = -0.13$), the difference between general and vocational programs has a small effect (Glass's $\Delta = 0.23$) in favor of the former, and the difference between public and private has a moderate effect (Glass's $\Delta = -0.63$) in favor of the latter. Thus, principal leadership among OECD Partners was more varied and obviously different between public and private schools.

## Mean comparisons

Between the OECD Members and OECD Partners, principal leadership was rather different, with those in OECD Partner countries being more actively engaged in school matters, all across different kinds of educational provisions. The effect sizes are all large for level (lower and upper secondary education), program (general and vocational), and governance (public and private), ranging from Glass's Δ = |0.90| (Lower secondary education) to Glass's Δ = |1.74| (Upper secondary education).

## Impact on student achievement

How principal leadership impacts student achievement is indicated in Table 4. As the analysis shows, where OECD Members are concerned, for every unit change in the principal leadership index, there is a reduction of −0.6 scale points for Reading. In contrast, where OECD Partners are concerned, for every unit change in the index, there is an increase of 3.65 scale points for Reading. The difference has an effect size of Glass's Δ = |0.51|, which is moderate in magnitude. Thus, for the same unit of change in principal leadership, there is a difference of 4.25 scale points in favor of the OECD Partners. Paradoxically, this suggests that active principal leadership has the opposite effect for the two sets of countries.

In view of the extremely high correlation among the three subjects, what has been observed for Reading can also be expected of Mathematics and Science; therefore, additional comparisons for the two subjects were not conducted.

Table 4. Principal Leadership Effect on Student Achievement.

|  | Members (N = 34) Mean | SD | Partner (N = 31) Mean | SD | Mean Diff. | Effect Size |
|---|---|---|---|---|---|---|
| Change in the reading scores per unit of this index | −0.6 | 8.46 | 3.65 | 8.30 | −4.25 | −0.51 |

*Source*: OECD (2011), Table IV.4.8
*Note*: Effect size was calculated as the difference divided by the OECD Members' standard deviation.

The finding of a *negative* effect of principal leadership on student achievement seems to go against the grain and thus calls for careful interpretation. Usually, and as suggested by the studies reviewed above, more active principal leadership leads to better student achievement, but it is the other way round here.

In view of the fact that OECD Members scored higher than OECD Partners in achievements (Table 1), it is possible that OECD Partner principals put in greater effort than did their OECD Member counterparts, with the purpose and hope of raising student achievement, thus resulting in a negative association between principal leadership and OECD membership. Thus, the causal direction is not the usually expected *stronger-leadership-to-better-achievement* but, on the contrary, *poorer-achievement-to-stronger-leadership*. In other words, it is not that weaker principal leadership (among OECD Members) leads to better achievement but poorer achievement causes principals (among OECD Partners) to exert greater influence with the aim of improving student achievement. This reversal of the relation between principal leadership and student achievement may look unusual at first sight, but it is a paradox which should not be too easily dismissed as invalid, when looking at international comparative studies. This is further discussed later.

## Principals' Views of Teacher Effect

Knowing how principals see their teachers may contribute to better understanding of how principals operate in their schools with the goal of enhancing student achievement.

### *OECD Member principals' views*

How principals viewed the effect of teacher behavior on student learning is shown in Table 5. As shown therein, more OECD Member principals believed that the following *negative* behavior of teachers would have an impact on student learning:

- Teachers' low expectation of students
- Teachers being late for classes
- Teachers being too strict with students

**Table 5.** Principals' Views of How Teacher Behavior Affects Learning.

| | Member (N = 34) Mean | SD | Partner (N = 31) Mean | SD | Mean Difference | Effect Size |
|---|---|---|---|---|---|---|
| Teachers' low expectation of students | 85.3 | 8.9 | 77.1 | 11.3 | 8.2 | 0.73 |
| Teachers being late for classes | 93.1 | 5.6 | 85.5 | 11.1 | 7.6 | 0.68 |
| Teachers being too strict with students | 90.0 | 6.6 | 83.7 | 9.9 | 6.3 | 0.64 |
| Teachers not being well prepared for classes | 91.5 | 6.3 | 83.5 | 12.7 | 8.0 | 0.63 |
| Poor teacher–student relations | 92.9 | 5.8 | 88.0 | 9.7 | 4.9 | 0.51 |
| Students not being encouraged to achieve their full potential | 78.6 | 11.9 | 70.2 | 17.7 | 8.4 | 0.48 |
| Teacher absenteeism | 86.5 | 9.2 | 79.9 | 18.5 | 6.6 | 0.36 |
| Teacher not meeting individual students' needs | 76.3 | 13.0 | 75.1 | 13.6 | 1.2 | 0.09 |
| Teachers having to teach students of heterogeneous ability levels within the same class | 45.1 | 15.9 | 45.1 | 15.0 | 0.0 | 0.00 |
| Staff resisting change | 74.4 | 10.9 | 76.5 | 14.0 | −2.1 | −0.15 |
| Teachers having to teach students of diverse ethnic backgrounds within the same class | 81.3 | 13.0 | 83.9 | 10.9 | −2.6 | −0.24 |

*Source*: OECD (2013), Figure IV.5.7: 178
*Note*: Effect sizes were calculated as the differences divided by the OECD Members' standard deviations.

- Teachers not being well prepared for classes
- Poor teacher–student relations
- Students not being encouraged to achieve their full potential
- Teacher absenteeism

### *OECD Partner principals' views*

At the same time, more OECD partner principals believed that teachers having to teach students of diverse ethnic backgrounds within the same class has an effect on student learning. However, the two groups of principals show no difference in their views regarding the effect on student learning of staff resisting change and teachers having to teach students of heterogeneous ability levels within the same class.

Thus, it is clear that OECD Member principals held a stronger view of teacher effect since more of them believed that many of the listed negative teacher behaviors would influence student learning. However, more than would their OECD Partner counterparts, OECD Member principals would expect teachers to encourage students to achieve their potential, to maintain good relations with students, to hold high expectation of students, to meet students' individual needs, not to be absent from school, not to be too strict with students, not to be late for classes, and to be well prepared for classes. On the other hand, OECD Partner principals would expect less of such behavior from their teaching staff.

For the observed differences, the effect sizes vary from a negligible Glass's $\Delta = |0.15|$ (Staff resisting change) to a moderate Glass's $\Delta = |0.68|$ (Teachers being late for classes). Although the effect sizes are not large in magnitude, the differences between the two sets of principals cannot escape attention.

## *Teacher involvement in management*

The opportunity for teachers to be involved in school matters of a managerial nature can be expected to be related to teacher morale as such involvement may heighten the teachers' sense of ownership. Table 6 shows the extent to which principals acknowledged involvement of their teachers in school management.

Responses to two of the three questions show that OECD Member principals provided fewer opportunities for teachers to be involved in managerial matters of the school. On the other hand, more OECD Partner principals indicated that they engaged teachers to help build a culture of continuous improvement in school and asked teachers to participate in reviewing the school's management practices. This shows a clear differentiation of the role of principals and that of teachers among the OECD Member principals. However, the effect sizes vary widely from a negligible Glass's $\Delta = |0.15|$ (Making decisions) to a nearly large Glass's $\Delta = |0.73|$ (Reviewing management practices). These, again, seem to show the greater differentiation of the respective roles of principals and teachers among OECD Members.

**Table 6.** Teacher Participation in School Management (More than once a week %).

|  | Member (N = 34) Mean | SD | Partner (N = 31) Mean | SD | Mean Diff. | Effect size |
|---|---|---|---|---|---|---|
| Provide staff with opportunities to make decisions concerning the school | 18.2 | 8.2 | 19.8 | 10.9 | −1.6 | −0.15 |
| Engage teachers to help build a culture of continuous improvement in the school | 23.3 | 11.0 | 26.9 | 12.1 | −3.6 | −0.30 |
| Ask teachers to participate in reviewing management practices | 5.5 | 5.5 | 10.6 | 7.0 | −5.1 | −0.73 |

*Source*: OECD (2013), Figure IV.4.6: 140
*Note*: Effect sizes were calculated as the differences divided by the OECD Members' standard deviations.

**Table 7.** Principals' Views of Teacher Morale.

|  | Member (N = 34) Mean | SD | Partner (N = 31) Mean | SD | Mean Diff. | Effect Size |
|---|---|---|---|---|---|---|
| Teachers work with enthusiasm | 94.0 | 5.3 | 93.1 | 7.0 | 0.9 | 0.13 |
| Teachers value academic achievement | 97.0 | 4.6 | 96.7 | 2.5 | 0.3 | 0.12 |
| Teachers take pride in this school | 95.1 | 3.3 | 95.4 | 3.9 | −0.3 | −0.08 |
| The morale of teachers in this school is high | 91.4 | 7.8 | 93.7 | 6.8 | −2.3 | −0.34 |

*Source*: OECD (2013), Figure IV.5.8: 179
*Note*: Effect sizes were calculated as the differences divided by the OECD Members' standard deviations.

### Teacher morale

Principals' views of teacher morale are shown in Table 7. Slightly more OECD Partner principals indicated that teachers in their school had high morale than did OECD Member principals; the effect size is a small

Glass's Δ = |0.34|. Other than this, there are negligible or no differences between the two groups regarding teachers' enthusiasm in work, taking pride in the school, and valuing academic achievement. However, the percentages for these are all very high for both groups, hovering around 95 percent. In sum, teacher morale was very high in all countries and somewhat higher in OECD Partner countries, as reported by the principals.

## Principals' Views of Student Effect

Knowing how principals see their students may also contribute to a better understanding of how principals operate in their schools with the goal of enhancing student achievement.

Being heads of schools, principals are normally held responsible for student achievement and behavior, and they therefore naturally are concerned with these. As shown in Table 8, generally, more OECD Member principals than OECD Partner principals believed that the following three misbehaviors of students will affect their achievement, although the differences are small between the two groups of principals, with effect sizes varying from Glass's Δ's of |0.24| to |0.33|:

- Use of alcohol or illegal drugs
- Truancy
- Not attending compulsory school events

On the other hand, more OECD Partner principals than OECD Member principals believed that disruption of classes would affect student achievement. The two groups of principals did not differ concerning skipping classes, arriving late for school, and lacking respect for teachers. However, for these misbehaviors, the percentages of principals with such beliefs are relative high at two-thirds or more of the principals surveyed.

With these responses, it may be concluded that OECD Member principals would be more actively demanding good behavior of their students than would OECD Partner principals.

Table 8. Principals' Views on Student Behaviors Affecting Learning.

| | Member (N = 34) Mean | SD | Partner (N = 31) Mean | SD | Mean Diff. | Effect Size |
|---|---|---|---|---|---|---|
| Student use of alcohol or illegal drugs | 94.0 | 4.8 | 90.8 | 9.7 | 3.2 | 0.33 |
| Student truancy | 68.1 | 13.9 | 60.8 | 23.7 | 7.3 | 0.31 |
| Students not attending compulsory school events | 86.9 | 5.9 | 84.9 | 8.7 | 2.1 | 0.24 |
| Students intimidating or bullying other students | 89.2 | 6.3 | 87.5 | 10.0 | 1.6 | 0.16 |
| Students skipping classes | 64.9 | 15.8 | 67.1 | 21.2 | 2.3 | 0.11 |
| Students arriving late for school | 68.8 | 9.9 | 68.1 | 16.2 | 0.7 | 0.04 |
| Students lacking respect for teachers | 80.9 | 6.8 | 80.1 | 12.3 | 0.9 | 0.07 |
| Disruption of classes by students | 67.6 | 11.6 | 72.6 | 16.3 | −5.0 | −0.31 |

*Source*: OECD (2013), Figures IV.5.5: 174

## Putting It Together

The findings of the comparisons between the two sets of principals can be summarized thus:

1. OECD Members as a group out-performed the OECD Partners in all three subjects assessed in PISA 2012. While the correlations among the subjects are extremely high for the OECD Members, they do not have the same pattern for the OECD Partners.
2. Principal leadership in OECD Members is more homogeneous but it is not as active as that of OECD Partners which is also more heterogeneous. Moreover, principal leadership has a greater impact on student achievement for OECD Partners than for OECD Members.

3. More OECD Member principals believe that certain *negative* teacher behaviors (e.g., low expectation of students, being late for classes, etc.) will ill-affect student learning.
4. Teachers of OECD Partners were given more opportunity to be involved in managerial matters of the schools.
5. Teacher morale is generally high for both sets of countries and there is not much difference between them, although it is somewhat higher among OECD Partners.
6. More OECD Member principals believe that certain *negative* student behaviors (i.e., use of alcohol or illegal drugs, truancy, not attending compulsory school events) will have an ill-effect on achievement.

When these findings are put together, it is obvious that principals of OECD Members and OECD Partners differ *in degree* in their beliefs about the impact of *negative* teacher and student behaviors on student achievement. The general impression is that principals of OECD Members are less active but more demanding where teacher and student behaviors are concerned. Moreover, school management is more concentrated in OECD Members and, correspondingly, more shared among teachers in OECD Partners.

It is interesting that such differences seem to be associated with student achievement and, paradoxically, *negatively* so. This seems contrary to the commonsensical expectation that more active principal leadership should lead to better student achievement — an expectation borne out by previous within-country studies of the past two decades. Specifically, it is paradoxical that change in principal leadership leads to minor negative change in student achievement in OECD Members but it leads to a sizable positive increase in OECD Partners. The ratio is as high as an astonishing six times (−0.6 compared with 3.65, Table 4 above) and this calls for an explanation.

Commonsense has it and past studies suggest that more active principal leadership should lead to better student achievement, albeit through a long chain of managerial actions and teacher behaviors. In other words, principal leadership is usually seen as a cause in the educating process within a school. Viewed this way, the finding of this study does not make good sense since OECD Partner principals are found to be more active while their students have poorer achievement, and a change in principal leadership in OECD Members is associated with a slight decrease in achievement, contradicting that in OECD Partners.

As is well-known, correlation is bi-directional because a correlation between two variables does not indicate which of them is the cause and which the effect. Principal leadership is always assumed to be the cause, causing the effect on student achievement. Thus, when the relationship between principal leadership and student achievement is reversed — that is, student achievement is the cause and principal leadership the effect — the above finding ceases to be paradoxical but logical.

This means that when student are doing well, principals feel safe with their leadership style and do not exert stronger leadership. On the other hand, when students are not doing well, the principals feel the need to exert stronger leadership. If this truly happened, it explains why OECD Member principals are less active in their leadership — their students are achieving — whereas the opposite situation is found with OECD Partner principals. Another understanding of the paradox is to evoke the concept of ecological fallacy. Of the four statistical ecological fallacies, we are interested here in *the confusion between ecological correlations and individual correlations.* The within-country studies reviewed above show a positive correlation between principal leadership and student achievement, and these are likely to lead to the expectation of the same result in international or between-country studies. However, while the national studies usually use the student as the unit of analysis, the re-analysis of PISA data in the present study uses the country mean as the unit of analysis. As such, to expect the same result might be committing the ecological fallacy, wherein the finding for individual data is transferred to aggregated or ecological data.

When individual correlation and ecological correlation are compared, two possible situations arise: (1) the correlations are consistent (i.e., both are positive or negative), or (2) the correlations are in opposite direction (i.e., one positive and the other negative). The present study falls into the second situation: positive correlations are expected (based on previous individual correlations) but they turn out to be negative. This is illustrated in Figure 1.

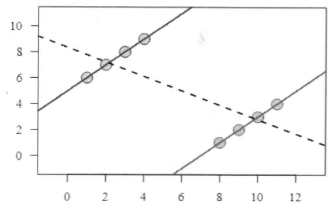

**Figure 1.** Ecological Fallacy.

In Figure 1, the two southwest–northeast lines represent two within-country studies which found positive individual correlations between high achievement (X) and principal leadership (Y); the lower-right line for an OECD Member and the upper-left an OECD Partner. When an ecological correlation is calculated using the two country means, the correlation between principal leadership and student achievement turns out to be negative. If this is what happened, then both positive and negative correlations are true representations of the situation, one at the individual level and the other ecological in nature.

In conclusion, if this makes sense, due caution is needed to interpret the causal relation between principal leadership and student achievement, when interpreting the results of international comparative studies such as PISA and the like.

## References

Hallinger, P., Bickman, L., and Davis, K. (1996). School context, principal leadership, and student reading achievement. *The Elementary School Journal,* **96**(5), 527–549.

Leithwood, K., Louis, K. S., Anderson, S., and Wahlstrom, K. (2004). *Review of Research: How Leadership Influences Student Learning.* Center for Applied Research and Educatioal Improvement, University of Minnesota, Ontario

Institute for Studies in Education at the University of Toronto, and The Wallace foundation.

Moffitt, J. R. (2007). *What Works: Principal Leadership Behaviors that Positively Impact Student Achievement in Elementary Schools*. Doctor of Education Dissertation. Electronic Theses & Dissertations. 264. Available at http://digitalcommons.georgiasouthern.edu/etd/264

OECD (2013). *PISA 2012 Results: What Makes a School Successful? Resources, Policies, and Practices (Volume IV)*, PISA, OECD Publishing.

OECD (2014). *PISA 2012 Results: What Students Know and Can Do: Student Performance in Mathematics, Reading and Science (Volume I, Revised edition February 2014)*, PISA, OECD Publishing.

Sebastian, J. and Allensworth, E. (2012). The influence of principal leadership on classroom instruction and student learning: a study of mediated pathways to learning. *Educational Administration Quarterly*, **48**(4), 626–663.

Shortridge, K. (2015). *Principals' Leadership Styles and the Impact on Student Achievement*. Doctor of Education Dissertation. Digital Repository at the University of Maryland. DOI: 10.13016/M25P84

Suskavcevic, M. and Blake, S. (2004). Principals' leadership and student achievement: An examination of the TIMSS 1999. University of Texas at El Paso, USA. Available at http://www.iea.nl/sites/default/files/irc/IRC2004_Suskavcevic_Blake.pdf

# Part III

# Reading, Science, and Mathematics

## Chapter 5

# PIRLS 2011 Reading and the Effects of Home, School, and Classroom Factors: Confirming and Contradicting Findings

There is no denying that reading is the most important subject in the school curriculum. Reading is the key to learning other subjects that require reading competence. Beyond the school years, reading is needed for handling many real-life tasks on and off the job. Besides, the development of a keen interest in reading affords an individual to access up-to-date information from print and digital sources as well as develop a pleasant pastime. It is not by chance that reading is a focus of international comparative studies such as the *Programme for International Student Assessment* (PISA; OECD, 2009) and *Progress in International Reading Literacy Study* (PIRLS; Mullis, Martin, Foy, and Drucker, 2012).

Both PISA and PIRLS recognize that reading is affected by a host of factors at home and in school. In addition to measuring the students' ability to read, these international surveys also gather (through questionnaires for students, teachers, and principals) information that is relevant to an understanding of reading performance. Specifically, in various chapters of its report, PIRLS covers home environment support, school resources, school climate, teacher preparation, and classroom instruction. In each of these aspects, there is a spectrum of indicators. All these are witness to the complexity of the seemingly simple ability to read.

This being the case, it is readily appreciated that any study, like the present one, will not be able to cover comprehensively all possible variables; it has to be selective. Basically, this study chooses mainly variables which are amendable or alterable by the teachers or principals. For example, PIRLS reports on the socioeconomic background of students. This is an important variable, as has been shown by numerous previous studies, that has an influence on reading. It, however, cannot be altered by teachers and principals, who can only accept it as a given condition. On the other hand, resources at home and in school, emphasis on reading, instructional practices — these are what parents, teachers, and principals can do to enhance student reading.

With specific reference to African American students who have consistently been found to be weaker in reading, Flower (2007) highlights promising areas of research and related educational practices, some of which are currently overlooked by reading researchers: (1) standardized testing, (2) teacher quality, (3) after-school programs, (4) parent involvement, (5) reading and study skills, and (6) computer games and simulations. After making specific recommendations, Flower (2007: 426) concluded thus,

> Improving reading achievement and enhancing reading skills…must remain a top priority for reading researchers…It is important to acknowledge that in addition to the issues discussed in this article, many other factors and variables require examination to gain a deeper understanding of how to improve students' reading achievement in schools, such as the educational environment, school setting, and physical and emotional characteristics of students.

Most of those areas identified by Flower (2007) are covered in PIRLS 2012 and the findings are reported in the various chapters of the PIRLS report (Mullis, Martin, Foy, and Drucker, 2012). The present secondary analysis is an attempt to bring together information scattered in the different chapters and present their relationships in a more integrated and compact manner for ease of comprehension and interpretation.

## Home Factors

It is a truism that home factors influence students' reading activity and hence reading achievement. To illustrate, a few articles are summarized below to highlight the importance of home factors that have been found to contribute to the development of the reading literacy of young students.

Using data from the earliest PIRLS 2001, Geske and Ozola (2008) re-analyzed the reading and other relevant scores of Fourth Grade students (N = 3,019) in Latvia (ranked fifth among the 35 countries, after Sweden, Netherlands, English, and Bulgaria). They found that the socioeconomic position of the family considerably influenced student reading achievement and that students usually had more books if their parents were well-educated. Collaboration between parents and children at the pre-school age also substantially influenced reading literacy. Moreover, children who read a wider variety of materials performed better.

In a secondary analysis of PIRLS 2006 data, Chan, Ko, and Tse (2008) compared students (N = 36,540) aged between nine and 10 from Chinese community (Hong Kong, Singapore, and Taiwan) and non-Chinese community (Canada and Russia). The two communities were matched for national means for PIRLS Reading. They examined family reading practices, including parents' evaluation of a child's early literacy skills, early home literacy activities, parent–child reading activities, parental reading attitudes and habits, books in the home, and children's books in the home. The results show that parents in the Chinese community held higher estimates of children's early literacy skills but there were lower reading activities between parents and children. Chinese parents' reading attitudes were moderate. By comparison, Chinese homes had *fewer* books; however, possession of books at home and children's books explained 1% to 9% of variance of students' reading achievement after controlling for children's early literacy skills. The patterns of regression are more similar than different between the two communities.

The complexity of home factors in reading was illustrated by Chatterji (2006). This study estimated reading achievement gaps in different ethnic, gender, and socioeconomic groups in the U.S., compared with specific reference groups with reference to correlates and moderators of early reading achievement. The data analysed was for a subset of kindergarten to First Grade students (N = 2,296) from 184 schools of the Early Childhood Longitudinal Study (ECLS). With child-level background differences controlled, significantly lower scores were found in African American children, boys, and children from high-poverty households when compared with White children. And the size of reading gaps increased with years of schooling. Reading level at kindergarten was a significant child-level correlate, related to poverty status. At the school level, class size and elementary teacher certification rate correlated with reading scores. Moreover, cross-level interactions indicated that reading achievement in African American children was moderated by the school they attended, with attendance rates and reading time at home explaining the variance.

Tse *et al.* (2010) re-analyzed data of Hong Kong Fourth Graders' data (N = 5,050) for PIRLS 2001. They examined the relations among family factors such as financial, human, and social variables on reading performance. Positive correlations were found for most family variables. Parents were found to be well placed to provide a stimulating home environment and served as positive role models for reading development. However, negative correlations were found for cultural idiosyncrasies such as unwillingness to be seen going to school to discuss their children's progress. It was concluded that the parents were able to provide a conducive home environment for developing reading but needed some guidance to maximize its effect.

While PIRLS and similar international comparative studies compare countries which understandably have very different social and educational contexts, Friedlander (2013) cautions that the local context should not be overlooked when considering reading achievement. His study examines associations between socioeconomic status, home literacy environment, and reading achievement in the developing world. Models that predict reading achievement were created and the patterns across countries were analyzed. Correlation coefficients for achievement and SES, as well as achievement and home literacy environment were compared. The author found significant between-country variations in both socioeconomic status and home literacy environment. Results from the study support the contention that education efforts in the developing world must consider local context to achieve their goals.

While studies of home factors contributing to reading development of young children vary in detail, they nevertheless consistently show their positive effects, especially parents' educational level, parental involvement in reading activities, and the availability of children's books at home.

Table 1. Home Factors.

| Variable | Home Support |
|---|---|
| Resources | 0.966 |
| Higher Education | 0.780 |
| Professional Job | 0.913 |
| Books > 100 | 0.907 |
| Room, Internet | 0.876 |
| Parent Reading | 0.727 |
| Total variance explained | 74.84% |

According the PIRLS, conditions at home that influence students' reading ability are resources, parental educational and job levels, number of books, facilities (study room and Internet), and parental reading habits.

As shown in Table 1, when the PIRLS 2011 data for such indicators was factor-analyzed, one general factor accounting for 75% of the total variance was obtained. The factor loadings are all very high, varying from 0.727 (Parent Reading) to 0.966 (Resources). The result suggests that for a country to score high on Reading, the students need to have the necessary resources, parents to hold high-level jobs, a large number of books, a study room, and access to the Internet. These factors may or may not directly facilitate the development of reading ability, but they help.

## School Factors

It is readily appreciated that school conditions influence students' development of reading over and beyond the influence of home factors. School factors may include the emphasis placed on reading, grouping of students for instruction, and resources (e.g., library, computer, and other materials needed for reading).

Using the Cyprus data of Fourth Graders (N = 3,001) from the PIRLS 2001, Papanastasiou (2008) found significant differences between high and low scoring schools on reading performance on several school factors: activities following reading instruction, reading outside school time, time spent on homework, attitude toward reading, activities during teaching, and school climate. Likewise, Kotte, Leitz, and Lopez (2005) conducted a multi-level analysis of data for Germany and Spain of the PISA 2000 Reading. Of particular interest here is the school-level analysis for which they found reading achievement to be influenced by assessment policy, access to reading materials, ratio of computer per student, instructional resources, and principal's perception of students' learning and disrespect for teachers.

It is a common notion that more reading leads to better reading and that more access to books results in more reading. This is where the school library can make its contribution to reading development. Making use of the reading scores and relevant questionnaire responses of 35 countries available in the PIRLS 2006 survey, Krashen, Lee, and McQuillan (2010) ran a multiple regression with reading score as the criterion. They found socioeconomic status to be the stronger predictor ($\beta = 0.42$) of reading achievement, thus confirming the importance of home influence mentioned above. This was followed closely by school library ($\beta = 0.34$), indicating the importance of one particular school factor beyond the influence of home resource. These two are the only statistically significant predictors out of four, while the two non-significant predictors are independent reading and average hours per week for reading instruction.

In her comprehensive review conducted for the Australian School Library Association, Lonsdale (2013) concluded that school libraries could have a positive impact on student reading as well as some other aspects of learning. She further noted that collaborative relationships between the teachers and librarians had a significant impact on learning, that a print-rich environment led to more reading, and that free voluntary reading was the best predictor of comprehension, vocabulary growth, spelling and grammatical ability, and writing style. It is also interesting to note that the extent to which books were borrowed from school libraries showed a strong relationship with reading achievement but not borrowing from classroom libraries.

Ability grouping is one of the most controversial issues in education, with proponents and opponents alike. Recently, Scharenberg (2012) presented findings within the context of a longitudinal study carried out in Germany. The study involved Eighth Graders (N = 5,941) in 331 classes. At the class level, a heterogeneous classroom composition was neither associated with a higher nor with a lower reading achievement. However,

Table 2. School Factors.

|  | Resources | Emphasis | Condition |
|---|---|---|---|
| Resources | 0.829 | — | — |
| Computer | 0.804 | — | — |
| Early Emphasis on Reading | 0.643 | 0.465 | 0.353 |
| Library | 0.560 | — | — |
| Emphasis by Principal | — | 0.960 | — |
| Emphasis by Teachers | — | 0.959 | — |
| Condition | — | — | 0.957 |
| Total variance explained | 29.85% | 30.24% | 15.65% |

*Note*: Factor loadings less than |0.3| are omitted.

high-ability and high-SES classes were found to be more effective in reading (again, confirming the importance of home influence). Further analyses showed that the class composition was highly confounded with the different tracks. Thus, classroom composition in itself does not seem to enhance reading development, and other factors need be considered as interacting conditions.

In PIRLS, school factors include resources, school library, condition for teaching, personal computer, principal and teacher emphasis on reading, and emphasis on reading in the earlier grades. Factor analysis of the data of these indicators yielded three orthogonal factors accounting for 76% of the total variance (Table 2). The first factor, which accounts for 33% of total variance, is formed by Resources, Library, Computer, and Early emphasis on reading. The second factor, which accounts for another 30% of total variance, is formed by three predictors of Emphasis. Lastly, the third factor, which accounts for 16% of total variance, is formed mainly by Condition and, to a lesser extent, by Early emphasis on reading. In PIRLS, Condition means proper school building, uncrowded classroom, adequate teaching hours, suitable workspace, and sufficient supply of instructional materials.

## Classroom Factors

While home conditions and school factors set the scene, so to speak, teaching and learning are possible only in the classroom where the action takes place. In this regard, the degree of active student involvement during reading lessons and the amount of time there is for learning to read can be critical to reading development.

It is a common belief that time for learning directly affects the outcome of learning and a linear relation between time and achievement is always assumed. As cited by Samuels and Wu (n.d.), the National Reading Panel concluded that it was hard to find clear evidence to support the idea that reading especially benefited students in reading achievement. The Panel made this conclusion based on a meta-analysis of 14 studies. However, the authors challenged the Panel's conclusion with an experiment involving Grade Three and Grade Five students (N = 72). The experimental students read books for 40 minutes a day while the control students read books for 15 minutes a day. The experiment lasted for six months and there was therefore an estimated difference of about 50 hours of reading between the two groups. Somewhat disappointed, the authors concluded that *"We do not have a simple answer regarding the question of how the amount of time spent on reading affects reading achievement because we failed to found a main effect for time"* (Samuels and Wu, n.d.: 16–17).

There are other classroom conditions of interest to reading educators, in the PIRLS context. Bellin, Dunge, and Gunzenhauser (n.d.), using the PIRLS 2006 data, explored the effects of class composition and teachers' instructional practices on reading achievement in German primary schools and considered the effects of class composition in terms of social and linguistic characteristics. They also investigated whether modified instruction by teachers met the needs of individual students and alleviated the effects of a disadvantageous class composition. The results indicated the importance of individual resources and also the effects of class composition in terms of language and educational resources on students' reading achievement. They found organizational approaches did not relate to reading achievement and did not reduce the effects of a disadvantageous class composition. Also, teachers in heterogeneous classes were already using a variety of instructional methods to accommodate the varying achievement levels. It was concluded that controlling for the variety of methods might not be a sufficient means of explaining the transmission processes of class composition: teacher and student interactions at the micro level might also be important factors.

Table 3.  Classroom Factors.

|  | Engagement | Time |
|---|---|---|
| Engagement (reported by teachers) | 0.884 | — |
| Engagement (reported by students) | 0.923 | — |
| Instructional Hours | — | 0.626 |
| Language Time | — | 0.787 |
| Reading Time | — | 0.690 |
| Total variance explained | 35.59% | 29.87% |

*Note*: Factor loadings less than |0.3| are omitted.

As shown in Table 3, three measures of classroom conditions of PIRLS 2011 were analyzed and the five measures formed two factors which together account for 66% of total variance. The first factor, which accounts for 36% of total variance, is formed by engagement as reported by teachers and by students, suggesting that active involvement in the reading lessons was one important aspect of classroom instruction. The second factor accounts for 30% of total variance and is formed by the time for language teaching and reading instruction.

## Clustering Countries

PIRLS ranked the 45 countries based on national means for Reading, thus yielding 45 'groups' of one country each. In fact, many of the adjacently ranked countries have very small differences in Reading. This creates an erroneous impression that the test is a very sensitive and precise measure which is able to discriminate finely. This creates the problem of spurious precision where miniscule differences in decimal values which have little substantive meanings are capitalized on for the purpose of ranking. The problem is partly due to the use of a very long scale with a mean of 500 and a standard deviation of 100 for such a small number of countries. Such a scale has theoretically 600 points (theoretically three standard deviations on each side of the mean) to spread across the 45 countries on the continuum and is unnecessarily long.

In all fairness, PIRLS does indicate that many of the countries do not differ with statistical significance on Reading (Mullis *et al.*, 2012,

Exhibit 1.3: 40); for example, Hong Kong, Russia, Finland, and Singapore are indicated as *not different from one another*. The four countries fall within a range of four scale points while their standard errors vary from 1.9 (Finland) to 3.3 (Singapore), and the four-point difference can well be attributed to sampling error. For this reason, the four countries are logically taken to be equivalent in Reading, in spite of the seeming differences of national means of 571 (Hong Kong), 568 (Finland and Russia), and 567 (Singapore). There are more countries which are found to be not statistically different from one another throughout the Reading scale. Unfortunately, these meaningless small differences are either carelessly overlooked or purposively ignored by commentators.

As the PIRLS ranking is based only on Reading, it is more meaningful and informative to group the countries on relevant indicators considered together. This was done by running a K-Means Cluster Analysis. Moreover, to facilitate presentation and interpretation, all national means were T-transformed to a common scale (with a mean of 50 and a standard deviation of 10, one-tenth of the original scale). It must be emphasized that this transformation does not change the relative positions of the countries on the various measures yet makes scores (means) comparable across variables.

As shown in Table 4, the analysis resulted in two clusters, with 22 in one group and 23 in another. The first group has a higher mean for Reading and hence is named High Cluster, the second group Low Cluster; the difference is 7.9, with a Glass's $\Delta = 1.20$, indicating a large difference.

Comparisons were hence made between the two Clusters. Countries in the High Cluster scored higher in Reading, Home Support, Emphasis, Condition, and Engagement, with large effect sizes (Glass's $\Delta > 0.80$) except Emphasis (Glass's $\Delta = 0.33$). On the other hand, Low Cluster scored higher on Resources (Glass's $\Delta = -0.67$), Condition (Glass's $\Delta = -1.03$), and Time (Glass's $\Delta = -2.04$); these seem to go against the common expectation that resources and time will make positive contributions to learning to read. This surprising difference will be discussed subsequently.

## Discussion and Conclusion

It must first be admitted that the findings may not add much to what is known about reading. However, the article integrates information that is

Table 4. Clusters of Countries.

| | High Cluster (N = 22) | Low Cluster (N = 23) | Difference | Effect Size |
|---|---|---|---|---|
| Reading | 54.0 (6.6) | 46.1 (11.1) | 7.9 | 1.20 |
| Home Support | 56.2 (7.6) | 44.1 (8.3) | 12.1 | 1.59 |
| Engagement | 53.9 (9.1) | 46.2 (9.3) | 7.7 | 0.85 |
| Emphasis | 51.7 (10.2) | 48.4 (9.6) | 3.4 | 0.33 |
| Resource | 47.3 (7.8) | 52.5 (11.2) | −5.2 | −0.67 |
| Condition | 48.5 (2.9) | 51.5 (13.5) | −3.0 | −1.03 |
| Time | 42.6 (7.1) | 57.1 (6.7) | −14.5 | −2.04 |
| Country | Hong Kong SAR<br>Finland<br>Singapore<br>Northern Ireland<br>Denmark<br>Chinese Taipei<br>England<br>Ireland<br>Canada<br>Netherlands<br>Czech Republic<br>Sweden<br>Germany<br>Israel<br>Italy<br>New Zealand<br>Austria<br>Australia<br>Norway<br>Belgium (French)<br>United Arab Emirates<br>Saudi Arabia | Russian Federation<br>United States<br>Croatia<br>Portugal<br>Hungary<br>Slovak Republic<br>Bulgaria<br>Slovenia<br>Lithuania<br>Poland<br>France<br>Spain<br>Romania<br>Georgia<br>Malta<br>Trinidad and Tobago<br>Azerbaijan<br>Iran, Islamic Rep. of<br>Colombia<br>Indonesia<br>Qatar<br>Oman<br>Morocco | | |

*Note*: (1) In each cluster, the countries are listed in descending order of Reading means. (2) Standardized mean difference (SMD) = Difference/Average SD. (3) SMD is evaluated by Cohen's (1988) criteria where 0.0–0.2 is trivial, 0.2–0.5 small, 0.5–0.8 moderate, and 0.8 and above large.

spread over several chapters of the voluminous PIRLS report (Mullis, Martin, Foy, and Drucker, 2012), turning that information into a compact and integral form. This will facilitate understanding a complex phenomenon by teachers, curriculum designers, and school administrators.

The 17 variables pertaining to home, school, and classroom conditions relevant to student reading fall into six independent factors that can be meaningfully interpreted. The finding that home support differentiates between countries of higher and lower Reading means does not come as a surprise. This is expected as tools and opportunity must be readily available before learning (of reading) can take place. Beyond this, that educational and job level of parents plays a role in students' reading is also expected, as parents in such favorable conditions are more likely to take reading seriously and their attitude to education can be subtly passed on to their children. This can be further enhanced by the parents' reading habits, serving a modelling function. In short, the importance of home support in various forms to students' reading cannot be over-emphasized.

The findings that High Cluster countries score higher on Emphasis and Engagement also match commonsense expectations. When principals and teachers emphasize reading, especially in the early grades, they naturally put more effort into developing reading among their students. This naturally leads to better performance. Likewise, when teachers engage their students in their lessons, students are actively involved in the learning process and are not put in a position of passive receiving. They will be actively processing linguistic input, which is fundamental to learning language and reading. This leads to the expectation of better reading performance.

The school and classroom form an arena where learning to read is played out constantly. The emphasis on reading by the principal and teachers, especially in the early years of schooling, may have two related effects on the student's reading development. First, the emphasis sends the message to youngsters that reading is valued by adults and hence is worthy of their effort — that reading will lead to praise, which satisfies the young learners' psychological need for recognition and encouragement. Secondly, the emphasis also means more time and resources will be allotted to reading, thus providing the necessary conditions for effective learning to occur.

In more concrete terms, the active engagement of students is the road to successful learning of reading (or any other subjects) for the simple reason that young students learn best by actively doing what they are supposed to learn. Traditional passive exposure to teacher talk may improve listening but reading requires active responses to the reading materials — taking it apart and putting the parts together, relating the parts to previous reading experience. Such active engagement in reading is further strengthened by having the computer around as another readily available source of reading materials and practice.

However, there are three factors (Resource, Condition, and Time) in which, contrary to the commonsense expectation, the Low Cluster countries score higher. Common sense has it that more instructional resources and curriculum time will lead to a better learning outcome. What has been observed here is just the opposite, and this calls for an explanation.

One possible explanation of the contradiction is *ecological fallacy*. In the studies reviewed, the individual student is the unit of analysis, but in the present study the country is the unit of analysis. While national means were used as though they were scores of the nations, they were in fact aggregated or ecological data. Ecological fallacy occurs when findings based on individual data is applied to aggregated data, and vice versa, and when analyses at the different levels yield different and even opposite results.

A study by Tainton (1990) illustrates this clearly. When the intercorrelations among 12 variables were calculated using individual teachers (N = 670) as the unit of analysis, as compared with when schools (N = 45) were the unit of analysis, many of the correlation coefficients changed not only in magnitude but also in direction, from being positive to negative and vice versa.

If this is a correct interpretation of the reversal, caution is necessary when reading the findings based on individual data (as done in the cited studies for which individual students form the unit of analysis) and expecting the same to happen when group data is analyzed (as done in the present study for which the country is the unit of analysis). This raises a further pertinent question.

PIRLS and other similar international comparisons (e.g., TIMSS and PISA) report national means and use these to rank the countries. Explicitly, the country is the *unit of analysis* and the national performance is the focus of the study, for which the students are *unit of observation* needed to estimate the national performance. As data of the individual students are available, many studies (e.g., those cited above) use student data for analysis at the level of individual students, literally treating students as the unit of analysis. Wouldn't doing this be committing ecological fallacy, thus rending the results doubtful and confusing?

Even more surprising is that Low Cluster countries assign more curriculum time for language and reading instruction; in fact, the correlation between Reading and Time is a negative r = –0.376. Time for learning is usually thought of as a contributing factor to learning; thus, a *linear positive* correlation is expected between time and reading achievement. With this expectation, the negative time-reading correlation is rather unexpected and counter-intuitive. However, it has been reported recently that the relation between time and achievement is more complex than previously assumed (Soh, circa 2013).

Common sense has it that there is a positive relation between the time available for learning and the outcome of learning. The international average of time spent on language and reading is 905 hours per school year, but the time for each country varies widely, from 643 (Lithuania) to 1297 (Indonesia), two countries which happen to be at the lower end of the Reading league table. The international average of instruction time devoted specifically to reading is only 70 hours per year, and the national means vary from 37 (Malta) to 131 (United States and New Zealand).

Although a direct relation between instruction time for reading and attainment in reading is usually expected, this assumption has recently been questioned (Soh, circa 2013) where PISA Science literacy (which has an extremely high correlation greater than r = 0.9 with PISA Reading) is concerned. It was found that the relation between time and achievement is better described as negative, where high-achieving countries have *less* time for instruction and low-achieving ones have more. This finding corroborates with the finding of the present study, albeit in different subjects.

It is possible that the positive relation between time and achievement works up to a point, beyond which the relation goes in the opposite direction, thus forming a curvilinear relation instead of a linear or straight one.

It is also possible that countries not doing well in reading decide to allot more time to reading as a way of coping with the problem. These explanations, however, call for due caution as instruction time is one factor, important though it may be, but not the only factor; the solution may have to be found elsewhere, especially in instructional strategies.

It appears that the causal direction from time to achievement has to be reversed to understand the negative correlation obtained for the PIRLS data. In other words, actual or expected low reading level is causing low-achieving countries to assign more curriculum time for the learning of language and reading as a coping strategy, while high-achieving countries do not see the need to do so. When this is done, a negative correlation between reading achievement and time for teaching and learning language and reading is understandable. The same argument (of reversing the causal direction) may be posited for the finding that High Cluster countries as a group have a lower mean for Resources and Condition. Low Cluster countries may find it necessary to invest more resources and to ensure conducive classroom conditions to inoculate against poorer reading performance.

The advantage of having a classroom condition conducive to learning to read is readily appreciated. In such a classroom, the teacher is able to focus on her main tasks without being distracted by ill-disciplined students using her and her student's time and effort on non-productive behavior. It is easy to imagine that when a teacher has to handle misbehaving students, the teaching of reading has to be withheld for some time, during which no learning takes place. On a different tack, a noisy, crowded, and uncomfortable classroom makes learning to read difficult as the classroom is distracting, to both the teacher and her students.

In conclusion, the present study, which re-analyzed PIRLS 2011 data at the national level, has produced findings confirming as well as contradicting earlier individual studies. Findings corroborating with previous studies lend further confidence to common notions where home influence and school conditions are concerned. Findings contrary to earlier findings serve to advise the careful reading of earlier studies, especially in terms of ecological fallacy and the need of low achieving countries to inoculate against possible poorer reading performance.

## References

Bellin, N., Dunge, O., and Gunzenhauser, C. (n.d.). The importance of class composition for reading achievement, migration background, social composition, and instructional practices: An analysis of the German 2006 PIRLS data. Available at www.ierinstitute.org/.../IERI_Monograph_Volume_03_Chapter_1.pdf

Chan, Y-L, Ko, H., and Tse, S. K. (2008). Family factors and reading achievement: Chinese community perspective. Available at http://www.iea.nl/fileadmin/user_upload/IRC/IRC_2008/Papers/IRC2008_Chan_Ko_etal.pdf

Chatterji, M. (2006). Reading achievement gaps, correlates, and moderators of early reading achievement: Evidence from the early childhood longitudinal study (ECLS) Kindergarten to First Grade sample. *Journal of Educational Psychology*, **98**(3), 489–507.

Cohen, J. (1988). *Power Analysis for the Behavioural Sciences*, 2$^{nd}$ Ed. Hillsdale: Erlbaum.

Flower, L. (July/August/September 2007). Recommendations for research to improve reading achievement for African American students. *Reading Research Quarterly*, **42**(3), 424–428.

Friedlander, E. (2013). Environmental factors associated with early reading achievement in the developing world: A cross-national study. *International Journal of Educational Research*, **57**, 2–38.

Geske, A. and Ozola, A. (2008). Factors influencing reading literacy at the primary school level. *Problems of Education in the 21$^{st}$ Century*, **6**, 71–77.

Kotte, D., Leitz, P., and Lopez, M. M. (2005). Factors influencing reading achievement in Germany and Spain: Evidence from PISA 2000. *International Education Journal*, **6**(1), 113–124.

Krashen, S., Lee, S., and McQuillan, J. (2010). An analysis of the PIRLS (2006) data: can the school library reduce the effect of poverty on reading achievement? *California School Library Association Journal*, **34**(1).

Lonsdale, M. (2013). *Impact of School Libraries on Student Achievement: A Review of the Research*, for the Australian School Library Association. Melbourne: Australian Council for Educational Research.

Mullis, I. V. S., Martin, M. O., Foy, P., and Drucker, K. T. (2012). Chestnut Hill, MA: TIMSS & PIRLS International Study Center, Boston College.

OECD (2009). Programme for International Student Assessment. http://www.oecd.org/pisa/

Papanastasiou, C. (2008). Factor distinguishing most and least effective schools in terms of reading achievement: A residual approach. *Educational Research and Evaluation*, **14**(6), 539–549.

Samuels, S. J. and Wu, Y-C. (n.d.) *How the Amount of Time Spent on Independent Reading Affects Reading Achievement: A Response to the National Reading Panel*. University of Minnesota.

Scharenberg, K. (2012). Do secondary students learn more in homogeneous or heterogeneous classes? The importance of classroom composition for the development of Reading achievement in secondary school. *Online Educational Research Journal*, **3**(12). Retrieved from www.oerj.org

Soh, Kaycheng (circa 2013). Is time NOT always a factor of achievement? A lesson from re-analyzing PISA data. *International Journal of TESOL and Learning*, **1**(1), 50–64.

Tainton, B. E. (1990). The unit of analysis "problem" in educational research. *Queensland Researcher*, **6**(1), 4–19.

Tse, S. K., Lam, R. Y. H., Ip, O. K. M., Lan, J. W. I., Loh, E. k. y., and Tso, A. S. F. (2010). Family resources and students' reading attainment: Capitalising on home factors. *Educational Studies in Language and Literature*, **10**(3), 27–54.

## Chapter 6

# Reading Achievement, Materials, Times, and Purposes in PISA 2010: Comparing OECD Members and Partners

Reading is important. That no one can deny. Reading is important educationally. The ability to read is needed not so much for its own sake but as a tool to effective learning of almost all other subjects in the school's curriculum. Without reading competence, students are handicapped in acquiring knowledge from print and their progress in schooling is handicapped. Reading is also important for social, economic, and political reasons. It is a common observation that the literacy level of a country is associated with its economic and political development. Countries improve their economic and political lots by first or concurrently improving their people in literacy.

### Educational Significance of Reading

Even in today's context, when electronic sources of information are so readily available, it is a well-known fact that before the days of televisions and computers, reading was the primary source of information and leisure. People in those days spent hour after hour reading in search of knowledge, to pass time in a pleasant manner, and to travel to far-away lands in their minds. Today, people have many exciting and thrilling options available to them other than books (Sofsian, n.d.). But still, reading offers a productive approach to improving one's vocabulary and word power. Moreover, reading involves greater levels of concentration and also adds to the reader's conversational skills. It enhances knowledge and helps readers decipher new words and phrases that they come across every day; through reading, readers acquire up-to-date information on various topics. It helps them to stay in-touch with contemporary matters and become better informed and more interesting people.

The importance of reading is resonated by Naik (2012) and others thus:

> The foremost thing — and undoubtedly the most important — is that reading improves your vocabulary, command on the language and, communication skills, as you regularly come across new words, phrases, idioms and, writing styles. Reading books of a variety of subjects helps you add to your knowledge, which, in turn, helps you with different attributes of life. Regular reading is also believed to boost creativity as it helps you think out of the box — look at the things from a different perspective. Studies have revealed that children who read often have better concentration ability than those who don't.

Harris (2006) goes further, suggesting that the literacy rate of a country is an indicator of her economic well-being. It reflects not only educational levels but also the country's economic power, government administration, corruption, and health. When literacy rate (an indicator of reading competence of a population) is low, the country is likely to be an economic backwater and inefficiently governed, with widespread corruption and a lack of universities, doctors, and other experts. Harris cited the situation in the African continent to illustrate the association between literacy rate and quality of life. It is argued that even in the age of multimedia, reading is still the most essential skill to acquire. The Internet means information is freely available to readers and with the advent of websites and e-books, reading continues to increase in importance. This reiterates the points made by Sofsian (n.d.) and Harris (2012) quoted above.

## Teen Reading

The importance of reading is reflected in society's interest in and concern for how youths read. Surveys on teen reading have been carried out by organizations and scholars over the years. A few are summarized below to illustrate the types of reading materials the young people are interesting in and the time they spend reading.

In early years, Shatter (1951) conducted a survey involving 16- to 19-year-olds. When the students were classified as low, normal, and advanced in academic achievement, the average numbers of books read within a six-month period by the three groups were less than one book, three books, and six books, respectively. The young people liked to read fiction more than nonfiction. Their reading list included magazines, novels, comics, and occasionally newspapers. Some gender differences were noticed: while boys read magazines related to sports, adventure, hobbies, mechanics, girls read magazines of romance, fashions, screen, and homemaking.

The 2003 *Report on Teen Read Week* (SmartGirl, n.d.) involved 3,677 respondents, of whom 3,489, or 95 percent, were between the ages of 11 and 18. Of the respondents, 63 percent made excellent or good grades in school and 48 percent reported that they enjoyed reading. To the statement "*I always read about things that I am passionate about*", 56 percent strongly agreed or agreed. But 50 percent strongly agreed or agreed with "*I did not have much time to read for pleasure, but I like to when there is the chance.*" There were, however, 22 percent who said they basically did not read non-assigned books at all, but 20 percent read 2–3 books not assigned by the school. The respondents had a wide range of daily reading: newspapers (24 percent), comic books (13 percent), and news magazines (13 percent). They also read daily magazines of special interests: fashion and beauty magazines (15 percent), sports magazines (15 percent), music and entertainment magazines (18 percent), and puzzle and game magazines (7 percent). Surprisingly, 32 percent even read daily cereal boxes or other product packaging.

Sainsbury (2004) conducted in 1998 and 2003 two surveys on attitudes of nine and 11 year olds towards reading, for the National Foundation of Educational Research, England. Results indicated that students who enjoyed reading more were generally better readers who preferred stories, magazines, and newspapers. Girls enjoyed stories, magazines, and poems whereas boys enjoyed comics, newspapers, and informational books. Of girls, 71 percent enjoyed reading and 10 percent found reading difficult.

In contrast, 66 percent of boys enjoyed reading and 14 percent found reading difficult. However, 4 percent of girls and 4 percent of boys never read at home. The findings show that gender differences in reading emerge as early as in the primary school years.

The Young Adult Library Services Association conducted yearly reading surveys for teens between the ages of 12–18 (Marra and Witteveen, 2005). The 2001–2003 results show that teens enjoyed reading adventure, mystery, fantasy, horror, and true stories, but they also liked to read about realistic characters. While 15 percent read "*just for the fun of it*", there was a large percentage indicating that they found reading boring. Moreover, a large percentage often had no time to read for pleasure. The survey concluded that teens should be encouraged to read through websites, blogs, e-books, and other online services.

As gathered from the above summaries, most young people do read and they read a wide range of materials relevant to their wide range of interests, although some have not developed the habit of reading beyond assigned reading. The fact that they cannot find time to read deserves attention, though.

## Social Significance of Reading

Reading acquires its social importance through its influence on economic and political development. The seriousness with which a government reacts to PISA survey results is reflected in national responses posted on the Internet. A few examples are sufficient to illustrate how serious the views are. From Portugal, with explicit competitive references to other countries:

> The results for Portugal indicated a very sizable improvement, when compared to 2006 and earlier results. For instance, the reading score increased from 472 to 489, placing Portugal at the OECD mean and above countries such as Spain, the Czech Republic, Slovakia or Austria. The government hailed these findings as vindication for all the reforms introduced since 2005, while many teacher blogs raised questions about the validity of the results. These questions became more vocal when the education ministry refused to release the list of presumely (*sic*) randomly-selected schools in the survey (Martins, 2011).

From the British front (Young, 2013), the PISA Reading results are taken with no less seriousness and the political overtone is hard to overlook, again with explicit competitiveness:

> British schoolchildren are now ranked... 25th for reading, according to the OECD's 2009 PISA report. That compares with a 2000 PISA ranking of ... 7th for reading... This is conclusive proof that Labour's claim to have "improved" Britain's schools during its period in office is utter nonsense. Spending on education increased by £30 billion under the last government, yet between 2000–09 British schoolchildren plummeted in the international league tables and are now ranked behind those of Poland, Estonia and Slovenia.

From down-under, the Australian response to the PISA results is stated in a matter-of-fact manner but the unhappiness in the commentary is obvious (Thomson and associates, 2010):

> The reading literacy of Australian 15-year-old students has fallen sharply over the past decade, results from the 2009 Programme for International Student Assessment (PISA) reveal... Australian students are still performing well above the OECD average but their results in reading literacy... have declined significantly over recent years. Australian students scored an average of 515 points on the 2009 reading assessments, compared to the OECD average of 493 points. Australia's overall performance declined by 13 score points from 2000 to 2009.

Response by government officials to the PISA results can sound like a national crisis as exemplified by the comment below from the USA:

> Here in the United States, we have looked forwardly eagerly to the 2009 PISA results. But the findings, I'm sorry to report, show that the United States needs to urgently accelerate student learning to remain competitive in the knowledge economy of the 21st century...Unfortunately, the 2009 PISA results show that American students are poorly prepared to compete in today's knowledge economy...The hard truth is that other high-performing nations have passed us by during the last two decades. Americans need to wake up to this educational reality — instead of napping at the wheel while emerging competitors prepare their students for economic leadership (Duncan, 2010).

A similar sense of a national crisis comes from Ireland (Education Matters, 2010), thus:

> The disappointing results of the PISA study released on December 7 were like salt on the wounds of an already smarting nation... The study places Ireland among the "average" performing countries in reading literacy, with a mean score of 495.6 (OECD mean is 493.4). Ireland's rank, based on its mean score, is 17th out of 34 OECD countries and 21st of 65 OECD and partner countries. Ireland's poor show in ... reading literacy brought an avalanche of comment from industry and education alike.

And lamenting the seemingly "*lost glory*" from Israel (Hartman, 2010):

> Israeli students' poor performance in a recent international exam shows the "colossal failure" of the country in its efforts to prepare its students for the future...This is a colossal failure that is all man-made. It wasn't like this once upon a time, and there's no justification for a country that's cleaning up in Nobel Prizes and has some of the best universities in the world to be in this situation...If the situation does not improve, Israel will not be able to compete internationally and socioeconomic gaps will only widen.

Even non-participation in the PISA has political sensitivity, as clearly shown in the case of India (Satya, 2011):

> The Indian Government seems to have been reluctant initially to participate in the Programme for International Student Assessment (PISA) tests. In reply to a question in Parliament... on the reasons for India not participating in the PISA tests,... the then Minister for HRD didn't answer the question...Subsequently, the government seems to have changed its mind and decided to participate in the PISA tests on a pilot basis.

As gathered from the quotes above, it is abundantly clear that the PISA results are given very serious thought by countries the world over. All that has been said about Reading applies equally well to Mathematics and Science, since there are extremely high correlations among the results for the three subjects (to be shown later). In a broader sense, Reading results are used as a proxy measure of the systemic effectiveness of education of the participating countries. The link between PISA results (especially Reading) and the future economic well-being of countries is explicitly assumed, although it is readily appreciated that from the students' reading achievement to their country's economic and political well-being, there are many intervening causal relations yet to be empirically demonstrated.

A common feature of the national responses is that the PISA results, in the form of national means or rankings, are accepted at face value with no questions asked about their trustworthiness in terms of reliability, validity, and measurement error. These are technical or statistical issues which cannot be discussed here and deserve separate treatments. However, a related problem is spurious precision in interpreting the scores (or national means). For example, in the Portuguese case cited above, the difference of 17 score points between 489 and 472 is said to show significant improvement; but in view of the standard deviation (SD) of 100 for the Reading scale, the difference is only 0.17 of a SD. Moreover, in view of the theoretical possible range of 600 point of the scale, the 17-point difference denotes only a change of about 3 percent score points. Likewise, the 22-point difference in the Australian case, and the 2.2-point difference in the case of Ireland are best seen in the same light.

Notwithstanding technical issues, it is clear that Reading (or PISA) has been of great concern to the participating countries as the results are taken, rightly or wrongly, as a barometer of national sustainability and international competitiveness.

## PISA and Reading

It is with such convictions that PISA (OECD, 2010: 18) takes Reading as its focus, although it also studies performance in Mathematics and Science. When justifying Reading as the focus of the mammoth international survey, it asks the following questions:

- Are students well prepared to meet the challenges of the future?
- Can they analyse, reason and communicate their ideas effectively?
- Have they found the kinds of interests they can pursue throughout their lives as productive members of the economy and society?

PISA seeks to answer the above questions by assessing the reading competence (more later) of 15-year-old students of 34 OECD Members and 31 OECD Partners. The choice of students at this age is guided by the idea that they are nearing the end of compulsory education and should have acquired knowledge and skills that are essential for full participation in modern societies. PISA purports to assess more than whether students can reproduce knowledge, but also how well they can extrapolate from what they have learned and apply it in unfamiliar settings, both in and outside of school. It is further argued that *"success in reading provides the foundation for achievement in other subject areas and for full participation in adult life"* (Ibid.: 18). While remaining cognizant that the ability to convey information is one of humankind's greatest assets transcending time and space, PISA also recognizes that learning how to read (and write) requires effort to master a collection of complex skills. In other words, becoming a proficient reader is a goal that requires practice and dedication. This is where schooling has a key role to play. For this reason, as PISA believes, the efficiency of a nation's education systems can be evaluated by way of assessing her students' reading competence.

PISA claims that it uses an innovative concept of *literacy*, referring to the students' capacity to apply knowledge and skills and to analyze, reason, and communicate effectively in a variety of situations. PISA also asks students to report on their own motivation to learn, their beliefs about themselves, and their learning strategies.

PISA collected data in 2009 from around 470,000 15-year-old students of 65 participating countries and economies and another 50,000 such students from nine additional OECD Partners. Each student spent two hours responding to pencil-and-paper tasks in Reading, Mathematics, and Science. In 20 countries, students answered additional questions on the computer and were assessed on their capacity to read digital texts. Both multiple-choice and constructed response questions were used. The constructed response questions involve texts and graphs much like those that students might encounter in real life. Moreover, the students also responded to a questionnaire which focused on their personal background, learning habits, attitudes towards reading, and engagement and motivation (Ibid.: 20). More specifically, PISA defines reading and its features as the following (Ibid.: 21):

The capacity of an individual to understand, use, reflect on and engage with written texts in order to achieve his/her goals, to develop his/her knowledge and potential, and to participate in society...In addition to decoding and literal comprehension, *reading literacy* also involves interpretation and reflection, and the ability to use reading to fulfill one's goals in life...PISA focuses on reading to learn rather than learning to read. Therefore, students are not assessed on the most basic reading skills.

As gathered from the above information culled from the PISA report (OECD, 2010), comprehensiveness and research rigor are assured. However, there are certain methodological details which often escape the attention of commentators and report readers alike. Such overlooked details have implications for the interpretation and use of PISA's survey results. In this regard, the following are worthy of note:

1. The total sample size is awesomely large and the average is 7,231 per country. An average sample size of this magnitude for each country assures that the estimate (country mean) is highly reliable with little error (fluctuation due to sampling), as borne out by the very small standard error (the greatest being 6.7). However, the actual numbers of students assessed vary from 329 (Liechtenstein) to 38,213 (Mexico). Relevant figures for the other countries are found in Table A2.3 and Figure I2.16 of the PISA report (OECD, 2010).
2. There are 131 items in the Reading test but not all students responded to all test items as is usually done in survey and school testing. PISA used matrix sampling to assess the students. The items were distributed into 13 different test booklets with some items overlapping to allow for horizontal equating. Thus, each student was tested on about 10 of the 131 items. Incidentally, there are much fewer items for Mathematics (35) and Science (53).
3. The testing time of two hours was not just for assessing Reading, but also Mathematics and Science. Thus, each student was given around 60 minutes to demonstrate what they have acquired as Reading *literacy* (a term used by PISA) for the past eight years of schooling. A typical Reading item takes the form of a passage followed by two to three MCQ and constructed response questions. For example,

sample item No. 10 consists of an excerpt of 1160 words adapted from a translation of Leo Tolstoy's *A Just Judge*. This is followed by one MCQ and two open-ended questions. More examples can be found on *PISA Sample Questions* (The Australian Council for Educational Research, 1999–2007).
4. PISA uses IRT scaling and plausible value methodology to derive the Reading scores for students and hence their respective country. The mixed coefficients multinomial logit model used is a generalized form of the Rasch model. This yielded scores which should not be mistaken as the traditional 'number/percent correct' scores. The imputed scores place the countries on a continuum of Reading *literacy*. The same estimating procedure was done for Mathematics and Science as well.
5. For reporting, the Reading scores were transformed to a scale with a mean of 500 and a standard deviation 100. Assuming normality, this scale will have scores varying from 200 to 800, allowing the countries to be distributed on a scale of 600 points. However, the actual scores range of 314 (Kyrgzstan) to 575 (Shanghai, China), covering only 261 points of the possible 600. Since the choice of scaling is arbitrary *a prior*, and as there are only 65 countries to be ranked, it might be more meaningful to use a scale with a mean of 50 and a standard deviation of 10. Just for the sake of discussion, had the scale chosen had a mean of 5,000 and a standard deviation of 1000, then the 65 countries would be distributed on a scale with 6000 points. This highlights the arbitrariness of the scaling and advises caution against the spurious precision by which countries with small differences are given different rankings, without taking into account the standard error.

It is not known how much the above conditions affect the reporting, but they are good to notice so as not to read too much meaning into small inter-country differences. In addition to assessing Reading, PISA also surveyed students through a questionnaire. It collected information about the students' personal backgrounds, learning habits, attitudes towards reading, and engagement and motivation. However, the responses were reported as descriptive statistics and little has been done to ascertain their correlations with Reading performance. Such correlations are of particular interest to the present study. More specifically, this analysis is concerned with the following background characteristics:

1. *Reading materials*: Magazine, Comics, Fiction, Non-fiction, Newspaper
2. *Reading time*: No reading, Up to 30 minutes, Up to 60 minutes, More than one hour, More than two hours
3. *Reading purposes*: Deep reading, Enjoyment.

## Correlates of Reading Achievement

First of interest is the correlation of reading achievement with reading materials, time, and purpose, these being likely contributing factors to reading achievement.

### Reading materials

It is reasonable that the types of materials young people read have an influence on their reading achievement. The question is whether reading a certain type of material contributes more to reading achievement than reading other types of materials. As Table 1 shows, for all 65 countries as a whole, Magazine has a moderate correlation with reading achievement, but Comics, Fiction, Non-fiction, and Newspaper all have very high correlations with reading achievement, with r = 0.95 and above. These indicate the relative importance of the various types of reading materials.

When the correlations were calculated for the OECD Members and OECD Partners separately, interestingly, coefficients for the OECD Members decrease somewhat but increase for the OECD Partners, especially for Magazine and Newspaper which now have practically perfect correlations with reading achievement. Although the differences between the two sets of coefficient may not be large (except for Magazine), the changes could indicate that types of reading materials predict reading achievement better for OECD Partners than OECD Members.

Table 1. Correlations between Reading Achievement and Reading Materials.

|  | **Magazine** | **Comics** | **Fiction** | **Non-fiction** | **Newspaper** |
| --- | --- | --- | --- | --- | --- |
| All (N = 65) | 0.685 | 0.977 | 0.974 | 0.950 | 0.973 |
| Members (N = 34) | 0.425 | 0.902 | 0.882 | 0.879 | 0.829 |
| Partners (N = 31) | 0.995 | 0.983 | 0.985 | 0.935 | 0.996 |

*Note*: All coefficients are statistically significant (p < 0.05).

Table 2. Correlations between Reading Achievement and Reading Time.

|  | No reading | Up to 30 minutes | Up to 60 minutes | More than one hour | More than two hours |
|---|---|---|---|---|---|
| All (N = 65) | **0.457** | 0.014 | **−0.254** | **−0.518** | **−0.438** |
| Members (N = 34) | 0.155 | −0.198 | 0.090 | −0.124 | 0.019 |
| Partners (N = 31) | 0.015 | 0.151 | 0.102 | −0.328 | −0.248 |

*Note*: Coefficients in bold are statistically significant ($p < 0.05$).

## *Reading time*

It is also reasonable to expect the time spent reading by students to influence their achievement in reading. In other words, do students who spend more time reading have better reading achievement? However, the correlations between these two variables are more complicated than expected. As shown in Table 2, for the 65 countries as a whole, the percentage of students reporting "*No reading*" is positively correlated with Reading and the percentages of students reported reading daily up to 60 minutes and more have *negative* correlations with achievement.

It is tempting to interpret the correlations as showing that more time spent reading has led to *poorer* Reading means, and that spending no time reading unassigned books has made for better Reading performance. Such an interpretation is not only puzzling but does not match the common belief that students who spend more time reading read better. A more reasonable alternative interpretation is that countries with poor Reading performance made their students spend more time reading as a way to compensate for this important shortcoming.

However, when correlations were calculated for the OECD Members and OECD Partners separately, all coefficients become non-significant, although the negative directions are preserved by some coefficients. These suggest that the amount of time students spend reading is not a good predictor of reading achievement, contrary to the common belief in the positive correlation between effort and achievement.

Note that the directions of correlations change in some cases when coefficients were calculated for the two groups of countries separately. Such directional changes are found for "*Up to 30 minutes*", "*Up to

Table 3. Correlations between Purposes of Reading.

|  | Deep reading | Reading for enjoyment |
|---|---|---|
| All (N = 65) | **0.300** | 0.149 |
| Members (N = 34) | 0.234 | 0.205 |
| Partners (N = 31) | **0.586** | −0.014 |

*Note*: Coefficients in bold are statistically significant ($p < 0.05$).

*60 minutes*", and "*More than two hours*". These are examples similar to those of Simpson' Paradox found for curriculum time and achievement in PISA data (Soh, 2013).

## *Reading purposes*

Basically, some students read with the purpose of gaining information, which requires deep-reading or reading for meaning, while other students read mainly for enjoyment, which supposedly does not require much thinking about meaning. Do these two approaches of reading for different purposes influence reading achievement?

As Table 3 shows, deep reading has a low positive correlation of $r = 0.30$ with Reading means for the 65 countries as a whole, but the correlation is much higher ($r = 0.59$) for OECD Partners but not OECD Members ($r = 0.23$). However, the correlations for reading achievement cannot be predicted from reading for enjoyment.

## Regression of Reading on Materials, Time, and Purposes

With the correlations reported above, the next logical question is which of the variables better predicts Reading means. To answer this question, the data for types of reading materials, reading time, and purposes of reading were submitted for a hierarchical multiple regression analysis. The three sets of variables were entered in *that* sequence as consecutive blocks. Three models resulted at shown in Table 4.

As shown by Model 1 in Table 4, four of the five types of reading materials made significant contributions to Reading, with the exception of Magazine. The four contributing types of materials predicted 98 percent

110   PISA and PIRLS: The Effects of Culture and School Environment

Table 4. Multiple Regression Models.

|  | Model 1 | Model 2 |
|---|---|---|
| Multiple R | 0.989 | 0.991 |
| Adjusted R-square | 0.977 | 0.980 |
| Increase in Adjusted R-square | 0.977 | 0.003 |
| **Type of reading materials** | | |
| Magazine | 0.010 | −0.002 |
| Comics | **0.265** | **0.276** |
| Fiction | **0.224** | **0.343** |
| Non-fiction | **0.192** | **0.152** |
| Newspaper | **0.321** | **0.267** |
| **Time for reading** | | |
| Up to 30 minutes | — | 0.015 |
| Up to 60 minutes | — | **0.057** |
| More than one hour | — | 0.050 |
| More than two hours | — | −0.034 |
| **Purpose of reading** | | |
| Deep reading | — | — |
| Enjoyment | — | — |

*Note*: Standardized regression coefficients in bold are statistically significant ($p < 0.05$).

of the criterion variance. This left very little variance to be further explained. However, of the four reading times, only "*Up to 60 minutes*" made a contribution to Reading, but it added only 0.3 percent more variance to what has already been predicted by reading materials. Finally, when the variables of purposes were entered, they did not change the prediction.

Based on the above findings, separate stepwise multiple regression analyses were run for the OECD Members and OECD Partners. The question to be answered here is whether types of reading materials predict Reading equally well for the two groups and whether the predictors are the same for them. Table 5 shows the final models obtained. For the

Table 5. Stepwise Regression Models.

|  | OECD | Partner |
|---|---|---|
| Multiple R | 0.952 | 0.997 |
| R-squared | 0.906 | 0.993 |
| Adjusted R-square | 0.896 | 0.993 |
| **Type of reading materials** | | |
| Magazine | — | — |
| Comics | 0.330 (1) | — |
| Fiction | — | 0.178 (2) |
| Non-fiction | 0.433 (2) | — |
| Newspaper | 0.174 (3) | 0.821 (1) |

Note: Figures show the steps variables entered the regression.

OECD Members, Comic was first entered, followed by Non-fiction, and then Newspaper. These three variables predicted 90 percent of the Reading variance. For the OECD Partners, Newspaper was first entered followed by Fiction. These two variables predicted 99 percent of Reading variance.

Thus, types of reading materials are better predictors for the OECD Partners than for the OECD Members, and the effective predictors for the two groups of countries are different. Newspaper is a common one but much more predictive for the OECD Partners.

## Comparisons between OECD Members and Partners

With the findings above, a question arises: how do OECD Members and OECD Partners compare in all the variables? Table 6 shows the results of comparing the two groups on Reading and relevant variables.

First of all, the OECD Members as a group outscored the OECD Partners by 61 points in Reading with a very large effect size of Glass's $\Delta = 2.66$. This difference represents 0.6 of the standard deviation (100).

Next, there are sizable differences in favor of the OECD Members in all five types of reading materials, with very large effect sizes, varying

112  PISA and PIRLS: The Effects of Culture and School Environment

Table 6. Comparisons between OECD Members and OECD Partners.

|  | OECD (N = 34) Mean | SD | Partner (N = 31) Mean | SD | Difference | Effect size |
|---|---|---|---|---|---|---|
| Reading | 493.4 | 22.9 | 432.5 | 55.6 | 60.9 | 2.66 |
| **Type of reading materials** | | | | | | |
| Magazine | 488.7 | 27.8 | 442.2 | 51.3 | 46.5 | 1.67 |
| Comics | 492.5 | 27.9 | 426.4 | 54.4 | 66.1 | 2.37 |
| Fiction | 532.7 | 61.6 | 447.9 | 62.3 | 84.8 | 1.38 |
| Non-fiction | 513.3 | 27.3 | 448.9 | 61.6 | 64.4 | 2.32 |
| Newspaper | 503.3 | 29.2 | 440.2 | 54.9 | 63.1 | 2.16 |
| **Time for reading** | | | | | | |
| No reading | 37.3 | 7.3 | 21.2 | 8.7 | 16.1 | 2.21 |
| Up to 30 minutes | 30.4 | 4.6 | 31.2 | 6.8 | −0.8 | −0.17 |
| Up to 60 minutes | 17.2 | 2.4 | 22.3 | 5.3 | −5.1 | −2.16 |
| More than one hour | 10.7 | 3.8 | 16.5 | 5.0 | −5.8 | −1.53 |
| More than two hours | 4.5 | 2.0 | 7.5 | 3.1 | −3.0 | −1.50 |
| **Purpose of reading** | | | | | | |
| Deep reading | 43.7 | 8.1 | 44.4 | 6.9 | −0.7 | −0.09 |
| Enjoyment | 0.5 | 0.02 | 0.4 | 0.02 | 0.1 | 0.5 |

*Note*: Cohen's $d$ was calculated as (Mean difference)/(Pooled SD).

from Glass's $\Delta$ = 1.38 (Fiction) to Glass's $\Delta$ = 2.37 (Comics). Such differences may reflect the availability of these reading materials in the two sets of countries.

Where time for reading is concerned, the OECD countries had 16 percent more students reporting that they did not read at all. However, there is no difference between the two sets of countries in the percentages of students reporting that they read only up to 30 minutes per day. Beyond this, OECD Partners have higher percentages, with sizable effect sizes of Glass's $\Delta$ = −1.53 to −2.16, and the differences vary from −3.0 to −5.8 percent. In short, students in the OECD Partners reported more time for reading.

As for purposes of reading, there is no difference in deep reading but there is a difference in reading for enjoyment in favor of the OECD Members. However, the means for this are rather small for them to be taken seriously.

## Discussion and Conclusion

No one can deny the importance of reading as a way to develop skills needed for the study of other subjects in the school curriculum. The PISA data attests to this: the correlations are near perfect, r = 0.95 between Reading and Mathematics and r = 0.98 between Reading and Science. These correlations are unusually high and, in that sense, unexpected. They nevertheless are strong evidence of the critical role reading plays in schooling. It is reasonable to assume that students doing well in reading are much more likely to do well in such important subjects as Mathematics and Science. This, again, underlines the importance of reading.

Although there is a visible difference in Reading between OECD Members and OECD Partners, it is interesting to note that, among the top 10 countries, there are three OECD Partners, namely Shanghai China (ranked 1), Hong Kong China (4), and Singapore (5). If these are grouped together with the two Asian countries which are OECD Members, namely Korea (2) and Japan (8), then there are five Asian countries topping the PISA 2009 Reading achievement. Incidentally, the other OECD Members among the top 10 are Finland (3), Canada (6), New Zealand (7), Australia (9), and Netherlands (10). In this case, it may be concluded that the top Asian countries are on par with the top Western countries in Reading, and by inference from the correlations reported above, also in Mathematics and Science.

The finding that 90 percent of Reading variance for OECD Members and 99 percent for OECD Partners are predicted by reading materials underscores the importance of these in the development of reading skills. While teachers may adopt different approaches to teaching reading in the classroom, students' reading beyond the curriculum is not to be overlooked. And it is safe to say that teachers (and parents, too) have been encouraging younger people to read and even mount special programs for reading (e.g., the Reading Week). However, it stands to reason that the choice of reading materials is critical to sustain students' reading interest as a motivational device. In this regard, the findings of the surveys summarized earlier and the finding of this analysis deserve attention.

For OECD Members, Reading is best predicted by Non-fiction followed by Comics, with Newspaper playing also a minor role. For OECD Partners, Newspaper is an overwhelmingly powerful predictor of Reading, with Fiction playing a minor role. This difference might be attributed to differences in resources and in culture. For instance, the OECD Members (perhaps excepting Japan and Korea, which are Asian countries) might have a more liberal view about reading comics, whereas the OECD Partners may take reading as a more serious business and discourage comics reading. That Non-fiction is a predictor for the OECD Members but not for the OECD Partners and that Fiction is a predictor for the OECD Partners but not the OECD Members might also reflect a difference in tradition and culture where out-of-school reading is concerned. Nevertheless, if this interpretation is reasonable, the question is whether a more balanced choice of reading materials should be attempted.

OECD Members have lower percentages of students spending time reading but still outscored OECD Partners in Reading. This is counterintuitive, even paradoxical, going against the common belief that more time learning leads to better achievement. This finding is similar to those reported in a re-analysis of PISA data for Reading, Mathematics, and Science (Soh, 2013) where Simpson's Paradox (Berman *et al.*, n.d.) was observed. It was concluded there that the relation between learning time and achievement is more complex than is usually assumed, that is, not linear but curvilinear. However, the finding of this study that, of the various time measures, only reading "*Up to 60 minutes*" daily is a significant predictor of reading performance is noteworthy. This implies that *that* is an optimum amount of time that contributes to reading achievement and students need be encouraged to spend this much time to develop their reading skills; more or less than that may not be beneficial.

The finding that almost no students in all 65 countries read for enjoyment should be a cause of concern. Two reasons may account for this unsatisfactory situation. Firstly, in the surveys cited above, an unspecified and supposedly sizable proportion of students claimed that they do not have time to read unassigned books and are not interested in reading. This might have been caused by an ever-increasing curriculum load, which affords students less and less time to read beyond the prescribed reading, and less opportunity to enjoy reading, which requires time and leisure. Secondly, in the multimedia context of today, there are more vivid images and information readily accessible to students, which make traditional books pale in comparison. However, reading competence will take students a long way in their studies, and even reading computer and iPad screens still requires reading skills. Thus, developing students' reading skills and interest remains an important educational task — one that is perhaps even more challenging in the present day.

## References

Berman, S., Dalle, Mule, L., Greene, M., and Lucker, J. (n.d.). Simpson's Paradox: A cautionary tale in advanced analytics. *Significance Statistics Making Sense.* Available at *http://www.significancemagazine.org/details/webexclusive/2671151/Simpsons-Paradox-A-Cautionary-Tale-in-Advanced-Analytics.html*

Duncan, A. (7 December 2010). Secretary Arne Duncan's Remarks at OECD's Release of the Program for International Student Assessment (PISA) 2009 Results. Available at http://www.ed.gov/news/speeches/secretary-arne-duncans-remarks-oecds-release-program-international-student-assessment

Education Matters (14 December 2010). *PISA Study Results: An Urgent Call to Action.* Available at http://www.educationmatters.ie/2010/12/14/pisa-study-results-an-urgent-call-to-action/

Harris, A. (12 June 2006) The Importance of Reading. Available at http://ezinearticles.com/?The-Importance-of-Reading&id=404734

Hartman, B. (9 December 2010) *PISA test results show colossal failure of Israel schools.* The Jerusalem Post. Available at http://www.jpost.com/NationalNews/Article.aspx?id=198640

Marra, T., and Witteveen, A. (2005). Trends in teen reading 2001–2003. *Young Adult Library Services,* **4**(1), 17–21.

Martins, P. S. (5 January 2011). *What explains the Portuguese PISA results?* The Portuguese Economy. Available at http://theportugueseeconomy.blogspot.sg/2011/01/what-explains-portuguese-pisa-results.html

Naik, A. (29 December 2012). *Importance of Reading.* Available at http://www.buzzle.com/articles/importance-of-reading.html

OECD (2010), *PISA 2009 Results: What Students Know and Can Do — Student Performance in Reading, Mathematics and Science (Volume I)*. http://dx.doi.org/10.1787/9789264091450-en

*Sample Questions: PISA Reading with Marking Guide.* http://pisa-sq.acer.edu.au/showQuestion.php?testId=2297&questionId=10

Sainsbury, M. (2004). Children's attitudes to reading. *Education Review,* **17**(2), 49–54.

Shatter, A. (1951). A survey of student reading. National Council of Teachers of English. Retrieved from www.jstor.org/pss/806821

SmartGirl (n.d.). Report on Teen Read Week 2003. Available at http://www.smartgirl.org/reports/2734196.html

Sofsian, D. (n.d.). *The Importance of Reading.* Available at http://ezinearticles.com/?The-Importance-Of-Reading&id=354498

Soh, K. C. (2013). Is time not always a factor of achievement? A lesson from re-analyzing PISA data. *International Journal of TESOL and Learning,* **1**(1), 50–64. Available at http://www.untestedideas.com/journals.php?journal=IJTL

Satya (28 December 2011). India's participation in PISA 2009+ cycle: The Process. Education in India. Available at http://prayatna.typepad.com/education/2011/12/india-in-pisa-2009-process.html

The Australian Council for Educational Research (1999–2007). *PISA Sample Questions.* http://pisa-sq.acer.edu.au/

Thomson, S., De Bortoli, L., Nicholas, M., Hillman, K. and Buckley, S. (2010). Challenges for Australian Education: Results From PISA 2009. Australian Policy Online. Available at http://apo.org.au/research/challenges-australian-education-results-pisa-2009

Young, T. (26 January 2013). *British schoolchildren now ranked 23rd in the world, down from 12th in 2000.* Available at http://blogs.telegraph.co.uk/news/tobyyoung/100067092/british-schoolchildren-now-ranked-23rd-in-the-world-down-from-12th-in-2000/

## Chapter 7

# Reading Competencies as Predictors of Science Achievement: Lessons from PISA 2009 Data

Science is one of the three core subjects, together with Reading and Mathematics, of the school curriculum worldwide. Reading ability is a tool for acquiring new knowledge and absolutely necessary for the learning of Science in the school context. It is no coincident that the *Programme for International Student Achievement* (PISA; 2010) places a premium on Reading as its key focus of international comparisons. This being the case, it is of theoretical and practical significance to find out the extent to and manner with which reading ability contributes to achievement in Science.

### Reading and Science: Past Studies

In spite of its importance, reading has never had much attention from science educators. After a review of articles published up to the year 1983, Sutrisno (n.d.) reported that science achievement was affected by student characteristics and socioeconomic status, etc., without any mention of reading. The same is true of Blosser's (1985) meta-analysis on science instruction research. No mention was made of the relation between reading and science learning. It thus appears that the science–reading relation was taken for granted or simply ignored.

In Volumes 21 to 23 (1999–2001) of the *International Journal of Science Education* (IJSE), with five to seven articles published in each of the 12 issues per year, only four out of 220 articles dealt specifically with some aspects of reading in connection with science learning. Likewise, 10 years later, in Volumes 33 and 34 (2011–2012) of IJSE, there are about 210 articles altogether but none deal with the science–reading relation. A search using *"language, reading, science, correlations, meta-analysis"* as search words on the Internet failed to surface any study dealing with the science–reading relation.

Even when reading data is readily available in such a large-scale survey as the PISA, researchers seem to have little interest in how reading relates to science learning. For instance, Sun, Bradley, and Akers (2012) re-analyzed PISA 2006 data for Hong Kong and investigated the factors that influenced science. The results at the student level indicated science achievement was associated with student gender (male), socioeconomic status, motivation, self-efficacy, and parental perception of science. At the school level, science achievement was associated with enrolment size, socioeconomic composition, and instruction time per week. Data about Reading in the PISA report was not included in the analysis.

The above is sufficient to suggest that the reading–science relation has been largely neglected, side-stepped, or ignored in science education research. While this may be true of reading in general, some researchers did consider reading in science as a special aspect of language learning. For instance, according to Kearsey and Turner (1999), science has a language of its own. Many science educators would agree that students need to learn and understand this *language of science* (a register specific to science) if they are to assimilate the material in science lessons, to communicate in science, and to think in a scientific way. Empirically, Clerk and Rutherford (2000) reported a study on the possibility that language confusion can be mistaken for misconception in science learning. They administered a written test of 20 multiple-choice items that diagnosed misconceptions in Physics to a sample of South African students who learned English as a first language. A sub-sample of these students was interviewed to explore the reasoning behind their test responses. It was found that language usage was frequently the reason behind the wrong choices in the Physics test.

Similarly, Unsworth (2001) argued that the quality of writing and explicit use of texts in science teaching warrant close attention. Without diminishing the importance of hands-on tasks and observation, the complementary use of effective texts has a significant role in science learning. The author demonstrated how language features in effective texts prepare students for scientific English. Key differences between different types of explanations were illustrated and an analysis of the sample text showed how language features index variation in explanation quality. Careful selection and use of texts was recommended and the role of knowledge of language in teaching critical comprehension and the composition of science explanations was stressed.

At a higher conceptual level in the context of science teaching, Rodrigues and Thompson (2001) discussed the key linguistic processes through which students learn. The authors used transcripts of videotaped lessons with teacher and student interviews. They illustrated the role of language in determining the effectiveness of science teaching and learning, using an integrated data set for one Australian Year 9 (14-year-old) science lesson. The data was analyzed for coherence and comprehension. The importance of communication skills in the classroom and the value of language analysis in determining the effectiveness of instructions were demonstrated. The authors then argued for the need for science teachers to consider the importance of learning in a linguistic milieu.

More recently, Ritchie, Tomas, and Tones (2011) studied the effects of science-writing on the development of students' scientific literacy. Students generated two Bio-Stories that merged scientific information with narrative storylines. In the exploratory phase, a qualitative case study of a Sixth-Grade class involving classroom observations and interviews informed the design of the confirmatory phase of the study conducted at a different school. The study involved two classes of Australian middle school students (i.e., Sixth Grade, 11 years of age). The results show that writing the stories helped the students become more familiar with biosecurity issues, develop a deeper understanding of related biological concepts, and improve their interest in science. The authors recommended that science teachers engage their students in the practice of science-writing in such a way that integrates scientific information into narrative storylines.

Rincke (2011) investigated how students developed an understanding of the concept of *force* and how they used the term *force*. The study related students' preconceptions to second language learning. Videotapes were taken of two lessons and were analyzed using a category system. Written tasks, students' logs, and tests provided additional data. Students were found to face difficulties in using the term *force* scientifically similar to those in a foreign language instruction. Reflecting on Lev Vygotsky's contention that there is a relationship between learning science and learning language, Rincke concluded that it might be useful to make reference to the research related to language learning when thinking about improving science education.

With a different perspective, Johnson (1998) considered the relation between reading and science learning — that of readability of science text. Four readability tests were used to evaluate texts for eight Physics topics in the UK national curriculum commonly taught in Years 10 and 11 (student age 14–16). It was suggested that if a book had a reading level of 14 years, an average 14-year-old student would score *only 50 per cent* on a comprehension test based on that text. This reading level is a long way from full comprehension. Moreover, it was pointed out that some Physics texts had sentences of over 50 words with one or more subordinate clauses and two or more new concepts. In such cases, Johnson argued, it would be very doubtful if many students, once they eventually reached the full stop, would be able to remember what the beginning of the sentence was about, let alone extract the essential meaning from the lengthy sentence. The author suggested that the reading level of the text should be *two years below* the students' reading level for them to be able to independently read with comprehension.

In the context of the present day, the effect of reading on science achievement may be further complicated by the prevalence of electronic devices available to students. Clark (2012) highlighted a recent study of international comparisons which shows that youngsters who owned iPhones and the like lost on average at least 20 marks in a reading test given to children in 45 countries and provinces. A linked study found that teenagers who spent hours on social networking sites did significantly worse in science and math tests.

However, the science–reading relation has also been given a non-statistical meaning in recent years, with science educators discussing the correspondence between science processes and reading skills. They suggest an approach to science teaching which integrates the learning of communication skills. Attempts have been made to align reading and science in terms of what science requires in understanding science texts and the corresponding reading sub-skills needed.

With this new perspective, Bowers (2000) aligned science skills with reading and writing skills. For example, students need to learn *classifying* in Science and this skill corresponds to the reading skill of *"identifying main idea or details"* and the writing of *"outline information"*. Bowers (2000: 3) advocated that *"Science and reading complement each other well because of the similarities between reading skills and science process skills, as can be seen in the table. The meshing of the skills in both subject areas makes them natural partners for integration."*

## Integrating Reading and Science: A New Trend

When discussing reading as a predictor of science achievement, the tacit assumption is that science learning can benefit from good reading skills. The integrated approach to science teaching goes further to suggest that the benefit is mutual in that reading can in turn benefit from learning science.

After a comparison of the goals set in 1996 by national curriculum bodies for the National Science Education Standards and the Standards for the English Language Arts, a conclusion is reached that *"Clearly, the goals of reading and science education are similar. They prepare students to acquire information and to use that information personally and globally"* (Science a-z.com, n.d., para. 2). It was further claimed that the integration *"helps educators use classroom time more efficiently, allowing students to reinforce science concepts during E/LA time and reinforcing good reading strategies and skills during science. The strategy of integrating the subjects has been found to increase achievement in both areas as well"* (Ibid, para. 4). Several recent research reports were cited in support of such assertions. In like vein, when promoting the *Seeds of Science/Roots of Reading* approach to science, it was suggested that the approach allows *"literacy activities support the acquisition of science concepts and inquiry skills, while inquiry science serves as a compelling context for literacy development"* (The Lawrence Hall of Science, n.d. para. 5).

Likewise, Yerrick and Ross (2001) noted an increasing disparity in science achievement among students as the classroom discourse became more constrained and prescriptive. They were also concerned that the practice of tracking at the secondary level was becoming more influential in the lower grades. Integrated teaching of science and literacy was then proposed as a solution to the problem. They used four strategies: (1) Expanding students' experiences and the science vocabulary available to them for their writing; (2) Stimulating creative writing and graphical representations through inquiry lessons; (3) Expanding students' knowledge of literary genres through the writing, editing, and production of public service announcements on scientific topics; and (4) Fostering development of students' voices and their understanding of audience through writing about science problems with societal impact. Thus, there is obvious enthusiasm in integrating science and reading for the mutual benefit to both subjects. A good example is the long-term project *Concept-Oriented Reading Instruction* (CORI) which was started in 1992 at the University of Maryland and the University of Georgia with the sponsorship of the National Reading Research Centre (Guthrie, 2005–2012). CORI aims to increase the integration of reading and science as the students use cognitive strategies common to both subjects more effectively.

By way of summary, while the reading–science relation has been neglected by researchers in science education in earlier years, it has gained attention in more recent years. Reading and science were seen as two different though related subjects in the past, but they have come to be seen as mutually benefiting and that the two subject could be taught integrally. The importance of improving reading and controlling the language demand of science texts has also been given due recognition. Above all, researchers in science education has begun to investigate specific aspects of reading in the context of science learning instead.

## Reading and Science in PISA 2009

The data of PISA 2009 afford a good opportunity to study the reading–science relation and an evaluation of specific reading sub-skills as they relate to science achievement. Over and above assessing students' reading in general, PISA 2009 gathered specific data pertaining to reading approaches, reading sub-skills, and reading time (OECD, 2010a). The rich information is useful for a more thorough understanding of the reading–science relation.

## Reading literacy

The PISA Reading test comprises 102 items, most of which are multiple-choice items scored dichotomously and some open-ended questions with score ranges. The items yield scores for five reading sub-skills and an overall Reading score. This overall Reading score was used to rank the 65 participating countries.

As conceptualized by the PISA, *Reading* is a generic term but in fact it entails three pairs of sub-skills each dealing with the materials in varied manners for different purposes. These are *aspects* defining the cognitive approach that determines how readers engage with a text. The three reading sub-skills include the following:

- *Access and Retrieve*: This involves skills associated with finding, selecting, and collecting information (Ibid.: 59).
- *Integrate and Interpret*: This involves processing what is read to make internal sense of a text (Ibid.: 67). Integrating tasks requires the reader to understand the relation(s) between different parts of a text (Ibid.: 64).
- *Reflect and Evaluate*: This involves engaging with a text while drawing on information, ideas, or values external to the text. In reflecting on a text, readers relate their own experience or knowledge to the text. In evaluating a text, readers make a judgment about it, either drawing on personal experience or on knowledge of a world that may be formal or content-based (Ibid.: 67).

These three reading sub-skills are supposed to be applied to both continuous and non-continuous texts. *Continuous texts* are typically composed of sentences that are organized into paragraphs, fitting into even larger structures such as sections, chapters, and books. *Non-continuous texts* are most frequently organized in matrix format, based on combinations of lists. Moreover, texts in continuous and non-continuous formats appear in both the print and digital media.

## Science literacy

There are 53 items assessing *science literacy* related to topics such as physical systems, living systems, earth and space, and technology. The items require competencies in identifying issues, explaining phenomena, and using evidence. PISA (OECD, 2010: 21) defines *scientific literacy* as:

> The extent to which an individual possesses scientific knowledge and uses that knowledge to identify questions, acquire new knowledge, explain scientific phenomena and draw evidence-based conclusions about science-related issues; understands the characteristic features of science as a form of human knowledge and enquiry; shows awareness of how science and technology shape our material, intellectual and cultural environments; and engages in science-related issues and with the ideas of science, as a reflective citizen.

## Literacy: A contentious term

PISA argues vehemently that its Reading, Mathematics, and Science tests are *literacy tests* which are future-oriented and process-based for assessing *literacies* related to the three subjects. In contrast, the conventional *achievement tests* are said to be past-oriented and content-based. For Reading, PISA asserts that reading literacy used in PISA is much broader than the historical notion of the ability to read and that it includes a broad set of cognitive competencies, from basic decoding, to knowledge of words, grammar, and linguistic and textual structures and features, to knowledge about the world, and includes metacognitive competencies such as the awareness of and ability to use a variety of appropriate strategies when processing texts. As for the preference of the term *literacy*, PISA explicates that *"historically, the term referred to a tool used to acquire and communicate information...the active, purposeful and functional application of reading in a range of situations and for various purposes"* (Ibid.: 37).

Notwithstanding the intention and persuasiveness, the concept of *literacy* as propounded by PISA has been contentious. Many researchers found the argument unconvincing (e.g., Sjoberg, 2007; Clark, 2011). For instance, Sjoberg (2007) questioned the possibility of assessing *real life challenges* (which PISA claims) by using paper-and-pencil tests as well as its cross-national validity, since such challenges vary from country to country. It was further pointed out that the PISA Science tests rely heavily on reading ability and require long reading times. This might have affected the students' performance and motivation levels.

Likewise, albeit on an earlier version, Bracey (2008) was highly critical of the PISA tests because the questions rambled discursively and sometimes contained irrelevant information and factually incorrect material. When administered to 15-year-olds, this means the assessment of science is heavily confounded with reading. With a different perspective, Mortimore (2009) summarized 10 criticisms of PISA. Of these criticism, the ones most relevant to the present study are test translation and disregard of national curriculum. On the latter issue, Mortimore (2008: 5) comments, *"The emphasis on asking questions which can be answered using common sense rather than knowledge of a particular curriculum has also been challenged."* Then, on the point that PISA tests claim to assess *literacies* but not what the students have learned in the school's curriculum, Mathews (2009) quoting test expert Loveless as asking *"Why not?"* This is in the same vein as Mortimore cited above.

These are only selected criticisms directed at the PISA tests and serve to caution against unquestioning acceptance of what the PISA team claims for their research output. Support for arguments for what the tests are needs to come from outside the arguments. Nevertheless, this article will continue to use *literacy* just to avoid confusion in terminology.

## Reading and Science: Present Study

### Research questions

Against the background and review above, the present study attempts to answer two specific questions using the PISA 2009 data:

1. How do reading and reading sub-skills correlate with science achievement?
2. Which reading sub-skills are most predictive of science achievement?

Answers to these questions will enhance the understanding of the influence reading has on the learning of and achievement in Science. The answers are of interest to educators in general and science educators in particular for curricular and instructional implications.

## *Data and analysis*

Data was gleaned from the relevant tables of the PISA report (OECD, 2010). These include the national means for Reading, Reading sub-skills, and Science. For analysis, correlations were first estimated as an exploration of the possible mutual influences among the variables. This was followed by multiple regression with Science mean as the criterion and Reading sub-skills as predictors.

## Results: What Has PISA 2009 Data Shown?

### *How do Reading and Reading sub-skills correlate with science achievement?*

As shown in Table 1, the correlation between Science and Reading is a very high $r = 0.98$, indicating 96% of shared variance between the two measures. The correlations between Science and Reading sub-skills are also high, varying from $r = 0.95$ (Reflect–Evaluate) to $r = 0.99$ (Integrate–Interpret).

Table 1. Correlations between Reading, Science, and Reading Sub-skills.

| | Reading | Science | Access–Retrieve | Integrate–Interpret | Reflect–Evaluate | Contin.-Text | Non-contin.-Text |
|---|---|---|---|---|---|---|---|
| Reading | 1.00 | 0.982 | 0.992 | 0.996 | 0.998 | 0.999 | 0.994 |
| Science | | 1.00 | 0.979 | 0.985 | 0.954 | 0.979 | 0.975 |
| Access | | | 1.00 | 0.988 | 0.968 | 0.990 | 0.988 |
| Integrate | | | | 1.00 | 0.971 | 0.995 | 0.986 |
| Reflect | | | | | 1.00 | 0.985 | 0.985 |
| Continuous Text | | | | | | 1.00 | 0.988 |
| Non-continuous Text | | | | | | | 1.00 |

*Note*: All coefficients are statistically significant ($p < 0.01$).

## Which Reading sub-skills are most predictive of Science achievement?

Multiple regression analyses were run with the Reading sub-skills as predictors and Science as the criterion. The results are shown in Table 2.

As shown in Table 2, the multiple correlation R = 0.99 indicates an effect size of 98% and the only significant predictor is Integrate–Interpret, with a beta-weight of 1.19, suggesting that an increase in one standard unit in Integrate–Interpret is associated with slightly greater than one standard unit in Science.

At the same time, it is interesting to note the effect of text type. As shown in Table 2, Continuous Text has a negative beta-weight of $\beta = -0.644$, sizable though statistically non-significant. A naïve interpretation is that countries where students scored higher on the sub-skill of reading Continuous Text tend to do poorer in Science! However, as Continuous Text in fact has an extremely high positive correlation with the criterion Science (Table 1), such an interpretation is not viable and an alternative is needed. The alternative is that Continuous Text functions as a 'negative net suppressor' which enhances the prediction when it is included. However, as the main concern of this study is the prediction of the criterion, in the words of Darmawan and Keeves (2006), such a multicollinearity problem has little effect. It is also interesting that Non-Continuous Text has a negligible negative beta-weight of $\beta = -0.054$, indicating that the sub-skill in reading such a text format has little or no impact on Science literacy.

**Table 2.** Multiple Regression on Science.

|  | Science |
|---|---|
| R | 0.987 |
| Adjusted R-squared | 0.971 |
| Predictors |  |
| Access–retrieve | 0.363 |
| Integrate–interpret | 1.188* |
| Reflect–evaluate | 0.136 |
| Continuous Text | −0.644 |
| Non-continuous Text | −0.054 |

*Beta-weight is significant (p < 0.05).

Since Integrate–Interpret, but not the other two Reading sub-skills, predicts a very large proportion of Science, the importance of this Reading sub-skill is not to be neglected in the teaching of Science. It is therefore reasonable to conclude that Integrate–Interpret is the single best predictor of performance in Science. The inclusion of additional Reading sub-skills as predictors did not add much to the prediction of Science literacy. This is most probably due to the very high correlations among the Reading sub-skills (Table 1) indicating a very high degree of multicollinearity, thus making the other predictors redundant.

## Discussion: Lessons Learned

The very high correlations among country means for Reading and Reading sub-skills (and, in fact, all variables as shown in Table 1) are surprising. If these measures assess something reasonably different from one another, such extremely high correlations are too good to be true. More importantly, this contradicts the intention of PISA to measure different aspects of learning — Reading, Mathematics, Science, and Reading sub-skills, which are supposed to be different constructs.

These lead to another interpretation. As suggested by Darmawan and Keeves (2006: 166), creating a latent variable may be an alternative when multicolinearity exists among predictors. Following up on this, scores for Science and the five reading sub-skills were factor-analyzed, resulting in one general factor explaining 98.4% of the total variance, with all variables having factor loadings of $\lambda = 0.95$ and above. In this case, it is tempting to interpret the pattern of extremely high correlations among measures as, when taken altogether, a measure of the effectiveness of national education systems or national education achievement at a very general level.

Controversy aside, on a positive note, respecting the contention of PISA in terms of the preferred concept of *literacy*, the very high correlations show a very high degree of consistency among the measures. In fact, the Reading sub-skills taken together as a scale (i.e., Reading) has a practically perfect internal consistency with a Crohbach's $\alpha = 0.99$. In this sense, the measures are trustworthy where reliability is concerned. On the other hand, the very higher correlations may in fact signal a hidden measurement problem — something like expressing a distance in miles and then in kilometers, that of information redundancy.

The more definitive finding of this secondary analysis is that the Reading sub-skill, Integrate–Interpret, is the single best predictor of Science literacy. PISA 2009 (OECD, 2010a: 34) describes the Reading sub-skill Integrate–Interpret as follows:

> Forming a broad understanding and developing an interpretation tasks focus the reader on relationships within a text. Tasks that focus on the whole text require readers to form a broad understanding; tasks that focus on relationships between parts of the text require developing an interpretation. The two are grouped together under integrate and interpret.

Thus, Integrate–Interpret requires the students to be able to do two separate but related processes when reading: (1) to focus on the whole text to form a broad understanding of what has been read and (2) to focus on relationships among parts of the text. This part–whole dual process resembles the required process when students solve science problems. In so doing, they need first to be able to comprehend the problems presented in words and this involves the usual reading comprehension. Next, they should be able to break down what they have read into its constituents and decipher the hidden connections among them. Then they need to translate these ideas into scientific terms and processes.

As shown in this re-analysis, there is a strong correlation between science and reading, especially the sub-skill of Integrate–Interpret. This implies that there is a need for science educators to ensure students have truly understood the science texts and problems before urging them to search for solutions. For this, some strategies, though not based on the data here second-analyzed, come readily to mind:

- Science teachers to work collaboratively with Language teachers to improve students' reading comprehension of texts involving science concepts, with focus on the science registers.
- Compile glossaries of scientific terms and familiarize the students with the ways such terms are used in Science texts, especially when their usages differ from the daily usages.

- Check, and simplify or modify when necessary, the language of Science texts to lower the demand on students' language competency.
- When setting assessment problems for Science, ensure that the language demand is suited to the language competency of the students, preferably lower, to avoid having the tests function as tests of language.
- As the first step of solving science problems, spend more time looking at them from different angles to ensure that they are properly understood by the students; that is, solve the reading problem before trying to solve the science problem. When necessary, re-phrase the problems to ensure student comprehension.

The call for science educators to help their students in reading comprehension (especially integration and interpretation) as the first step to solve science problems is certainly not new. The finding based on the world-wide PISA data reiterates this oft-neglected procedure and serve as a reminder. However, it is necessary to mention that the PISA data was trusted at face value, with no questions asked about its reliability and validity.

## References

Blosser, P. E. (1985). Meta-Analysis Research on Science Instruction. *ERIC/ SMEAC Science Education Digest No. 1.* Ericae.net Clearinghouse on Assessment and Evaluation. Available at http://ericae.net/edo/ED259939.htm

Bowers, P. (2000). *Reading and Writing in the Science Classroom.* Houghton Mifflin Company. Available at http://www.eduplace.com/science/profdev/articles/bowers.html

Bracey, G. W. (August 2008). *The leaning (toppling?) tower of PISA: facts and doubts about international comparisons in education.* Dissent Magazine. Available at http://www.dissentmagazine.org/online.php?id=128

Chang, A. (2012). Tables of sample size for multiple regression. *StatTools.net.* http://www.stattools.net/SSizmreg_Tab.php

Clark, D. (15 March 2011). *Leaning Tower of PISA — 7 Serious Skews.* Available at http://donaldclarkplanb.blogspot.sg/2011/03/leaning-tower-of-pisa-7-serious-skews.html

Clerk, D. and Rutherford, M. (July 2000). Language as a confounding variable in the diagnosis of misconceptions. *International Journal of Science Education*, **22**(7) 7, 703–717.

Clark, L. (12 December 2012). *Children's reading skills suffer if they have TVs in their bedroom and own mobile phone.* Mail Online. Available at http://www.dailymail.co.uk/news/article-2246724/Childrens-reading-skills-suffer-TVs-mobile-phones-bedroom.html?ITO=1490&ns_mchannel=rss&ns_campaign=1490

Darmawan, I G. N., and Keeves, J. P. (2006). Suppressor variables and multilevel mixture modelling. *International Education Journal, 2006*, 7(2), 160–173.

Guthrie, J. T. (2005–2012). CORI Concept-Oriented Reading Instruction. Available at http://www.corilearning.com/

Johnson. K. (1998). Readability. Available at http://www.timtabler.com/reding.html#4

Kearseym, J. and Turner, S. (October 1999). The value of bilingualism in pupils' understanding of scientific language. *International Journal of Science Education*, **21**(10), 1037–1050.

Kenny, D. A. (10 September 2011). *Multiple Regression.* Available at http://davidakenny.net/cm/mr.htm

Mathews, J. (October, 2009). *Test that makes U.S. look bad may not be so good.* Available at http://voices.washingtonpost.com/class-struggle/2009/10/politicians_and_pundits_are_us.html

Mortimore, P. (2009). Alternative Models for Analysing and Representing Countries' Performance in PISA. Brussels: Education International Research Institute.

OECD (2010). *What Students Know and Can Do: Student Performance in Reading, Mathematics, and Science. (Volume I).* Organisation for Economic Co-operation and Development. Accessed on December 1, 2011 from http://dx.doi.org/10.1787/9789264091450-en

Rincke, K. (January 2011). It's rather like learning a language: development of talk and conceptual understanding in mechanics lessons. *International Journal of Science Education,* **33**(2), 229–258.

Ritchie, S., Tomas, L., and Tones, M. (March 2011). Writing stories to enhance scientific literacy. *International Journal of Science Education,* **33**(5), 685–707.

Science a-z.com (n.d.). *The importance of integrating science and literacy.* Available at http://www.sciencea-z.com/scienceweb/research.do

Sjoberg, S. (2007). PISA and "real life challenges": Mission impossible? In Hopmann, G. Brinek, and M. Retzl, Eds.(2007). *PISA According to PISA.*

Vienna: LIT-Verlag. Available at http://folk.uio.no/sveinsj/Sjoberg-PISA-book-2007.pdf

Sun, L., Bradley, K. D. and Akers, K. (September 2012). A multilevel modelling approach to investigating factors impacting science achievement for secondary school students: PISA Hong Kong Sample. *International Journal of Science Education*, **34**(14), 2107–2125.

Sutrisno, L. (n.d.).Science performance: A meta-analysis results. Available at http://www.scribd.com/doc/4776475/Students-Achievement-in-Science-A-Meta-Analysis-Results.

The Lawrence Hall of Science, University of California Berkeley (n.d.). *Science/Literacy Integration.* Available at http://scienceandliteracy.org/about/howisitdifferent/integrated

Unsworth, L. (1 June 2001). Evaluating the language of different types of explanations in junior high school science texts. *International Journal of Science Education*, **23**(6), 585–609.

Yerrick, R.K. and Ross, D.L. (2001, July/August). I read, I learn, iMovie: Strategies for developing literacy in the context of inquiry-based science instruction. *Reading Online,* **5**(1). Available at http://www.readingonline.org/articles/art_index.asp?HREF=/articles/yerrick/index.html

## Chapter 8

# Reading Competencies as Predictors of Mathematics Achievement: Lessons from PISA 2009

Reading, Mathematics, and Science are three core subjects in the school curriculum all over the world. It is therefore not a coincidence that the *Programme for International Student Achievement* (PISA; OECD, 2010) places a premium on Reading as its key focus of international comparisons, together with Mathematics and Science. While mathematics itself is a special form of language, reading as one aspect of natural language plays a critical role in the learning of mathematics, since so many mathematical concepts are described and conveyed through language, especially reading. In other words, language (or more specifically, reading) is a thinking tool by which mathematical thinking is conducted. Thus, the extent to which and what kind of reading contributes to mathematics learning is not a trivial question to mathematics educators.

### Reading and Mathematics: Past Studies

Admittedly, the relation between reading and mathematics achievements is not a new issue. Early studies on this dated back to Hansen's (1944) paper published some 70 years ago. Since then, a plethora of such studies appeared one after another, culminating in Aiken's (1972) now classic review. The relation is conceived not only as correlational but causal — reading ability influences mathematics achievement. This causal assumption has been made explicit by titles such as *A Study of the **Dependence*** *of Mathematics Achievement on Reading Achievement* (Smith, 1976; emphasis added).

Mathematics is a special kind of language which has its own register; many mathematical terms are commonly used and have specialized meanings different from their daily usage. Based on this conception, Cox and Poe (1991) developed a list of graded mathematical terms which purported to yield a quick estimate of a child's *reading ability in mathematics*. They asserted that the list of mathematical terms was able to identify students who needed instruction in mathematical vocabulary and who had difficulty reading their mathematics textbooks. A high correlation between teacher estimates and results obtained with this instrument was reported. This implies that for effective learning of mathematics, students need to be able to read mathematical terms with proper understanding before they can solve mathematical problems involving such terms. Similarly, Loo and Fong (1996) studied the relation between mathematics and reading achievements of Fifth Graders in Singapore. They designed a test of 'mathematics language' using English words which had special mathematical usages. The authors found a correlation of $r = 0.71$ between knowledge of mathematics language and mathematics achievement scores.

In similar vein, Larwin (n.d.) conceived reading as a predictor of mathematics achievement. Using data for Tenth Graders extracted from the Educational Longitudinal Study, the author studied the relations of mathematics achievement, reading proficiency, computer-assisted instruction, mathematics self-efficacy, and teacher expectation. Of all the correlation coefficients calculated, the one between reading and mathematics scores was the highest ($r = 0.75$) and, as would be expected, reading was most predictive of mathematics performance, with a standardized regression weight of $\beta = 0.68$.

The predictive power of reading in mathematics learning is illustrated in another manner. Lamb (2010) found increased reading difficulty of mathematics assessment items to have negatively affected mathematics performance of elementary and middle school students. Using analysis of covariance, the author analyzed the effects of reading grade level of mathematics assessment items on student performance on the *Texas Assessment of Knowledge and Skills*. For mathematics items which had an above-level reading demand, students performed worse as compared with those items with a lower reading demand. This corroborates with the literature, which shows that students who struggle in reading also struggle in mathematics. Here, students are called to acquire mathematical skills that are grounded not only in computation but also in complex problem solving (NCTM, 2000; cited in Lamb, 2010). Lamb cited other researchers in support of his argument that mathematical problem solving unavoidably required a great deal of reading, as mathematics test items continued to include reading passages to present the mathematical problems. Lamb urged that the dual nature of mathematics assessment involving reading was inevitable and should be attended to by mathematics teachers, school administrators, and writers of mathematics tests and textbooks.

The issue of the relation between reading and mathematics achievements is not specific to a particular language, although many of the relevant studies have been conducted involving English Language. For example, Innabi (2005) studied undergraduates in an Arabian university and found Arabic reading comprehension to correlate with $r = 0.38$ with total mathematics score, $r = 0.38$ with story problems, and $r = 0.27$ with mathematics symbols test. This illustrates that the relation question transcends language specificity. In a sense, this is similar to the study by Loo and Fong (1996), conducted in Singapore where the students learned Mathematics using the English Language which was *not* the home language of most students (whose first languages could be Chinese, Malay, or Tamil). Singapore could well be the only country participating in *Trends of International Mathematics and Science Study* (TIMSS) where most students are taught and tested in Mathematics in a language that may not be their first language.

While most studies in this area are correlational in approach, Abedi and Lord (2001) conducted a series of experiments. One of the experiments involved Eighth Graders (N = 1147) classified as proficient English speakers and English Language Learners (ELL). Students were given released items from the *National Assessment of Educational Progress* mathematics assessment. These were items that had been judged most likely to impede the student's performance because of their language — language that could be misunderstood, could confuse the student, or could present difficulties that might interfere with the student's focus on the mathematic content of the items. A different version of the test was created by simplifying the language but retaining the quantities, numerals, and visuals in the original items. In general, the authors found the modifications had greater impact for low-performing students. Specifically, ELLs benefited more than proficient speakers of English Language, low SES students benefited more than others, and students in low-level and average mathematics classes benefitted more than those in high-level mathematics and algebra classes. It is evidence like this that shows unequivocally that reading does impinge on mathematics achievement and the casual direction is clearly established.

However, the effect of reading on mathematics learning can be confounded by students' social backgrounds. Beal's (2010) study focused on the relationship of English Language proficiency and mathematics performance in a sample of high school students, including 47% English Language Learners (ELLs). Variables included scores for a state-based mathematics test, a study-specific pretest and posttest, online mathematics problem-solving, and mathematics self-concept. The students were also assessed for English Language in conversational and reading proficiencies. Results showed that mathematics performance for the ELLs increased with English-reading proficiency in a nonlinear manner, suggesting a more complex relation between reading and mathematics achievement. Nevertheless, the ELLs' English Language reading proficiency predicted mathematics scores, progress in the online mathematics problem-solving, and mathematics self-concept. These findings indicate that the relation between reading and mathematics achievement has ramifications beyond mathematics learning alone. For a thorough discussion on the effects and problems of learning mathematics using a second language (e.g., the Singapore case), see Cuevas (1984) who cited previous studies that showed correlations ranging from a moderate $r = 0.40$ to a high $r = 0.86$ between reading and mathematics achievement.

The ways in which students low in reading ability are disadvantaged in mathematics learning are more clearly shown by comparing students with equal mathematics performance but with different reading abilities. This calls for analysis of differential item functioning (DIF). A study which illustrates this well is by Adams and Le (2009). The data used in their DIF analysis came from five groups of countries that participated in PISA 2003: English-speaking, German-speaking, Eastern European, Top mathematics achievement, and Low mathematics achievement groups. Students differing in reading ability but equivalent in mathematics performance were compared on their performance at the item level. Adams and Le (2009) found mathematics items which were harder than expected for low reading ability students had such characteristics as (1) in open constructed response format; (2) containing a formula; and (3) requiring selecting or ordering important information among number of different sources. On the other hand, advantaging lower reading students were items (1) in multiple-choice format; (2) requiring a simple answer without explanation; (3) based on few events or information; (4) requiring a simple computation or comparison; and (5) containing a simple formula and requiring only a direct substitution. It is obvious from the findings that when students take a mathematics test, it tests not only their mathematics understanding but also their reading ability.

Likewise, Walker, Zhang, and Suber (2008: 1) argued that *"many teachers and curriculum specialists claim that the reading demand of many mathematics items is so great that students do not perform well on mathematics tests, even though they have a good understanding of mathematics."* The authors verified this contention empirically by conducting a DIF analysis and found indeed that students' performance on some mathematics items was influenced by their reading ability, such that students of low reading ability were less likely to answer correctly. They further argued that instead of eliminating such items from the test, attempts should be made to control the reading demand to avoid its confounding effect while maintaining the construct validity of the test as a test of mathematical understanding.

It stands to reason that while reading and mathematics achievements correlate, they both also correlate with measures of intellectual or cognitive ability. This does not seem to have been discussed in most studies on the relations of reading and mathematics learning. However, Floyd and Evans (2003) studied a large national sample of school-age children and adolescents and found mathematics achievement to correlate with various tests of cognitive functioning. Kovas, Harlaar, Petrill, and Plomin (2004) recently studied 2,825 pairs of seven-year-old same-sex twins in the United Kingdom. They found strong correlations between reading and mathematics ($r = 0.70$), moderate correlations between mathematics and intelligence (r = 0.43), and between reading and intelligence (r = 0.47). Interestingly, they also found substantial genetic overlap between mathematics, reading, and intelligence, with correlations ranged between r = 0.62 and r = 0.76. Thus, it is obvious that when estimating the reading–mathematics correlation, it is necessary to partial out the influence of cognitive ability where possible and, when this is not done, at least be aware of the confounding effect of the third variable.

The review above is not comprehensive but selective for the purpose of putting the present study in context. As such, the positive correlation between reading ability and mathematics achievement is conclusive as found in the articles reviewed (and many like studies). Moreover, the reading–mathematics relation is not simply a statistical confirmation but more complex because of other confounding or moderating variables. This complication deserves further investigation. It is also reasonable to conclude, albeit tentatively, that most previous studies treated reading as a global or holistic ability without finer specifications of the kind of reading abilities involved. Factors related to reading may need to be considered, such as the students' approach to reading, their reading sub-skills, and the amount of time they read independently beyond formal instruction.

## Reading and Mathematics: PISA 2009

Over and above assessing students' reading competency globally or holistically, PISA 2009 also gathered data pertaining to reading approaches, reading sub-skills, and reading time (OECD, 2010a). This information is useful for a more thorough, in-depth understanding of the reading–mathematics relation, which is the focus of this secondary analysis. A brief review on these reading factors follows.

It needs be highlighted that the PISA researchers assert that their tests for Reading and Mathematics are future-oriented and competency-based, in contrast with the conventional achievement tests which are past-oriented and content-based, and they purport to assess the mathematical and linguistic literacies (or competencies) required in real-life situations of the 15-year-olds who are nearing the end of their high-school education. Whether this conception has been actualized (i.e., imagined or real) remains contentious (Sjøberg, 2007; Mathews, 2009; Mortimore, 2009).

## Mathematics literacy

PISA 2009 defines *mathematical literacy* as the students' ability to analyze, reason, and communicate effectively, and to solve and interpret mathematical problems that involve quantitative, spatial, probabilistic or other mathematical concepts (OECD, 2010: 122). There are 35 items assessing mathematical literacy related to topics such as quantity, space and shape, change and relationships, and uncertainty. The items require competencies in reproduction, connection, and reflection. The items are couched in different contexts, including personal, public, occupational, educational, scientific, and intra-mathematical (OECD, 2010, Table A5.2: 188). The Mathematics raw scores were transformed to a scale of a mean of 500 with a standard deviation of 100.

## Reading literacy

The PISA Reading test comprises 102 items, most of which are multiple-choice items scored dichotomously and some open-ended questions with score ranges. The items yield scores for the five reading sub-skills. For each sub-skill test, the raw scores were transformed to a scale of a mean 500 with a standard deviation 100.

## Reading sub-skills

*Reading* is a generic term but in fact the activity called *reading* entails several sub-skills which deal with the materials in varied manners for different purposes. While PISA 2009 ranks participating countries almost exclusively based on their Reading means, the test in fact comprises sub-tests for several reading sub-skills applied to continuous reading and abilities to access and retrieve, integrate and interpret, and reflect and evaluate (OECD, 2010). These are *aspects* defining the cognitive approach that determines how readers engage with a text. The abilities are explicated thus:

> Proficient readers have a repertoire of approaches and purposes for reading. They approach texts in order to access and retrieve information. They are able to interpret texts at the level of words, sentences and larger sections, and integrate information within texts and across *multiple texts*.

Proficient readers reflect on texts in order to better understand and extend their own experiences, and in order to evaluate the relevance, utility and quality of the texts themselves (OECD, 2010: 39).

## Mathematics and Reading: Present Study

### Research questions

Armed with the review above, this secondary analysis attempted to answer the following specific questions:

1. How do Reading and reading sub-skills correlate with Mathematics achievement?
2. Which reading sub-skills are most predictive of Mathematics achievement?

It is readily appreciated that answers to these questions will enhance understanding of the influence reading has on the learning and achievement in mathematics. The answers are of interest to educators in general and mathematics educators in particular, with implications for curriculum design and instructional procedures.

### Data and analysis

Data re-analyzed in this study were gleaned from the relevant tables of the PISA report (OECD, 2010). These include the country means for Reading, Mathematics, and five Reading Sub-skills (i.e., Access–Retrieve, Integrate–Interpret, Reflect–Evaluate, Continuous Text, and Non-continuous Text). Correlations were first estimated for the variables as a preliminary exploration of the possible mutual influences among them. This was followed by a multiple regression analysis with the PISA Mathematics mean as the criterion and Reading and Reading Sub-skills means as predictors.

### How do reading and reading sub-skills correlate with Mathematics achievement?

As shown in Table 1, the correlation between Mathematics and Reading is a very high $r = 0.95$ indicating 90% of shared variance between the two

**Table 1.** Correlations between Mathematics Achievement and Reading Sub-skills.

| | Mathematics | Reading | Access–Retrieve | Integrate–Interpret | Reflect–Evaluate | Continuous Text | Non-cont. Text |
|---|---|---|---|---|---|---|---|
| Math | 1.00 | 0.948 | 0.951 | 0.959 | 0.903 | 0.943 | 0.941 |
| Reading | | 1.00 | 0.992 | 0.996 | 0.998 | 0.999 | 0.994 |
| Access | | | 1.00 | 0.988 | 0.968 | 0.990 | 0.988 |
| Integrate | | | | 1.00 | 0.971 | 0.995 | 0.986 |
| Reflect | | | | | 1.00 | 0.985 | 0.985 |
| Continuous Text | | | | | | 1.00 | 0.988 |
| Non-continuous Text | | | | | | | 1.00 |

*Note*: All coefficients are statistically significant ($p < 0.01$).

achievement measures. It is of note that all reading sub-skills also have very high correlations with Mathematics, varying from $r = 0.90$ (Reflect) to $r = 0.96$ (Integrate), indicating shared variances from 81% to 92%. Moreover, the ability to read continuous and non-continuous texts both correlate highly with Mathematics. Besides, as would be expected, all reading sub-skills have very high correlations with Reading as well as among themselves.

As Reading score was derived from the scores for the reading sub-skills and these are different aspects of reading, the high correlations may not be unexpected. However, the correlation between Reading and Mathematics is unusually high in view of the magnitudes of correlations reported in the studies reviewed above, which have an upper bound of around $r = 0.75$.

A methodological implication of such high correlations is that there is very high multicollinearity when Reading Sub-skills are used to predict Mathematics. This renders some of the reading sub-skills redundant in prediction. Statistically, with such high correlations, any one of the several sub-skills will be a good predictor even though the sub-skills conceptually differ in nature. For example, the ability to read continuous text and non-continuous text may require different set of mental processes although there is a very high correlation suggesting that students good in one are mostly also good in the other, as the PISA results show.

## Which reading sub-skills are most predictive of Mathematics achievement?

When scores for the five reading sub-skills were submitted for a stepwise multiple regression analysis using the forward method, three models resulted (Table 2). The first model shows that Integrate–Interpret predicts 92% of Mathematics achievement. Model 2 picks up Reflect–Evaluate, but the *negative* beta-weight indicates that this predictor functions as a suppressor while the prediction of Integrate–Interpret increases. Model 3 adds Non-continuous Text to the prediction with a positive beta-weight. However, it is of note that Models 2 and 3 add very little to the prediction, explaining only 1% and then another 0.5% more of Mathematics variance.

As suspected earlier when the very high correlations were noted, there is high multicollinearity among the reading sub-skills when used as predictors of mathematics achievement. In fact, even the three entered into the regression analysis have variance inflation factors (VIF) varying from 33.5 to 71.5 when VIF > 5 is considered as showing a redundancy problem (Kenny, 2011). Since Integrate–Interpret predicts a very large proportion (92%) of Mathematics achievement and the inclusion of additional

Table 2. Models of Multiple Regression.

|  | Model 1 | Model 2 | Model 3 |
|---|---|---|---|
| R | 0.959 | 0.965 | 0.968 |
| R-square | 0.919 | 0.932 | 0.937 |
| Adjusted R-square | 0.917 | 0.930 | 0.934 |
| Increase in R-square | 0.919 | 0.013 | 0.005 |
| Predictor beta-weight |  |  |  |
| Integrate–Interpret | 0.959 | 1.420 | 1.097 |
| Reflect–Evaluate | — | −0.475 | −0.768 |
| Non-continuous text | — | — | 0.616 |
| Access–Retrieve | — | — | — |
| Continuous test | — | — | — |

*Note*: All beta-weights are significant at the $p < 0.05$ level.

predictors does not contribute much to the prediction, it is reasonable to conclude that Integrate–Interpret is the single best predictor of performance in Mathematics.

## Lessons Learned

The very high correlations among country means for the PISA tests on Mathematics, Reading, and Reading sub-skills are surprising. No doubt these measures are the outcome of learning in the school context and should therefore be correlated to a large extent, but correlations beyond $r = 0.9$ are not always found nor expected. It is hard to say whether these are a boon or a bane.

On a positive note, they show a very high degree of consistency of the measures. In fact, the five reading sub-skills taken together as a scale (i.e., Reading) has practically perfect internal consistency as indicated by a Cronbach's coefficient $\alpha = 0.996$! In this sense, the measures are totally trustworthy where reliability is concerned. On the other hand, the far higher correlations are too good to be true and may in fact signal a hidden measurement problem — something like expressing a certain length in inches and then in centimeters.

It is well-known that body height and weight have a very high correlation in the region of $r = 0.8$ and both also correlate with prowess in some sports. However, it does not make good sense to equate height with weight as they measure different aspects of the body. Analogously, it does not make much sense to equate Reading with Mathematics on the grounds of the near perfect correlation. But then, they can both be expected to correlate highly with a third measure, that of intellectual ability. This is an issue awaiting further research to show one way or another.

The more definitive finding of this secondary analysis is that one of the reading sub-skills is the single best predictor of mathematics achievement. PISA 2009 (OECD, 2010a: 34) describes the reading sub-skill Integrate–Interpret as follows:

> Forming a broad understanding and developing an interpretation tasks focus the reader on relationships within a text. Tasks that focus on the whole text require readers to form a broad understanding; tasks that

focus on relationships between parts of the text require developing an interpretation. The two are grouped together under integrate and interpret.

Thus, the reading sub-skill Integrate–Interpret requires the students to be able to do two separate but related processes while reading: (1) To focus on the whole text to form a broad understanding of what has been read and (2) to focus on relationships among the constituent parts of the text. This whole-and-parts dual process resembles the required process when students solve mathematical problems, be these presented in words (e.g., story sums) or as mathematical sentences (e.g., equations). In so doing, they need first to be able to comprehend the problems presented in words and this involves the usual reading comprehension which reading instruction is about. Next, they should be able to break down what they have read into its constituents and decipher the connections among them. Then they need to translate these ideas into mathematical terms and operations. This is the initial step propounded in Polya's four-step problem-solving which has been widely adopted by mathematics educators (Wilson, Fernandez, and Hadaway, 1993).

When the high school curriculum is compartmentalized into a conglomeration of well-circumscribed subjects to be taught by different specialized teachers, teaching of the various subjects tend to go in different directions. There is, then, a fragmentation of instruction and hence learning. Teachers of language and teachers of mathematics tend to see their instructions as having different purposes and play down or even ignore the link between the subjects. Mathematics teachers tend to see reading comprehension *not* as part of their job but language teachers'. They may also rush themselves and their students into getting the correct answers to the mathematical problems (be these story sums or mathematical equations). In such a situation, students are urged to quickly solve mathematical problems that they do not really understand, leading to unsatisfactory achievement levels.

As shown in this re-analysis, there is a strong correlation between mathematics and reading, especially the reading sub-skill of integration and interpretation. Correlation does not necessarily indicate a causal direction, but in the context of this study, it stands to reason that poor mathematic achievement could have been caused by poor reading competency, at least partly, and not the other way round. This implies, in a general manner, that there is a need for mathematics teachers to ensure students have truly understood the problems before plunging into the relevant mathematical operations.

More specific strategies may include the following, depends on the students' needs:

- Mathematics teachers work collaboratively with language teachers to improve students' reading comprehension, particularly texts involving mathematics concepts.
- Compile a set of mathematical terms and familiarize the students with the mathematical register and the conventions of mathematics problems.
- Check, and modify when necessary, the language of problem sums and mathematical problems to reduce the demand on students' language competency.
- As the very first step of solving any mathematical problem, spend more time to look at it from different angles to ensure it is well-understood by the students; solve the reading problem before trying to solve the mathematical problem.
- If found to be necessary, have lessons on reading comprehension of mathematical problems, focusing on reading without doing the mathematics.

## Caveats

This call for mathematics teachers to help their students in reading comprehension (especially integration and interpretation) as the first step to solve mathematical problems is not new. The findings based on worldwide data reiterate this oft-neglected procedure and serve as a reminder of its importance. However, it is necessary to mention that the PISA data here was trusted at face value, *bona fide,* with no question asked about its reliability and validity.

PISA asserts that its tests are process-oriented assessing 'literacy' and not product-oriented for assessing acquired knowledge (OECD, 2010). This has been doubted (e.g., Sjoberg, 2007; Clark, 2011). For instance, Sjoberg (2007), while discussing the political significance of PISA, questioned the possibility of assessing *real life challenges* (which PISA tests claim to assess) by using paper-and-pencil tests as well as its cross-national validity. It was further pointed out that the PISA tests rely heavily on reading ability. In the context of the present study, the language dependency of the tests might have grossly inflated the correlations between Mathematics, Reading, and reading sub-skills found for the data.

Another concern is the small number of countries involved in the multiple regression analysis, for which usually far more than 65 cases are needed. In fact, sample size is not a simple question as it is related to several statistical conditions such as the *alpha* level, the number of predictors, the required power, and the expected effect size. However, for this study, when the conditions are taken into account, the relevant table of the *StatTools.net* (Chang, 2011) suggests that a size of as small as 12 (which is far below 65) would suffice. Thus, the findings for the analysis here can be trusted.

## References

Abedi, J. and Lord, C. (2001). The language factor in mathematics tests. *Applied Measurement in Education*, **14**(3), 219–234.

Adams, R. and Le, L. *Effects of Student Reading Proficiency on PISA Mathematics Items — A DIF Study Across Countries.* Paper presented at the PISA Research Conference. Kiel, Germany. Sep. 2009.

Aiken, L. W. (1972). Language Factors in Learning Mathematics. *Review of Educational Research*, **42**(3), 359–385.

Beal, C. R. (January 2010). Reading Proficiency and Mathematics Problem Solving by High School English Language Learners. *Urban Education*, **45**(1), 58–74. doi: 10.1177/0042085909352143

Chang, A. (2012). Tables of sample size for multiple regression. *StatTools.net.* http://www.stattools.net/SSizmreg_Tab.php

Clark, D. (15 March 2011). *Leaning Tower of PISA — 7 Serious Skews.* Available at http://donaldclarkplanb.blogspot.sg/2011/03/leaning-tower-of-pisa-7-serious-skews.html

Cox, J. M. and Poe, V. L. (Summer 1991). The math-reading connection: a graded word list to estimate mathematics ability. *Reading Improvement*, **28**(2), 108–112.

Cuevas, G. J. (March 1984). Mathematics learning in English as a second language. *Journal for Research in Mathematics Education*, **15**(2), 134–144.

Floyd, R. G. and Evans, J. J. (2003). Relations between measures of Cattell-Horn-Carroll (CHC) cognitive abilities and mathematics achievement across the school-age years. *Psychology in the Schools*, **40**(2), 155–171.

Hansen, C. W. (1944). Factors associated with successful achievement in problem solving in 6th grade arithmetic. *Journal of Educational Research*, **38**, 111–117.

Innabi, H. (2005). The relationship between mathematical skills and Arabic reading comprehension among United Arab Emirates University Students. *Journal of Faculty of Education*, **18**(22), 37–50.

Kenny, D. A. (10 September 2011). *Multiple Regression*. http://davidakenny.net/cm/mr.htm

Kovas, Y., Harlaar, N., Petrill, S. A. and Plomin, R. (2004). Mathematics, reading and IQ: a multivariate genetic analysis in 7-year-old twins. *Behavior Genetics*, **34**(6), 646.

Lamb, J. H. (2010). Reading grade levels and mathematics assessment: an analysis of Texas Mathematics Assessment Items and their reading difficulty. *The Mathematics Educator*, **20**(1), 22–34.

Larwin, K. H. (n.d.) Reading is fundamental in predicting math achievement in 10th graders. *International Electronic Journal of Mathematics Education*, **5**(3), 131–145.

Liu, J. (April 2011). The geek's dilemma: breadth vs. depth of interests. *GeekDad: Raising Geek Generation 2.0*. Accessed on January 6, 2012 from http://www.wired.com/geekdad/2011/04/the-geeks-dilemma-breadth-vs-depth-of-interests/

Loo, C. P. and Fond, H. K. (1996). Variables associated with mathematics achievement of primary five pupils in Singapore schools. *The Mathematics Educator*, **1**(1), 1–16. Accessed on January 20, 2010 from http://repository.nie.edu.sg/jspui/bitstream/10497/41/1/ME-1-1-1.pdf

Mathews, J. (October, 2009). *Test that makes U.S. look bad may not be so good*. http://voices.washingtonpost.com/class-struggle/2009/10/politicians_and_pundits_are_us.html

Mortimore, P. (2009). Alternative models for analysing and representing countries' performance in PISA. Paper commissioned by Education International Research Institute, Brussels. http://download.ei-ie.org/Docs/WebDepot/Alternative%20Models%20in%20PISA.pdf

OECD (2010). *What Students Know and Can Do: Student Performance in Reading, Mathematics, and Science. (Volume I)*. Organisation for Economic Co-operation and Development. Accessed on December 1, 2011 from http://dx.doi.org/10.1787/9789264091450-en

Smith, L. M. (1976). *A Study of the Dependence of mathematics Achievement on Reading Achievement.* Ann Arbor, Michigan: University Microfilms, Order No. 76–21.913MF.

Sjøberg, S. (October 2007). PISA and "Real Life Challenges": Mission Impossible? Contribution o Hopman (Ed): PISA according to PISA Revised Version Oct 8 2007 http://folk.uio.no/sveinsj/Sjoberg-PISA-book-2007.pdf

Walker, C. M. , Zhang, B., and Suber, J. (April 2008). Using multidimensional differential item functioning framework to determine if reading ability affects student performance in mathematics. *Applied Measurement in Education*, **21**(2), 162–181.

Wilson, J. W., Fernandez, M. L., and Hadaway, N. (1993). Mathematical problem solving. In Wilson, P. S., Ed. (1993). *Research Ideas for the Classroom: High School Mathematics.* New York: MacMillan.

## Chapter 9

# Collaborative Problem Solving in PISA 2015: Highlights and Reflections

In the present day, collaborative problem solving is gaining importance as development projects require the cooperation of people with different expertise and capabilities. It is timely that PISA included collaborative problem solving as one domain of its 2015 survey, in which Singapore topped the list of more than 50 participating countries and economies. This article highlights some of the key findings and reflects on their interpretation. In addition, results of the re-analysis of the two sets of relevant attitudes (valuing relationship and teamwork) are presented and discussed.

There are two basic approaches to problem solving: individual and collaborative (or group). In the typical, traditional educational context, problem solving is undertaken by an individual student to find answers to textbook-based problems, which by and large are closed-ended and have standard answers. Such textbook-based problem solving serves to consolidate what has been learned and, in today's sense of problem solving, does not constitute problem solving, strictly speaking. In the present day context, problem solving is more likely to involve open-ended problems which have no fixed answers, the pursuit of which may extend beyond textbooks. And, perhaps more often than not, solving the problem involves more than reading prescribed texts but entails model construction of sort, and such problem solving may take the form of project work. Moreover, students have been increasingly involved in solving problems together, that is, collaboratively in student-centered teaching (McKenna, 2017).

Collaborative problem solving is not only a pedagogical strategy; it has been shown to have a therapeutic function for children with oppositional behaviors (Stetson and Plog, 2016).

PISA studied 15-year-olds' ability in individual problem solving in the 2012 survey, and it is a logical extension to cover collaborative or group problem solving in the next round in the 2015 survey. Both surveys involved the assessment of such soft skills or 21$^{st}$ century skills, as compared with PISA's conventional concern for the hard skills in the three subjects of Reading, Mathematics, and Science. PISA 2015 justifies the assessment of collaborative problem solving thus:

> Today's workplaces demand people who can solve problems in concert with others. But collaboration poses potential challenges to team members. Labour might not be divided equitably or efficiently, with team members perhaps working on tasks they are unsuited for or dislike. Conflict may arise among team members, hindering the development of creative solutions. Thus, collaboration is a skill in itself (OECD, 2017: 18).

A total of 52 countries (and economies) were involved in this survey, of which 32 were OECD Members and 30 OECD Partners. Computer-based problem solving tasks were presented in several units, each requiring between five and 20 minutes to complete. Individual students worked through the problem in two ways, involving programmed computer agents as partners and also their peers as partners. The involvement of computer agents in place of human partners was decided upon after a successful trial which compared both types of agents, showing only negligible differences of no practical consequence (OECD, 2017).

## Collaborative Problem Solving Tasks

In the PISA 2015 survey, there are three different types of tasks: (1) Jigsaw or hidden-profile tasks where group members need to pool different information to solve the problem; (2) consensus-building tasks where group members consider partners' views, opinions, and arguments to come to an agreed solution; and (3) negotiation tasks where group members negotiate to reach the group's goals. For these, 12 problem solving skills were assessed. These resulted from merging the 2012 individual problem solving processes (*exploring and understanding, representing and formulating, planning and executing,* and *monitoring and reflecting*) and the 2015 collaborative problem solving competencies (*establishing and maintaining shared understanding, taking appropriate action to solve the problem,* and *establishing and maintaining team organization*). It is noted here that the problem solving tasks, as illustrated by the released task (Xandar), entailed the extensive reading of texts used to present the problems and options in the form of multiple-choice questions. Moreover, as the tasks are presented on the monitor, a certain degree of familiarity with computer skills is required of the student.

## Interesting Findings

Some interesting findings are highlighted in the PISA 2015 report (OECD, 2017: 17). These are cited below with integration and comments added by the present writer.

### *High scorers*

*Students in Singapore score higher in collaborative problem solving than students in all other participating countries and economies, followed by students in Japan...On average across OECD countries, 28% of students are able to solve only straightforward... collaborative problems, if any at all...Across OECD countries, 8% of students are top performers in collaborative problem solving.*

Except for Singapore and Japan, which scored 561.5 and 551.7, respectively, the findings cited above do not seem to be very encouraging in view of the importance placed on the ability to collaboratively solve problem in the present day, when problem solving capacity and collaboration in the work force is critical to social and economic development. Singapore and Japan may congratulate themselves on being the two top-scoring countries. Their impressive achievement might be attributable to their educational practices, which emphasize group project work (Cult of Pedagogy, 2016; Ministry of Education, 2015) in which students have

Table 1. Comparisons on Collaborative Problem Solving.

| | Mean | SD | Difference | Pooled SD | Effect size |
|---|---|---|---|---|---|
| OECD Members | 500.0 | 31.2 | 38.3 | 42.8 | 0.9 |
| OECD Partners | 461.7 | 49.4 | | | |
| OECD Members minus* | 497.0 | 29.8 | 35.3 | 41.9 | 0.8 |
| OECD Partners | 461.7 | 49.4 | | | |
| East Asia Top 5 | 545.2 | 11.2 | 11.5 | 9.7 | 1.2 |
| Europe Top 5 | 533.7 | 1.7 | | | |

*Minus Japan and Korea.

ample opportunity to solve non-textbook problems collaboratively working with their peers.

Table 1 shows the results of comparisons between collaborative problem solving means. Firstly, OECD Members as a group scored 38.3 higher than did OECD Partners, with a large effect size of Cohen's $d = 0.9$. However, when Japan and Korea, the two East Asian countries, were excluded, the difference is reduced somewhat to 35.3, which is still a sizable difference with a large effect size of Cohen's $d = 0.8$.

It is interesting to see if there is a sizable difference between the top five East Asian and European countries. The top five East Asian countries are Singapore (561.5), Japan (551.7), Hong Kong–China (540.8), Korea (538.3), and Macao–China (533.8). On the other hand, the top five European countries are Canada (535.4), Estonia (535.2), Finland (533.9), New Zealand (532.8), and Australia (531.4). It is obvious that the East Asian countries are heterogeneous (SD = 11.2) whereas the European countries are rather homogeneous (SD = 1.7).

There is a large difference in favor of the East Asian countries, with a difference of 11.5 and a large effect size of Cohen's $d = 1.2$. This difference leads to an interesting paradoxical conclusion that the East Asian countries are *heterogeneously more group-minded* while the European countries are *homogeneously more individual-minded*. This seems to go against the commonly held stereotype that Asians are collective and that Europeans are individualistic (e.g., Hopper, 2015; Triandis, 1993).

## Correlations with hard skills

*Collaborative problem-solving performance is positively related to performance in the core PISA subjects (science, reading, and mathematics), but the relationship is weaker than that observed among those other domains.*

Correlation coefficients of r = 0.74, r = 0.70, and r = 0.77 are reported (OECD, 2017, Figure V.3.7: 77) between collaborative problem solving scores and, respectively, Reading, Mathematics, and Science scores. As alluded to earlier, the collaborative problem solving tasks are highly verbal and therefore require a high level of reading comprehension. With such high correlation, it is not surprising that Reading alone accounts for 55 percent of the criterion variance. A similar observation was made by Sjøberg (October 2007) on PISA tests 10 years ago.

Moreover, there seems to be under-reporting on the inter-correlations among Reading, Mathematics, and Science as shown in Table 2 below. In Table 2, correlations above the principal diagonal are reported by PISA and those below are calculated by the present writer using the data (i.e., country means) from the PISA 2015 report (OECD, 2016, Figure I.1.1). It can be seen that those reported by PISA vary from r = 0.80 to r = 0.88, while those newly calculated vary from r = 0.94 to r = 0.98. These discrepancies indicate that between 16 and 24 percent of the shared variances among the three subjects are under-estimated. By inference, the correlations between collaborative problem solving and the three subjects are also under-estimated. In view of these, the dependence of collaborative problem solving ability on the three subjects is even more obvious.

Table 2. Correlations among Reading, Mathematics, and Science.

|  | Reading | Mathematics | Science |
|---|---|---|---|
| Reading | — | 0.80 | 0.87 |
| Mathematics | 0.94 | — | 0.88 |
| Science | 0.96 | 0.98 | — |

## Attitudes to collaborative problem solving

*Students in every country and economy have generally positive attitudes towards collaboration...Girls in almost every country and economy tend to value relationships more than boys...Boys agree more often than girls that they prefer working as part of a team to working alone.*

The general positive attitude towards collaboration is to be celebrated as this has practical implications for instruction while the students are still in the school as well as in the long term (to their benefit and that of the economic development of their countries) when they enter the national and even the international work force. The gender difference may reflect the different lifestyles of the boys and the girls; and it is of note that while girls are more relationship-oriented, boys are more task-oriented. With a stretch of mind, it might be argued that such difference is a reminiscence of inheritance from time forgotten as far back as the hunter–gatherer culture (e.g., Hopkins, 2009).

## Contributing factors

*The more students value relationships, the better they perform in collaborative problem solving. A similar relationship is observed the more that students value teamwork...Attitudes towards collaboration are generally more positive as students engage in more physical activity or attend more physical education classes per week...Students who play video games outside of school score slightly lower in collaborative problem solving than students who do not play video games...Students who work in the household or take care of other family members value both teamwork and relationships more than other students.*

The importance and hence the need to develop collaborative problem solving capacities in students is too obvious to require further elaboration. The advocacy and efforts to train students in the 21$^{st}$ Century skills, of which collaborative problem solving is one such competency, are well-documented (e.g., Ministry of Education, 2015; Rotherham and Willingham, 2009). Such skills can be, and are being, trained explicitly and directly in the classroom and through specific programs. They can also be developed or acquired implicitly and indirectly through other activities which may and may not target at the skills in the first place.

What has been reported above in PISA 2015 in this regard is more of the latter type. It is readily appreciated that taking part in physical activities has a positive correlation with collaborative problem solving, since team games (like basketball and soccer and even doubles table tennis) are in reality collaborative problem solving tasks in their own right. The same case may be argued for involvement in household work and care. On the other hand, the slight negative correlation for video games is also understandable, since most such games pit an individual player against another, thus imperceptibly developing ego-centrism (e.g., Zamani *et al.*, 2010).

## Revisiting Attitudes to Collaborative Problem Solving

PISA 2015 measured attitudes towards collaborative problem solving using two sets of items.

Items for valuing relationships include the following:

1. I am a good listener.
2. I enjoy seeing my classmates be successful.
3. I take into account what others are interested in.
4. I enjoy considering different perspectives.

At the same time, items for valuing teamwork include the following:

1. I prefer working as part of a tem to working alone.
2. I find that teams make better decisions than individuals.
3. I find that teamwork raises may own efficiency.
4. I enjoy co-operating with peers.

PISA derives a score for valuing relationships by combining the item scores for the first four items above, having assumed that these items are a measure of the same construct (valuing relationships) so the item scores are therefore additive. The same idea goes for the items valuing teamwork. When the country means for the items are submitted for factor analyses, one for relationship items and the other for teamwork items, results shown in Table 3 are obtained.

**Table 3.** Factor Analyses.

|  | Factor 1 | Factor 2 |
| --- | --- | --- |
| Valuing relationships |  |  |
| I am a good listener. | 0.265 | 0.774 |
| I enjoy seeing my classmates be successful. | 0.831 | −0.072 |
| I take into account what others are interested in. | −0.063 | 0.810 |
| I enjoy considering different perspectives. | 0.779 | 0.288 |
| Total variance predicted | 34.3% | 33.9% |
| Inter-factor correlation | −0.25 | |
| Valuing teamwork |  |  |
| I prefer working as part of a team to working alone. | 0.769 | |
| I find that teams make better decisions than individuals. | 0.928 | |
| I find that teamwork raises my own efficiency. | 0.837 | |
| I enjoy co-operating with peers. | 0.788 | |
| Total variance predicted | 69.3% | |

As shown in Table 3, the four items for valuing relationships form two oblique (correlated) factors. The first factor is heavily loaded by "*I enjoy seeing my classmates be successful*" and "*I enjoy considering different perspectives*", and the second factor by "*I am a good listener*" and "*I take into account what others are interested in*". The two factors are of about the same 'size' in terms of the total variance explained (68.2 percent) and, more importantly, they have a low *negative* correlation of r = −0.25. Going by the item content, the first factor seems to be more concerned with the outcome of collaborative problem solving whereas the second is more reflective of the relation between self and partners. The negative correlation suggests, of course, that students who value outcome tend to de-value relationships, and vice versa.

More critical is the negative correlation, low though it is. This is contrary to the PISA's practice of summing item scores for the attitude of valuing relationships. As such, PISA's conception of a single dimension formed by the four items is not actualized in the data. Also, it may be useful to split the four items into two subscales and see how they correlate with collaborative problem solving competence.

Also shown in Table 3 is the factor analysis result for the four items for valuing teamwork. The one factor (explaining 69.3 percent of total variance) confirms the validity of PISA's conceptualization that there is one dimension.

It is interesting to note that the internal consistency reliability of the four-item scale is Cronbach's $\alpha = 0.98$, and the reliabilities of the two-item subscales are both $\alpha = 0.97$. Thus, the split subscales yield comparable reliability and yet are able to provide more information.

The Cronbach's $\alpha$ is a high 0.97. However, taking these together, such high reliabilities for such short scales is unusual, and one possible explanation is that they rely to a large extent on verbal proficiency.

Factor scores generated for the three factors reported above were then correlated with the country means for collaborative problem solving. The results show that collaborative problem solving means have a negative correlation of $r = -0.40$ with the factor focusing on outcome, a positive correlation of $r = 0.52$ with the factor focusing on self–partner, and a negative correlation of $r = -0.30$ with valuing teamwork. Thus, it appears that countries where students were more concerned with outcome and with teamwork tend to be poorer in collaborative problem solving and, at the same time, countries where students were more interested in the relation between self and partners tend to do better. This suggests that for collaborative problem solving to be effective, relation is more critical than task; obviously, this paradox deserves further investigation since relation-orientation and task-orientation seem to be somewhat antagonistic.

Table 4 shows the result of multiple regression. When country means for collaborative problem solving were regressed on the factor scores for outcome, self–partner, and teamwork, only self–partner was found to be a

Table 4.  Multiple Regression.

|  | Beta | b | S.E. | t | p |
| --- | --- | --- | --- | --- | --- |
| Outcome | −0.186 | −7.703 | 5.816 | −1.324 | 0.192 |
| Self–partner | 0.496 | 20.862 | 4.925 | 4.236 | 0.001 |
| Teamwork | −0.213 | −9.256 | 6.012 | −1.540 | 0.130 |
| Intercept | 0.000 | 483.705 | 4.819 | — | — |

Adjusted R-square = 0.358 (d.f. 3:47, F = 10.290, p < 0.001).

significant predictor; outcome and self–partner have negative regression coefficients and were not statistically significant. As collaborative problem solving has two aspects, relationship (collaboration) and problem solution (task), this results suggest that relationship is most critical.

## Conclusion

As the title of this article indicates, it is to provide a summary of the PISA 2015 survey on collaborative problem solving of 15-year-olds of the participating countries. It also provides some observations based on secondary analyses of the data available from the PISA report. This article might have raised some points worthy of further analysis and research. As this is the first time PISA expended itself to study soft skills internationally, it will be interesting to wait for the next round to see how the competence in collaborative problem solving has developed and changed in the participating countries.

## References

Cult of Pedagogy (26 June 2016). *Project Based Learning: Start here.* https://www.cultofpedagogy.com/project-based-learning/

Hopkin, Whitney (22 October, 2009). *Hunter vs. Gatherer: Gender Differences on the Mind.* Fast Company. Available at https://www.fastcompany.com/1369824/hunter-vs-gatherer-gender-differences-mind

Hoper, E. (30 January 2015). Individualist or Collectivist? How Culture Influence Behavior. *Healthypsych.* Available at https://healthypsych.com/individualist-or-collectivist-how-culture-influences-behavior/

McKenna, J. (14 September 2017). Collaborative Problem Solving in the Classroom. *Robo Matter.* Available at https://www.robomatter.com/blog-collaborative-problem-solving/

Ministry of Education, Singapore (2015a). *Project Work.* Available at https://www.moe.gov.sg/education/programmes/project-work

Ministry of Education, Singapore (2015b). *21$^{st}$ Century Competencies.* Available at https://www.moe.gov.sg/education/education-system/21st-century-competencies

OECD (2017). *PISA 2015 Results (Volume V): Collaborative Problem Solving.* PISA, OECD Publishing, Paris. http://dx.doi.org/10.1787/9789264285521-en

OECD (2016). *PISA 2015 Results (Volume I): Excellence and Equity in Education.* PISA, OECD Publishing, Paris. http://dx.doi.org/10.1787/9789264266490-en

Rotherham, A. J., and Willingham, D. (September 2009). 21$^{st}$ Century Skills: The Challenges Ahead. *Educational Leadership*, **67**(1), 16–21.

Sjøberg, S. (October 2007). PISA and "Real Life Challenges": Mission Impossible? Contribution to Hopman (Ed): *PISA according to PISA Revised Version Oct 8 2007.* Available at http://folk.uio.no/sveinsj/Sjoberg-PISA-book-2007.pdf

Stetson, Erica A., Plog, Amy E. (2016). Collaborative Problem Solving in Schools: Results of a Year-Long Consultation Project. *School Social Work Journal,* **40**(2). Available at https://www.questia.com/library/journal/1P3-4060103011/collaborative-problem-solving-in-schools-results

Triandis, H. (1993). Collectivism and individualism as cultural syndromes. *Cross-Cultural Research: The Journal of Comparative Social Science,* **27**, 155–180.

Zamani, E., Kheeraadmand, A., Cheshmi, M., Abedi, A., and Hedayati, N. (Summer–Autumn 2010). Comparing the social skills of students addicted to computer games with normal students. *Addict Health*, **2**(3–4), 59–66.

## Chapter 10

# PISA's New Venture in Creative Thinking: Some Conceptual and Methodological Concerns

PISA started with assessment of Reading, Mathematics, and Science, rotating the three subjects in consecutive surveys. These are always referred to as *hard skills*. Then, in 2015, PISA added soft skills such as information and communication technology as well as financial literacy as additional domains to the three subjects. Doing this reflects the concerns of present day education. Continuing this line, PISA will include creative thinking in its 2021 survey. To educationists in the world, this is definitely a welcome new development of PISA.

### Creativity Research in the Past

The world's interest in creativity in the educational context started in the USA, with J. P. Guilford working, after the World War II, on assessing the intelligence and creativity of army recruits. Interest in creativity and its research got a booster when America lost the space race to Russia, which sent the Sputnik up into the sky in 1957. This prompted the passing of the National Defense Education Act of 1958, with which came a huge source of funding. This enabled the American educational system to meet the demands posed by national security needs. In this context, Guilford became the kingpin in creativity research, leading to his creation of a model called Structure of Intellect (SI; Guilford, 1967) which influenced much of creativity research in the subsequent decades. As time passed, as

162    PISA and PIRLS: The Effects of Culture and School Environment

is true of many things educational, interest in creativity gradually waned into a low tide.

Guildford's SI Model has three dimensions (Contents, Products, and Operations). Basically, the SI Model enables researchers to think about *what we do to what, to produce what*. In the SI Model, *Contents* include the visual, auditory, symbolic, semantic, and behavioral. *Products* include units, classes, relations, systems, transformation, and implications. And *Operations* include cognition, memory, divergent production, convergent production, and evaluation. This $5 \times 6 \times 5$ model yields a total of 150 different kinds of components. (See Figure 1.)

Of immediate relevance to creativity are the 30 divergent components, e.g., divergent-auditory-system (such as a piece of music newly composed). Elaborating on the components, Guilford created some tests for measuring creativity which are widely used by creativity researchers. A well-known example of such test is his *Alternative Uses Test*. An item of this test, for instance, asks the respondent to think of as many ways of using an empty Coca-Cola can. The respondent has to think of many ways, applying the divergent thinking process, to transform the empty can

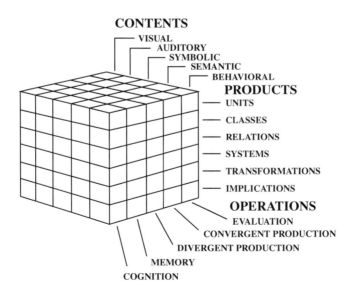

**Figure 1.**    Structure of Intellect Model.

to suit a variety of purposes (e.g., to hold up a lit candle — not the original purpose of the can); each use (idea) is an assessment unit. The responses are then assessed for (1) *fluency* (numbers of ideas), (2) *flexibility* (categories of ideas), (3) *originality* (infrequency of the idea), and (4) *elaboration* (details of the idea).

Subsequent to Guilford's efforts, there are many other theories (models). For instance, Synectics (Gordon, 1961) and Geneplor (Finke, Ward, and Smith, 1992) are interesting models which have spawned much of creativity research. Kozbelt, Beghetto, and Runco (2010) provide a comprehensive summary and comparisons of the major theories of creativity available to date. And for the measurement of creativity, *Creativity Based Information Resources: Assessment of Creativity* (International Centre for Studies in Creativity, n.d.) list no less than 162 creativity tests published in 1994–2004; by now, the list would have been extensively extended. Specifically well-known and widely used tests are exemplified by the ubiquitous *Torrance Tests of Creative Thinking* (Torrance, 1966) which has verbal and figural versions, and the *Remote Association Test* based on Mednick's (1962) theory of association, which has adult and high school versions.

Skimpy though the above summary may be, it goes to show that creativity research has had a long enough history, during which much of our understanding of creativity was accumulated, and, above all, that there is a very large number of tools for its assessment. This being the case, it stands to reason that it would be prudent and economical to base further studies of student creativity by adopting or integrating some of the tested models and relevant validated measurements, instead of reinventing the wheel. The accumulated knowledge of creativity research and measurement may now be considered as classic; they form the knowledge base from which future research can take off. Nevertheless, to be creative, by definition, is to do things differently.

## Creativity Research in PISA's Pipeline

### *Motivation*

In view of the trend of the past summarized above, it may be said that PISA's interest in creativity is nothing new but a revival in a different context — globalized need for survival in the present day world. In fact, OECD justifies PISA's plan to include creativity with the following statements (OECD, n.d.):

> There is a growing consensus that formal education should cultivate the creativity and critical thinking skills of students to help them succeed in modern, globalised economies based on knowledge and innovation.

It further justifies the intent by pointing to the inadequacy of schools and teachers where development of student creativity is concerned:

> However, teachers' (and countries') ability to foster and monitor progress is limited by the lack of understanding of how some of these skills materialise at different development stages.

## *Objectives*

Thus, the OECD aims to further develop and refine the understanding of how creative (and critical thinking) skills can be assessed in an educational setting. The following four specific aims are set for this project:

1. Take stock of how countries or institutions explicitly assess creative and critical thinking skills (when they do so), or some aspects of them;
2. Prototype and pilot an assessment tool that will help teachers and students monitor their acquisition, and articulate a language that appears easily understandable and usable internationally;
3. Produce a set of pedagogical activities and exemplars of student work describing what students at different levels of mastery of these skills could do and thus give concrete examples of progression (or standards) in these skills; and
4. Provide a platform for knowledge exchange on practices and ideas around the fostering and assessment of creative and critical thinking skills.

The need for the PISA's creativity survey is further supported by Lucas (2017) who asserts that the "*national curricula are becoming increasingly expansive making aspects of critical and creative thinking mandatory. In Australia, New Zealand, Finland and Singapore, for example, this is the case."*

## Preparation

Preparatory work is well underway. An advisory group, led by Bill Lucas (Professor of Learning at the University of Winchester) and Jack Buckley (Senior Vice-President for Research and Evaluation at the American Institutes of Research), has been tasked to define creative thinking and work on its assessment, with the ultimate aim, as would be expected, to enable ranking (incidentally, can PISA do without ranking?) the participating countries and economies (Ward, 2017).

There is no dearth of definitions of creativity and Batey (2012) provides a selected list of such definitions by influential creativity researchers such as Beghetto, Sternberg, Simonton, and Barron. Leading the PISA team to work on creativity, Lucas adds to the huge conglomeration of definitions his own: *"Creative thinking is a multi-faceted concept involving the generation and refining of ideas as well as the processes by which such thinking can be improved."*

Guided by this definition, the advisory group will work out a set of assessment tools with reference to Lucas's (22 November 2017) *creativity wheel* (literally reinventing a wheel) which has five components: *inquisitive, persistent, collaborative, disciplined,* and *imaginative*. It is interesting that, in Lucas's conceptualization, each of these five creative dimensions (or "*habits of mind*") has three sub-components, thus:

1. Inquisitive: wondering and questioning, exploring and investigating, and challenging assumptions.
2. Persistent: tolerating uncertainty, sticking with difficulty, and daring to be different.
3. Collaborative: cooperating appropriately, giving and receiving feedback, and sharing the product.
4. Disciplined: crafting and improving, developing techniques, and reflecting critically.
5. Imaginative: catering and improving, playing with possibilities, and making connections.

In view of the accumulated knowledge of creativity research, it may be argued that, of the five components of Lucas's creativity wheel, only Imaginative has immediate relevance to the intended PISA survey, while the others are simply correlates supporting behavioral characteristics of a creative person and their processes. When seen in the context of the classical model of the four-Ps of creativity (Rhodes, 1961), the fourth P (Press) seems to be overlooked.

## Research plan

It should be correct to say that all international comparisons of student achievement such as PISA are surveys. They describe the current status of the participating countries in terms of achievements in selected subjects (mainly, Reading, Mathematics, and Science). They also, however, collect data on conditions from which they can infer the probable causes of achievements or the lack thereof. Being surveys, they do not allow bona fide, clear-cut interpretations of cause-and-effect relationships between achievements and the presumed casual factors, like the causal relationship between a country's Science achievement and its teaching resources such as science labs and perhaps computers. Basically, the inferences that are frequently made are merely correlational, which is equivocal where cause and effect are concerned.

PISA 2021 will study creative thinking using an experimental approach. This is not only a deviation from its past practice but, more importantly, a brave undertaking that is very challenging and ambitious in terms of planning and implementation, for several reasons to be discussed later. Nonetheless, OECD (n.d.; emphases added) describes the procedures thus:

> ...the project is a controlled pedagogical intervention that will engage research teams and school networks in 15 countries. The school network within each country will be split into **intervention and control groups**... the project will focus on two areas: Science, Technology, Engineering and Mathematics (*STEM*) subjects, on the one hand, and **arts** education (either visual arts or music), on the other, but will also leave room to interdisciplinary or project-based approaches.

...the project will use **a pre- and post-design** to collect a range of contextual data that will serve to better understand and interpret findings, including potential differences between countries. Instruments for the contextual data collection include subject-specific standardised assessment tests, background questionnaires, and the Evaluation du Potentiel Créatif des élèves (EPoC), a **standardised assessment tool** for creativity.

It is commendable that the team has planned the experiment with build-in methodological rigor in terms of the experimental design: intervention and control groups, pretest and posttest.

## *Research design*

As highlighted in the quote above, PISA promises a lot in the planned experiment, which is, even at the national or localized levels, difficult to actualize. To attempt this at the international level is indeed a great challenge and a bold undertaking. Hopefully it is correct that, even until today, the only large-scale true experiment in the context of education is Tennessee's STAR Project (Mosteller, 1995) which looked into the effect of class size on achievement of younger children, and it was conducted within a state, not even a nation.

A true experiment like the one PISA has planned entails randomization to assign students into experimental and control groups. If the students are truly randomized, the two groups are theoretically equivalent and subsequent interpretation of the experimental outcome (be it positive, neutral, or negative) is unequivocal. This is an ideal situation. However, it is not clear in the PISA statement cited above whether randomization will be practiced. From the school's perspective, randomization will involve pulling out students from their classes to form new classes, and this is operationally clumsy and would disrupt the natural flow of events in the school. Moreover, doing this jeopardizes the contextual validity of the experiment since it is a contrived situation and not a natural one. Additionally, if randomization is not done at the individual level but at the class level (i.e., randomizing a whole class), then the unit of analysis will be the class and not the individual; this critical difference will have to be made clear when analyzing the data, interpreting the outcome, and reporting the result.

Moreover, if there is true randomization (be it of individual or class), the experimental and control groups are at least theoretically justified, equivalent in creative thinking to be begin with — there is then no need for the pretest. Then the experimental design is turned into one of *posttest only control group design* which is as strong as the originally chosen design but with the added benefit of not having to worry about pretesting effect. Understandably, the need for only the posttest means saving resources (e.g., assessor manpower, student class time).

Furthermore, PISA surveys always involve a very large number of students. When there are pretest and posttest, with a reasonable time interval in between them, the problem of motility threat may set in with some students being absent at the posttest, thus reducing the sample size. Since the number of students is large, the reduction may not cause much of a problem as the number of remaining students will still be quite high. However, there is a need to watch out if the absent students 'drop out randomly' and not systematically in some ways that have implications for the interpretation of outcome.

Besides, the need for a control group as planned may be another cause of concern. Teachers are often found to be unwilling and resistant having their students serve as controls in teaching experiments. They see putting students in the control group unethical and unfair, since the intervention is supposed to be beneficial, especially when there are additional resources given to the experimental group. Moreover, they foresee that their students (when put in the control group) are, by definition, going to achieve less and looks inferior, and this may inevitably reflect on the teacher's reputation. To the researcher, such worries may not be necessary, but to the teachers they are real issues.

## *Assessment*

As the statement cited above shows, the *Evaluation du Potentiel Créatif des élèves* (EPoC; Lubart, Besancon, and Bartbot, 2011) will be used to collect data of creative thinking. This is a newcomer to the whole lot of available creativity tests. It is said to assess creative skills by detecting children with high creative potential and provides a creative profile for guiding their creativity development. At the time of writing, EPoC has verbal and graphic forms (like many other creativity tests preceding it) and will later expand to include a third form for 'other areas' (i.e., musical, social, technical inventions, etc.). In this sense, EPoC is *not* a test of general creativity but specific to different domains. For administration, the two forms will take between one to one-and-a-half hours to complete and they can be administrated by non-psychologists after training.

The assessment outcome is a profile (in the form of a Rada Chart) with 10 dimensions: Divergent thinking, motivation to create, openness, ambiguity tolerance, risk taking, intuitive style, analytical style, selective combination, associative capacity, and mental flexibility (Lubart, Barbot, and Zenasni, 2013). Obviously, these dimensions cover three of Rhode's (1961) four-Ps of creativity: person, process, and press (environment), using product as the source for assessment.

From the above information, a few questions arise. First, it is stated that the EPoC is a standardized assessment tool. The test was developed in France and naturally was standardized with a French sample of students. This however does not automatically make it a standardized test for any other country, let alone for so many countries, since the responses of students of other countries are most likely not the same as of French students. This means that for the EPoC to be a valid test across countries and a truly international standardized test, it needs re-norming.

The need to re-standardize leads to the second question. PISA has been developing its assessment tools using English and French as prototypes, which were then translated into the participating countries' languages of instruction. When a test is translated, test equivalence has to be verified and demonstrated. So, the second question is what and how the verification will be done to ensure equivalence among translated versions since, as a normal practice, PISA will compare countries on performance. To this end, differential item functioning analysis may be necessary to check and ensure cross-country comparability of the items making up the EPoC.

It has long been established that different countries do things differently and favor different behaviors (Hofstede, 1980, cited in Soh, 2017a). In other words, they have different cultures. PISA has been ranking the participating countries on one-dimensional measures such as Reading, Mathematics, or Science. These three subjects, especially Mathematics and Science, can be argued to be culture-free. This may not be the case for creativity for two reasons. Creativity is culture-based; what is considered creative in one culture may not be considered so in a different culture. For instance, a painting by Salvador Dali or Pablo Picasso may be seen as 'absurd' when evaluated with a conventional Eastern (e.g., Chinese, Japanese) standard. Moreover, creativity is multi-facet or multi-dimensional (as both Lucas's creativity wheel and Lubart *et al.*'s EPoC show). How are countries to be ranked, as was done for the three more conventional subjects? This requires careful consideration.

And, lastly, while Lucas's five dimensions for the creativity wheel and Lubart's 10 dimensions for EPoC have some overlaps, they are not totally the same conceptualizations. A question can be asked as to how the differences can be resolved so that theory and practice are consistent and cohesive with each other. Supposedly, this also requires careful consideration.

Ken Robinson (Hicks, 2015) was reported to suggest five ways teachers can foster student creativity: Don't limit assignments to one format, set time aside for creativity, use tech to broaden idea of assignments, introduce unconventional materials into class, and encourage discussion.

## Teachers' Role in Student Creativity

The important role the teacher plays in developing student creativity cannot be over-emphasized. Esquivel (1995: 185) reviewed literature on teacher behaviors that influenced the development of creative abilities in children and concluded that *"Teachers who show a humanistic philosophical orientation, have developed their own creative competencies, and implement specific creative methods and techniques in their classroom are more effective in enhancing students' creative abilities than teachers who follow more traditional instructional approaches."* And, with reference to the *Investment Theory of Creativity* (Sternberg and Lubart, 1995), Sternberg and Williams (2003) offer 24 tips to teachers to develop their students in creativity. Moreover, Davies, Jindal-Snape, and Digby (2014) found and reviewed 35 articles published between 2005 and 2011 pertaining to creativity and teachers. They concluded that the evidence suggested that teacher skills, attitudes, willingness to act as role model, awareness of learner needs, flexible lesson structure, and particular types of classroom interaction were important for teaching for creativity.

However, there seems to be some confusion or uncertainty about creativity. Beghetto and Kaufman (2013: 15), in their response to the call for creativity in education, clarified some common issues and confusion about creativity, especially for the teachers. They concluded:

> As parents, educators, and creativity researchers, we are encouraged by the increased attention being paid to creativity and the recognition that it has a role to play in schools and classrooms. It's essential, however, that education leaders develop a thorough understanding of creativity and that they take the time and care necessary to ensure that the benefits of creativity are realized in schools and classrooms.

While the teacher's role in fostering student creativity cannot be denied, how this is to be done is equivocal. One oft-heard call is for the teachers to be creative themselves or to show creativity in their teaching. Another is for the teachers to reward students when they show creativity. As argued by Soh (2017b), each of these approaches has its own problems and there is a need for teachers to create a *creativity ecology* in the classroom so that student creativity can emerge.

The ecological approach to fostering student creativity is based on a list of nine teacher behaviors which Cropley (1997) identified after summarizing a large number of articles pertaining to teacher behavior and student creativity. The nine behavioral principles were operationalized into the *Creativity Fostering Teacher Behavior Index* (*CFTIndex*; Soh, 2000) which has been translated into several languages and even used for PhD theses in Canada, Chile, and America. More recent articles, from Hong Kong, Turkey, Greece, and other countries, on the use and adaptation of the *CFTIndex* are compiled in a monograph (Soh, 2018).

In short, earlier and recent research provide ample evidence that teachers do influence students in their creativity development. In view of this, to study student creativity without looking into how teachers influence its development is like minting a one-sided coin without the other.

However, in the PISA statement cited above, there is no explicit indication whether teachers of the participating countries will be involved in providing information about what they have and have not done to foster student creativity — their teaching behaviors which might have impact on the development of creativity in the students as, for example, those measured by the *CFTIndex*. In all fairness, the team might have considered conducting a teacher survey using questionnaires as it has customarily done in the previous PISA surveys.

## Conclusion

Creativity research has almost all been localized and on a small scale. PISA's intention to include creative thinking is its 2021 survey is rather ambitious and brave. Although the history of creativity research is not long, it has nevertheless accumulated a tremendous amount of knowledge and a wide range of measuring tools. In the spirit of building future research on past experience, these tools obviously deserve attention in terms of conceptualization and instrumentation for the study. With reference to the available information of the PISA's plan, several questions on conceptualization and methodology have been discussed, with suggestions for their possible solutions.

## References

Batey, M. (2012). The measurement of creativity: from definitional consensus to the introduction of a new heuristic framework. *Creativity Research Journal*, **24**(1), 55–65.

Beghetto, R. A. and Kaufman, J. C. (February 2013). Fundamentals of Creativity. *Educational Leadership*, **70**(5), 10–15.

Davies, D., Jindal-Snape, D., and Digby, R. (2014). The roles and development needs of teachers to promote creativity: A systematic review of literature. *Teaching and Teacher Education*, **41**, 34–41. DOI: 10.1016/j.tate.2014.03.003

Esquivel, G. B. (1995). Teacher behaviors that foster creativity. *Educational Psychology Review*, **7**(2), 185–202.

Finke, R., Ward, T. B. and Smith, S. M. (1992). *Creative cognition: Theory, Research, and Applications*. MIT Press.

Gordon, W. J. J. (1961). *Synectics: The Development of Creative Capacity.* New York: Harper and Row.

Guilford, J. P. (1967). *The Nature of Human Intelligence.* New York: McGraw-Hill.

Hicks, Kristen (17 March 2015). *Why Creativity in the Classroom matters more than Ever.* Edudemic. Available at http://www.edudemic.com/creativity-in-the-classroom/

Hofstede, G. (1980). *Cultural Consequences: International Differences in Work-Related Values.* Sage. Cited in Soh (2017): 51, 60.

International Centre for Studies in Creativity (n.d.). *Creativity Based Information Resources: Assessment of Creativity.*

Kozbelt, A., Beghetto, R. A., and Runco, M. A. (2010). Theories of creativity. In J. C. Kaufman and R. J. Sternberg (Eds.), *The Cambridge handbook of creativity* (20–47). New York, NY, US: Cambridge University Press. http://dx.doi.org/10.1017/CBO9780511763205.004

Lubart, T., Baarbot, B., and Zenasni, F. (2013). Creative potential and its measurement. *International Journal for Talent Development and Creativity,* **1**(2), 41–50.

Lubart, T., Besancon, M., and Bartbot, B. (2011). *EPOC: Evaluating the Creative Potential of Children.* Editions Hogrefe France.

Lucas, B. (13 November 2017a). *Why PISA is Moving towards Creativity.* Available at http://www.mitchellinstitute.org.au/opinion/pisa-moving-towards-creativity/

Lucas, B. (22 November 2017b). *The power of creative thinking. Royal Society for the encouragement of Arts, Manufactures and Commerce.* Available at https://www.thersa.org/discover/publications-and-articles/rsa-comment/2017/11/the-power-of-creative-thinking

Mednick, S. A. (1962). The associative basis of the creative process. *Psychological Review,* **69**(3), 220–232.

Mosteller, F. (1995). The tennessee study of class size in the early school grades. *The Future of Children: Critical Issues for Children and Youth,* **5**(2), 113–127.

OECD (n.d.). *Teaching, assessing and learning creative and critical thinking skills in education.* Available at http://www.oecd.org/education/ceri/assessingprogressionincreativeandcriticalthinkingskillsineducation.htm

Rhodes, M. (1961). An analysis of creativity. *Phi Delta Kappan,* **42**, 305–310.

Soh, K. (2017a). *PISA Ranking: Issues and Effects in Singapore, East Asia and the World.* NJ: World Scientific.

Soh, K. (2017b). Fostering student creativity through teachers behaviors. *Thinking Skills and Creativity*, **24**, 58–66. DOI: 10.1016/j.tsc.2016.11.002

Soh, K. (2018). *Creativity Fostering Teacher Behavior: Measurement and Research*. NJ: World Scientific.

Soh, K. C. (2000). Indexing creativity fostering teacher behavior: a preliminary validation study. *Journal of Creative Behavior*, **34**, 118–134.

Sternberg, R. and Williams, W. M. (1 January 2003). Teaching for Creativity: Two Dozen Tips. The Center for Development and Learning. Available at http://www.cdl.org/articles/teaching-for-creativity-two-dozen-tips/

Sternberg, R. J., and Lubart, T. I. (1995). *Defying the Crowd: Cultivating Creativity in a Culture of Conformity*. New York: Free Press.

Torrance, E. P. (1966). *The Torrance Tests of Creative Thinking-Norms-Technical Manual Research Edition-Verbal Tests, Forms A and B-Figural Tests, Forms A and B*. Princeton, NJ: Personnel Press.

# Part IV

# Trustworthiness of International Comparisons

## Chapter 11

# Readability of PISA Reading Tasks as a Predictor of Reading Performance

*To do a good job, sharpen your tools first.*

Chinese Proverb

Data collection tools are critical to research. The validity of results of international surveys like PISA depends on the tests (and questionnaires) they use to collect the needed data. There are important qualities for these tests, such as reliability and validity of the data collected; one quality that seems to be taken for granted is the readability of the data collection tools.

Readability, simply put, is what makes some texts easier to read than others. Educators discovered in the 1920s a way to predict the difficulty of a text by using vocabulary difficulty and sentence length. This information was used to build readability formulas which have proven their worth in the past 100 years or so. Reading researchers like Rudolf Flesch, George Klare, Edgar Dale, and Jeanne Chall popularized the formulas during the 1950s. Since then, readability formulas have been widely used in journalism, research, health care, law, insurance, and industry; even the U.S. Army developed its own set of formulas for technical training materials. By the 1980s, there were more than 200 readability formulas and over a thousand relevant studies. These attest to the strong theoretical and statistical validity of readability formulas and related research (DuBay, 2004: 2).

An author's intent when writing reading materials (be it a textbook, a worksheet, or an examination paper) is to transmit information to the targeted readers. The success of such an effort depends to a large extent on the readability of the text. Thus, the objective of ensuring readability is to maximally match the demand of the text and the reader's competence in reading. A mismatch between the two will discourage reading and leads to failure in communication.

Several methods have been commonly used to establish readability (*Readability*, n.d.). First, there is the *question and answer technique* by which students of different ages are given the text to read and are then questioned on the text to gauge the level of comprehension. This enables the establishment of the reading age of the text. Secondly, there is the *sentence completion* or *'cloze' technique* whereby every nth (say, the fifth or seventh) word of a text is omitted and the mutilated text is to be completed by the target reader to gauge the text's readability; there are also variants of the original *cloze* procedure. The third method is by *comparison of text with a standard word list*, whereby the percentage of words not included in the word list is used to calculate reading age. This method presupposes the availability of a suitable word list; the compilation of such word lists is an area of reading research in its own right. The Dale-Chall Word List is a well-known one in common use. The fourth method to establish the readability of a text is the *calculations of a readability index* using one or more of the readability formulas.

## Readability Indices

Almost all achievement tests involve reading. A typical procedure for the assessment of reading comprehension requires the students to read a chosen passage and then respond to questions the answers of which can be found or, more often, inferred from the given passage. It stands to reason that if the student does not understand the passage, he cannot answer the questions correctly, barring chance correctness.

Many readability indices have been proposed and in fact used to predict the extent to which reading materials can be read with understanding by a target group of students. These are useful for textbook writers who need to ensure that their texts are at a level suitable for the target readers. Such indices are, in the main, analogs or outcomes of multiple regression based on a corpus of texts analyzed for their characteristics such as total number of words, number of unique words, number of syllables, number of sentences, and some variations and combination of such raw counts as the predictors. Nonetheless, the use of readability formulas has been applied mainly to textbooks and training materials. The readability of tests seems to have escaped the attention of test designers, even though tests normally use language extensively and the readability of test items can be expected to influence test performance.

Oakland and Lane (2004), citing some relevant studies, extensively discuss the impact of language, and more specifically of reading, on test performance, by dealing with the use of readability formulas in the development, adaptation, use, and evaluation of tests. They first point out that a test has several components of which readability is a concern: test directions, text, item stems, and options. They further point out that all tests that require reading items or directions inherently rely on the readability of these portions of the test. Moreover, when testing knowledge and skills other than reading (e.g., Science and Mathematics in PISA surveys), the readability of test items should not influence the measurement of subject-matter knowledge or skills. The readability of tests therefore is enhanced through careful consideration of word choice, clarity, and density of ideas, as well as complexity of sentence structure. More recently, Liu (2011) discusses various formal and linguistic aspects that affect reading and testing of reading, including text topic and content, type and genre, linguistic variables, typographical features, and others. The author points out that researchers have long been concerned with identifying features that make text readable in order to adjust difficulty to the intended readership and that this has resulted in readability formulae which could be used to estimate text readability, based on empirical research into difficulty.

The present study uses the *Free Text Readability Consensus Calculator* which takes a sample of writing and calculates the number of sentences, words, syllables, and characters in the sample. These numbers are plugged into the seven popular readability formulas described below. These readability formulas help to find out the reading level and grade level of reading materials and determine if the student can read them with ease and comprehension. A sufficient sample size consists of 200–500 words in total. The calculator uses sample sizes of up to 600 words; text over 600 words are automatically truncated. The output of this calculator includes seven reading indices and two indices derived from them. These are described briefly below.

1. *Flesch Reading Ease Formula* will output a number from 0 to 100 and a higher score indicates easier reading. An average document has a Flesch Reading Ease score between 60 and 70. As a rule of thumb, scores of 90–100 can be understood by an average Fifth Grader. Eighth and Ninth grade students can understand documents with a score of 60–70; and college graduates can understand documents with a score of 0–30.
2. *Gunning FOG Formula* is similar to the Flesch scale in that it compares syllables and sentence lengths. A Fog score of 5 is readable, 10 is hard, 15 is difficult, and 20 is very difficult. Based on its name, 'Foggy' words are words that contain 3 or more syllables.
3. *Flesch-Kincaid Grade Level* outputs a U.S. school grade level; this indicates the average student in that grade level can read the text. For example, a score of 7.4 indicates that the text is understood by an average student in Seventh Grade.
4. *Coleman-Liau Index* relies on characters, instead of syllables per word, and sentence length. This formula will output a grade. For example, 10.6 means the text is appropriate for 10–11 Graders.
5. *SMOG Index* outputs a U.S. school grade level; this indicates the average student in that grade level can read the text. For example, a score of 7.4 indicates that the text is understood by an average student in Seventh Grade.
6. *Automated Readability Index* outputs a number which approximates the grade level needed to comprehend the text. For example, if the output is the number 3, it means students in the Third Grade (8–9 years old) should be able to comprehend the text.
7. *Linsear Write Formula* is a readability formula for English text, originally developed for the United States Air Force to help them calculate the readability of their technical manuals. This formula is specifically designed to calculate the United States grade level of a text sample based on sentence length and the number of words used that have three or more syllables.
8. *Consensus Grade* is based on the various reading indices described above and *Consensus Age* is an estimate of the age of students who can read the materials with ease, based on the Consensus Grade.

## PISA Reading Tasks

According to OECD (2009: 3), *Programme for International Student Assessment* (PISA) provides parents, students, teachers, school leaders, governments, and the general public good information on how well their education systems prepare students for life, and there is a growing commitment by governments to monitor the outcomes of education systems in terms of student achievement on a regular basis. Then, in 1997, within an internationally agreed framework, PISA was launched, to be repeated every three years.

PISA assesses Reading, Mathematics, and Science of 15-year-olds (mainly Eighth Graders) of the participating countries. The PISA team asserts that the three subject tests are different from the conventional assessment procedures: PISA tests assess *literacy* and are therefore future-oriented and competence-based, in contrast with the conventional assessments which are past-oriented and content-based. However, this is a contentious point as many researchers disagree with the claim of PISA (Bracey, 2008; Mathews, 2009; Sjoberg, 2007). As this issue is beyond the scope of the present study, it is not pursued further here.

The PISA tests have been criticized because their questions rambled discursively and sometimes contained irrelevant information and factually incorrect material (Bracey, 2008). When administered to 15-year-olds, this means the assessment of Science and Mathematics is heavily confounded with Reading. Mortimore (2009), with a different perspective, summarized 10 criticisms on PISA in seven documents published from the year 2003 onwards. Two of the most relevant criticism are test translation and disregard of national curriculum. On the latter issue, Mortimore (2008: 5) comments, *"The emphasis on asking questions which can be answered using common sense rather than knowledge of a particular curriculum has also been challenged."* In the same vein, on the claim by PISA that its tests assess *literacies* but not what the students have learned through the curriculum, Mathews (2009) quoted Loveless, a test expert, as asking *"Why not?"*

Secrecy in methodology has been a criticism of PISA (Sjoberg, 2007). Perhaps as a response to this, sample questions for the three subject tests were released as a monograph *Take the Tests* (OECD, 2009). It contains all the publicly available questions for the three subjects. Some of the questions were used in the 2000, 2003, and 2006 PISA surveys and others were used in developing and trying out the assessment. *Take the Tests* makes available 17 Reading Units, 50 Mathematics Units, and 34 Science Units. Of interest to the present study is the set of 17 Reading Units. As the sample questions are mainly from the three first PISA surveys, it is safe to take them as representative of PISA Reading tests. (See Appendix for more information of the Reading Units.)

Reading is defined for PISA as *"Understanding, using and reflecting on written texts, in order to achieve one's goals, to develop one's knowledge and potential, and to participate in society"* (OECD, 2009: 16). A primary distinction in the test materials is in *text formats* between *continuous* and *non-continuous* tests. Continuous text refers to prose organized in sentences and paragraphs, and includes descriptions, narrations, and argumentations amongst others, whereas non-continuous text includes lists, maps, graphs, and diagrams.

As can be expected, reading units (tasks) using continuous text will have more words and hence are more extensive in structure. In contrast, reading tasks of non-continuous text will used words sparingly and are therefore shorter and less complex in structure. Although both text formats have their place in reading, continuous texts are nevertheless the prototype of reading materials. For this reason, the present study focuses only on the 10 reading tasks involving continuous texts. Doing so also fits the requirement of the readability calculator, as the five reading tasks using non-continuous texts have less than 100 words each and their readability indices cannot be estimated.

## Readability Indices of the PISA Reading Units

Table 1 shows for each of the 10 reading tasks the length and readability indices, with Grade representing the consensus of them and the student age estimated for each reading task. As each reading task has two to five questions, the last column Score shows, each reading task's mean of the OECD average percentages for the questions. However, this information is available for only eight of the 10 reading tasks.

**Table 1.** Readability Indices (N = 12).

| Task | Words | FL | GF | FK | CL | SMOG | Auto | LW | Grade | Age | Score |
|---|---|---|---|---|---|---|---|---|---|---|---|
| 2  | 366  | 53.9 | 13   | 9.6  | 10 | 9.6  | 8.8  | 10.6 | 10 | 14.5 | 48.6 |
| 3  | 285  | 68.5 | 9.5  | 6.1  | 11 | 7    | 6.3  | 5.2  | 7  | 12   | 32.5 |
| 6  | 627  | 72.5 | 9.8  | 6.9  | 8  | 7.1  | 6.5  | 8.1  | 7  | 12   | 70.0 |
| 7  | 383  | 58.5 | 13.8 | 10.7 | 10 | 9.8  | 11.9 | 14.1 | 11 | 16   | 79.3 |
| 8  | 1711 | 87.2 | 7.5  | 5.2  | 7  | 3.9  | 6.4  | 7.7  | 6  | 10.5 | 84.0 |
| 9  | 870  | 79.3 | 8    | 5.4  | 7  | 6.3  | 4.5  | 6.5  | 6  | 10.5 | 93.0 |
| 10 | 334  | 46.3 | 13.6 | 10.4 | 13 | 10.2 | 10.4 | 9.3  | 10 | 14.5 | 58.5 |
| 11 | 472  | 58.6 | 11.2 | 8.9  | 11 | 8.5  | 8.9  | 8.8  | 9  | 14   | 37.0 |
| 13 | 172  | 53.2 | 12   | 10.2 | 10 | 9.9  | 9.2  | 11.7 | 10 | 14.5 | —    |
| 14 | 1178 | 88.1 | 6.3  | 4.5  | 4  | 3.9  | 3.4  | 6.5  | 5  | 8.5  | —    |

*Note*: Words = Word count of the passage; FL = Flesch Reading Ease formula; GF = Gunning FOG formula; FK = Flesch-Kincaid Grade Level; CL = Coleman-Liau Index; SMOG = the SMOG Index; Auto = Automated Readability Index; LW = Linsear Write Formula; Grade = Consensus Grade; Age = Consensus age of reader.

As defined, lower Flesch scores indicate lower readability and that the reading task is more demanding or difficult, that is, more suited to students of higher grade. (This reversal needs be borne in mind when interpreting the Flesch ratings.) The other six indices indicate directly the grades each reading task is estimated as being suitable for, with greater values indicating greater demand and being more suited for higher grades.

A cursory inspection of the different columns shows that the different indices are fairly consistent, in spite of their different conceptualizations and formulas. For example, when the score for Gunning Fog (GF) goes down from one reading task to the next, the score for Flesch-Kincaid (FK) also goes down, and vice versa.

## Correlations Among the Indices

Table 2 shows the inter-correlations among the readability indices and also their correlations with task length (Words) and student performance in the PISA Reading test (Score).

Table 2. Correlations.

|  | Words | FL | GF | FK | CL | SMOG | Auto | LW | Grade | Age | Score |
|---|---|---|---|---|---|---|---|---|---|---|---|
| Words | 1.00 | | | | | | | | | | |
| FL | 0.81 | **1.00** | | | | | | | | | |
| GF | −0.72 | **−0.94** | **1.00** | | | | | | | | |
| FK | −0.66 | **−0.92** | **0.99** | **1.00** | | | | | | | |
| CL | −0.75 | **−0.89** | **0.75** | **0.72** | **1.00** | | | | | | |
| SMOG | −0.85 | **−0.97** | **0.96** | **0.94** | **0.77** | **1.00** | | | | | |
| Auto | (−0.49) | **−0.79** | **0.92** | **0.95** | **0.67** | **0.80** | **1.00** | | | | |
| LW | (−0.27) | **−0.83** | **0.78** | **0.82** | (0.23) | **0.64** | **0.86** | **1.00** | | | |
| Grade | −0.65 | **−0.90** | 0.98 | 0.99 | 0.70 | 0.92 | 0.95 | 0.84 | 1.00 | | |
| Age | −0.69 | −0.88 | 0.97 | 0.98 | 0.71 | 0.92 | 0.95 | 0.83 | 0.99 | 1.00 | |
| Score | (−0.61) | (0.53) | (−0.33) | (−0.28) | −0.71 | (−0.39) | (−0.21) | (0.17) | (−0.30) | (−0.34) | 1.00 |

*Notes*: (1) Words = Word count of the passage; FL = Flesch Reading Ease formula; GF = Gunning FOG formula; FK = Flesch-Kincaid Grade Level; CL = Coleman-Liau Index; SMOG = the SMOG Index; Auto = Automated Readability Index; LW = Linear Write Formula; Grade = Consensus Grade; Age = Consensus age of reader. (2) Coefficients in parentheses are statistically *non-significant* (p > 0.05) for their corresponding degree of freedom (i.e., 8 for Score and 10 for the others).

As shown in Table 2, firstly, with the exception of r = 0.23 (between LW and CL), the inter-index correlations (in bold) vary from r = |0.64| (between LW and SMOG) to r = |0.97| (between SMOG and FL). The pattern of correlations indicates a high degree of consistency among the readability indices. In other words, the result shows a high reliability for it to be trustworthy. As cautioned above, the lower the Flesch score, the more difficult the reading task, hence the negative correlations of Flesch with the other six indices.

It is of note that Words (passage lengths), generally, has negative correlations with all readability indices. The positive correlation with Flesch has been explained above. These indicate that longer passages with more words are easier to read and comprehend, and vice versa. One way to understand this relation is that a longer passage with more words provides more cues for students to decipher the meanings of the words and the meaning of the passage as a whole. In this sense, this is consistent with Goodman's (1967) conceptualization that reading is a psycholinguistic guessing game in which a reader tries to piece together information given the words to form a cohesive meaning.

The correlations for Score with the reading indices are generally in the expected direction in that the more demanding the reading task the poorer the reading performance, although the coefficients fail to be statistically significant, with the exception of r = |0.71| for Coleman-Liau Index.

## Readability of PISA Tasks as a Whole

Table 3 presents the statistical summaries of the information of Table 1 for a general indication of the readability of the PISA Reading Test as a whole.

Firstly, it can be seen that the reading tasks have a mean length of 600 words, but with a large standard deviation of 427 words. More specifically, the long task has 1711 words (Gift) and the shortest 172 words (Warranty), giving a range of 1539 words.

Secondly, the Flesch index has a mean of 66, indicating that the reading tasks taken together as a whole has a readability suited to Eighth and Ninth Graders. This is consistent with the PISA's intention to assess the reading ability of the 15-year-olds, although slightly more difficult

Table 3. Means and Standard Deviations.

|       | Words | FL   | GF   | FK   | CL   | SMOG | Auto | LW   | Grade | Age  | Score |
|-------|-------|------|------|------|------|------|------|------|-------|------|-------|
| Mean  | 600.8 | 66.4 | 10.7 | 8.1  | 8.8  | 7.8  | 8.0  | 9.5  | 8.3   | 13.0 | 62.9  |
| SD    | 427.2 | 13.6 | 2.5  | 2.4  | 2.4  | 2.2  | 2.7  | 3.0  | 2.2   | 2.5  | 20.9  |
| Max   | 1711  | 88.1 | 13.9 | 11.9 | 13.0 | 10.4 | 12.5 | 15.9 | 12.0  | 17.5 | 93.0  |
| Min   | 172   | 46.3 | 6.3  | 4.5  | 4.0  | 3.9  | 3.4  | 5.2  | 5.0   | 8.5  | 32.5  |
| Range | 1539  | 41.8 | 7.6  | 7.4  | 9.0  | 6.5  | 9.1  | 10.7 | 7.0   | 9.0  | 60.5  |

*Note*: Words = Word count of the passage; FL = Flesch Reading Ease formula; GF = Gunning FOG formula; FK = Flesch-Kincaid Grade Level; CL = Coleman-Liau Index; SMOG = the SMOG Index; Auto = Automated Readability Index; LW = Linsear Write Formula; Grade = Consensus Grade; Age = Consensus age of reader.

for them. This is supported by the various indices using other formulas: the means vary from 7.8 (SMOG) to 10.7 (Gunning Fog) and most indices are on the higher end of 8.0. It is therefore safe to conclude that the PISA reading tasks involving continuous text format are, on the whole, slightly more difficulty for the target students, although the Consensus Age of 13 is younger than the 15-year-olds targeted by the PISA.

As shown in Table 3, the ranges (i.e., the differences between the maximums and the minimums) are sizable. More specifically for example, the Flesch scores have a range of 41.8 (out of a 100) because the maximum is 88.1 and the minimum 46.3. In other words, there is a passage scoring near 90 and hence can be understood by Fifth Grader but there is another scoring near 30 which requires nearly the reading competence of college graduates. The ranges for the other six indices attest to this very wide variability. The most and least demanding tasks vary from 6.5 grades (SMOG) and 10.7 grades (Linsear Write Formula). On average, the difference is slightly greater than eight grades.

In terms of Consensus Grade, the difference between the most and the least demanding tasks is seven grades, varying from the Fifth to the Twelfth Grades. And, in terms of Consensus Age, the variability is nine grades, from age 8.5 to age 17.5.

For the eight tasks for which information is available, the mean is 63 percent, with a standard deviation of 21 percent. It is also interesting to note the variation in performance (Score) which can be assumed to have been affected to some extent by the readability of the tasks. Specifically, the difference between the most demanding task (33 percent for Graffiti) and the least demanding one (93 percent for Amanda and the Duchess) is as much as 61 percent.

## Discussion and Conclusion

The finding that, as a whole, the PISA reading tasks (which use continuous text format) have been pitted at the Eighth Grade level, albeit slightly on the higher side, is reassuring. This is consistent with the expected level of reading competence of the 15-year-olds who are the targeted students of this international survey over the past decade. The variety in content topics and styles (see Appendix) should be a plus point of the reading tests as the varied topics and styles inoculate against possible knowledge and linguistic biases. The issue of what the PISA reading tests really assess — *literacy* as claimed or otherwise — can only be settled by further research. Pending this, the PISA reading tasks, which represent the reading tests used in the past surveys, have shown face and content validities as tests of reading by the inclusion of a wide variety of topics and styles.

The wide variability in readability or estimated grade levels of the reading tasks, however, gives rise to some degree of concern. Recall that the 10 tasks differ as much as from seven grades (following the SMOG range) to eleven grades (following Linsear Write range), as shown in Table 3. The difference between the easiest and the most difficult tasks is, on average, seven grades.

A test of reading has to have sufficient rooms to accommodate the wide variation in reading competence among the students, so as to avoid the possible *floor* and *ceiling* effects. A sufficiently wide possible range allows both weak and strong students to show their 'true colors', so to speak, and thereby yields a realistic representation of their reading competence. Depending on the particular education system, students of different countries and within the same grade level may have different ranges of reading competence. However, it is highly unlikely that students of a country within the same grade level span as many as seven grades in their reading competence, as allowed by the PISA reading tasks.

It is not known how students taking the PISA Reading tests have responded to the readability of the reading tasks — in other words how readability has influenced their responses. It is readily appreciated that highly capable students will find the unusually easy tasks (15-year-olds being tested as if they were in the Fourth Grade) unchallenging, boring, and even meaningless. On the other hand, the unusually difficult tasks (testing 15-year-olds as if they were Twelfth Graders) can cause frustration, bewilderment, and defeatism among the weak students. In short, being assessed far below or above their actual competence level may have undesirable motivational effects and this deserves further study. Though supporting empirical evidence is needed, it may be intuitively ventured to suggest a more realistic, shorter range of two grades above and below the Eighth Grade, allowing the tests to span a five-grade range.

Although the correlations between the readability indices and performance on the reading tasks are in the expected direction, with higher demand correlating negatively with reading scores, the magnitudes of the correlations are mainly low and statistically non-significant. This could partly be due to the limitation of small data set of only eight tasks. But it is also likely due to some other critical factors not considered. As pointed out by Oakland and Lane (2004), there are other linguistic features affecting the readability of a passage; and these are not included in readability formulas. Besides, familiarity with content or topics is not part of the conceptualization of readability. Moreover, the present study is based on the readability of the passages and the readability of the options offered for the multiple-choice questions, but the ability to write answers for the constructed response questions are not considered. In such a situation, the low correlations are not surprising. In short, performance in the PISA reading tests depends more than the readability of the tasks.

In the context of international surveys, PISA compares the 15-year-old students of an increasing number of countries, starting with some 30 countries in the early years to now 65 or so. This requires the translation of reading tasks into many different languages. PISA did take good care to ensure equivalence among the translated versions (OECD, 2012: 84). The procedures include development of two source versions (in English and French), double translation, detailed instructions for the translation, translation/adaptation guidelines, training of national staff in charge of the translation/adaptation of the instruments, and verification of the national versions by international verifiers. Notwithstanding these, there remains the questions of comparability in readability cross-language. It is not impossible that a translated version, in spite of its content equivalence, is easier or more difficult for students of the target language than for those of the source languages (English and French) due to the peculiarities of the languages. This obviously is a topic worthy of further research.

By way of summary, the PISA reading tasks have been found to be close, on average, to the reading level of its target students: 15-year-olds or Eighth Graders, albeit slightly on the higher side. The tasks have a wide coverage in content and format and thus minimize possible topical and stylistic biases. Correlations between readability and performance are low, though in the correct direction; this could be due to linguistic features and content familiarity not included in readability formulas. However, the range of seven grades among the tasks may be too wide to affect motivation of the students when taking the tests; for this, a more realistic range of five grades is suggested. Care has been taken to ensure translation equivalence, but this does not rule out the possibility that having different versions in so many languages means different readability levels, which in turn affects performance. Further research is needed in this area.

## References

Bracey, G. W. (August 2008). The leaning (toppling?) tower of PISA: Facts and doubts about international comparisons in education. *Dissent Magazine.* Available at http://www.dissentmagazine.org/online.php?id=128

DuBay, W. (2004). *The Principles of Readability.* Costa Mesa, California: Impact Information. Available at http://www.nald.ca/library/research/readab/cover.htm

*Free Text Readability Consensus Calculator.* http://www.readabilityformulas. com/free-readability-formula-tests.php

Kenneth S. Goodman, K. S. (1976). *Reading: A Psycholinguistic Guessing Game: Theoretical Models and Processes of Reading.* International Reading Association.

Liu, F. (2011). A short analysis of the text variables affecting reading and testing reading. *Studies in Literature and Language,* **2**(2), 44–49.

Mathews, J. (October, 2009). *Test that makes U.S. look bad may not be so good.* Available at http://voices.washingtonpost.com/class-struggle/2009/10/politicians_and_pundits_are_ us.html

Mortimore, P. (2009). *Alternative Models for Analysing and Representing Countries' Performance in PISA.* Brussels: Education International Research Institute.

Oakland, T. and Lane, H. (2004). Language, reading, and readability formulas: Implications for developing and adapting tests. *International Journal of Testing,* **4**, 239–252.

OECD (2009). *Take the Tests: Sample Questions for OECD's PISA Assessment.* Available at http://www.oecd.org/pisa/pisaproducts/pisa2000/41943106.pdf

OECD (2012), *PISA 2009 Technical Report.* http://dx.doi.org/10. 1787/9789264167872-en

*Readability* (n.d.). http://www.timetabler.com/reading.html

Sjoberg, S. (October 8 2007). PISA and "Real Life Challenges": Mission Impossible? Contribution to Hopman (Ed): *PISA according to PISA Revised Version.* folk.uio.no/sveinsj/Sjoberg-PISA-book-2007.pdf

# Appendix

**Table A1.** Descriptions of the Reading Tasks.

| Unit | Title | Test Format | Reading Level |
|---|---|---|---|
| 2 | Flu | Continuous prose, followed by three multiple-choice questions and two constructed response questions. | Fairly difficult |
| 3 | Graffiti | Continuous prose, followed by one Multiple-choice question and three constructed response questions. | Average |
| 6 | Police | Continuous prose with inserts, followed by four multiple-choice questions. | Fairly easy |
| 7 | Runners | Continuous prose with illustration, followed by two multiple-choice questions and three constructed response questions. | Fairly difficult |
| 8 | Gift | Continuous prose, following by three multiple-choice questions and four constructed response questions. | Easy |
| 9 | Amanda and the Duchess | Text 1 is a scene from a play. Text 2 defines some theatrical occupations. These are followed by one multiple-choice question, one constructed response question, and one table to be completed. | Fairly easy |
| 10 | Personnel | Itemized descriptions, followed by two constructed response questions. | Difficult |
| 11 | New Rules | Continuous prose in the form of an editorial, followed by two constructed response questions. | Fairly difficult |
| 13 | Warranty | Text 1 is a receipt. Text 2 is a warranty card. These are followed by four constructed response questions. | Fairly difficult |
| 14 | Just Judge | A story with conversation, followed by three multiple-choice questions and one constructed response question. | Easy |

# Chapter 12

# Ecological Fallacy in Predicting Reading Achievement: The Case of PIRLS

*There are two kinds of statistics, the kind you look up and the kind you make up.*

—Rex Stout

Just as the adage goes, there is more than one way to skin a cat, there is more than one way to analyze a set of data. That is why we have two kinds of statistics — the individual and the aggregate. The question is, which one do we look up and which one do we make up? And, more importantly, do they tell the same story and, if not, why?

International comparative studies like the *Programme for International Student Assessment* (PISA; OECD, 2013), the *Trends in International Mathematics and Science Study* (TIMSS; Mullis, Martin, Foy, and Arora, 2012) and the *Progress in International Reading Literacy Study* (PIRLS; Mullis, Martin, Foy, and Drucker, 2012) all collect data from individual students, teachers, parents, and principals. The individuals are the *unit of observation* since the individuals are the source of data, but the countries are the *unit of analysis* since they are the entity for reporting. The individuals' statistics are summed and averaged to make up the countries means (or percentages, which is a special kind of mean) for reporting and ranking. This is in contrast with many within-country studies for which the individuals (students, teachers, principals, and parents) are both the unit of observation and the unit of analysis at the same time.

Teachers, principals, and policymakers may know some research findings about learning and its relations with relevant background factors gained from public media or professional publications. Most of the time, these are based on individual data. For international surveys, what they usually read are *aggregated, grouped,* or *ecological* data (which are, of course, collections or averages of individual data). When we relate findings of studies based on individual data with findings of surveys reported as group data, ecological fallacy may be committed. Ecological fallacy may not be a white-collar crime, but it definitely is an intellectual sin.

In a recent article, Sjoberg (2017) points out some unexpected results of PISA:

> It seems that pupils in high-scoring countries also develop the most negative attitudes to the subject. ...PISA scores also seems to be **negatively related** to the use of active teaching methods, inquiry based instruction, doing experiments and the use of ICT. **Whether one believes in PISA or not, such intriguing results need to be discussed** (330; emphasis added).

Although not made explicit in the above quote, Sjoberg (2017) implies that positive correlations are expected where negative ones are found in PISA, contradictory to logical expectations and common sense. As will be made clear later, one possible explanation is that most *within-nation* studies at the local or even school level, positive correlations are indeed found. The problem is related to *ecological fallacy*, a fallacy that occurs when findings at a higher level are transported to a lower level or vice versa.

## Ecological Fallacy

Ecological fallacy, as a statistical phenomenon, is when a research finding is applied from one level to a higher or lower level, from individual to group or from group to individual. For example, it is a well-established fact that students' academic achievement correlates moderately with their socioeconomic background. This is a research finding obtained by analyzing the data at the individual level when students are the unit of analysis.

When, by faulty inference, it is predicted that countries' academic achievement correlates with their economic conditions, the research finding for individual data is generalized to a different (higher) level where countries are now the unit of analysis, ecological fallacy may be committed.

Ecological fallacy as a methodological (essentially, statistical) issue was first raised by W. S. Robinson (1950) more than half a century ago, although the idea was mentioned much earlier by Karl Pearson in the late 19$^{th}$ century. Robinson analyzed illiteracy data of the 1930 US Census and found that correlations for the same two variables were different at the individual and the state levels. However, Robinson's idea was neglected for quite some time and his seminal paper was seldom cited (Oaks, 2009). Only in the recent years have epidemiologists begun to pay attention to ecological fallacy, trying to sort out conflicting findings of individual and ecological correlations.

Recently, Subramanian, Jones, Kaddour, and Krieger (2009) re-analyzed the same data used by Robinson, using multilevel techniques (which were not available or, at least, unpopular in Robinson's time). These authors found that different approaches to modelling state-effects yielded considerably attenuated associations at the individual level. They therefore concluded that multilevel thinking is thus a necessity, not an option.

This being the case, the situation in education research is not any better. Hamilton (1996) raised the issue of ecological fallacy in school effectiveness research where correlations between aggregate measures are extrapolated to the performance of individuals. Not long ago, Connolly (2006) was critical of the uncritical labelling of a whole group of pupils as 'under achievers' or 'overachievers' when group-level data are simply applied to individual students, thus committing the ecological fallacy. This problem was demonstrated earlier by Berninger and Abbot (1990) who reported a study examining whether conclusions about constructive processes in reading based on an analysis of group data were consistent with those based on an analysis of individual data. Subjects (N = 45) were First Graders in a longitudinal study on the acquisition of linguistic procedures for printed words. They were from a variety of ethnic and cultural backgrounds and were relatively homogeneous in socioeconomic indicators. The same data of reading scores was analyzed in four different ways.

Relevant to the present study is the finding that the results depended on how the data was aggregated. Differences in conclusions were attributed to the ecological fallacy in which inferences about one unit of analysis are based on analyses at another, higher or lower, level.

In another education example, Tainton (1990) studied the correlations of organizational structure and organizational climate. Correlations of 12 variables were calculated for the teachers (N = 670) and for their schools (N = 45). Of the possible 66 correlation coefficients, practically all changed in magnitude and 14 (21%) changed in direction, from positive to negative and vice versa. Obviously, how the relations among variables are to be understood depends on the level at which the correlations are calculated.

A more recent example is provided by May, Boe, and Boruch (2003). The authors used data of Eighth Grade students (N = 147,000) from 41 nations from TIMSS 1995. The data was re-analyzed at the individual and then national level using multilevel modelling. Responses to seven background questions related to learning Mathematics were included. It was found that 31 percent of the variance exists at the national level but 69 percent at the individual level. Most relevant to the present study is the findings that, of the seven correlations between background variables and Mathematics achievement, three change from positive at the individual level to negative at the ecological level, one changes the other way around, two remain negative, and one remains positive across levels. The authors urged educators to be acutely aware of ecological fallacy, because *"many factors that influence student achievement warrant completely different interpretations when analysed at different levels"* (11).

Most recently, re-analyzing PISA 2009 data for Reading, Mathematics, and Science of 65 countries, the present writer observed that the correlations between achievement and instruction times are largely negative when countries were the unit of analysis. However, when countries were grouped according to their performances in the three subjects, correlations are all positive for countries in the Highs (i.e., at and above international medians), but all negative for those in the Lows (i.e., below international median). Thus, while the positive correlations between instruction time and achievements for Highs match the commonsense expectation (that more time leads to better learning), the negative correlations for Lows contradict intuition and do not seem to make sense. The existence of ecological fallacy is evident.

## PIRLS and Follow-up Studies

The *Progress in International Reading Literacy Study* (PIRLS; International Association for the Evaluation of Educational Achievement, 2013) was started in 2001 with the aim to collect data to provide information on trends in reading literacy achievement of Fourth Graders of the participating countries. Thirty-five countries participated in the first survey and the number increases in its five-year cycle to 49 in 2011. In addition to reading, PIRLS also gathered information pertaining to the students, the teachers, the principals, and their schools. The usefulness of and hence the need for the background information was explicitly argued for in the first cycle of PIRLS by Kelly (2003: 29):

> Children are exposed to language and print at home and at school; receive formal reading instruction; and see others reading for recreation and to perform tasks. These and other experiences and activities at home and school combine to influence how well children read and how they feel about reading by the end of fourth grade. Beyond influences within the home and at school are those in the wider environments in which children live and learn. Community size and resources, organization of the educational system, and educational decision-making affect homes and schools, and thus children's literacy development.

The point is reiterated in later PIRLS report (TIMSS & PIRLS International Study Center, 2013: 1), thus,

> There are numerous contextual factors that affect students' learning, for example, type of school, school resources, instructional approaches, teacher characteristics, student attitudes, and home support for learning contribute heavily to student learning and achievement. For a fuller appreciation of what the PIRLS...achievement results mean and how they may be used to improve students learning in reading, it is important to understand the contexts in which students learn.

The PIRLS reports give detailed descriptions of how the background questions were crafted but are silent on the rationale for choosing the context factors. It is reasonable to assume that they were chosen based on reviews of studies in the pertinent literature which show positive relations between reading and background conditions such as socioeconomic status, availability of books at home and in school, active engagement during lessons, etc.

Following the PIRLS reports, some countries published their in-country follow-up reports, including Hong Kong (Tse, 2012), South Africa (Howie, Venter, van Staden, Zimmerman, Long, du Toit, Scherman, and Arher, 2008), Scotland (Scottish Government, 2007), and the United States (Baer, Baldi, Ayotte, Green, and McGrath, 2007). These follow-up reports are mainly highlights of the PIRLS findings and do not involve further analysis, although causal relations between reading performance and background conditions are occasionally hinted at without formal statistical analysis, tacitly assuming that within-country correlations are equally applicable across-country.

## The Present Study

In the educational arena, international comparative studies such as the PIRLS, TIMSS, and PISA use practically the same approach to data collection, analysis, and reporting. They gathered data from the students at the individual level, the teachers at the classroom level, and the principals at the school level. To facilitate better understanding of test performance, in addition to testing the students for achievements, they also conduct surveys asking many questions on conditions and factors that are tacitly assumed to have influence on learning and hence test scores. Presumably, the assumed positive correlations are based on previous within-country studies for which a positive correlation between achievement and home background is a typical finding.

In the case of international comparative studies like PIRLS, TIMSS, and PISA, data was aggregated for the countries and the findings are reported at the country-level in terms of country means. This implies that ecological fallacy is not seen as an issue or a problem of interpretation. Without due caution, countries may interpret the findings as though they were analyzed at the individual level. Moreover, secondary analysis may also be carried out by national researchers using the database to study interesting phenomena at the individual level. Irrespective of whether the country-level and individual-level findings are consistent or otherwise, ecological fallacy is committed in making cross-level comparisons. When the findings at the individual and country levels do not corroborate, they may puzzle and even confuse.

The present study re-analyzed data of the PIRLS 2011 to find out the correlations of Reading with some relevant background factors to see how such factors contributed to reading performance, *at the country-level*. This will enable an evaluation of whether the correlations are consistent with what would have been tacitly assumed by the PIRLS study. If the findings are *not* consistent with the within-country studies for which positive relations have been found, ecological fallacy may be committed when trying to reconcile the correlations observed at the two levels.

## Methodology

### Data

The data re-analyzed here were gleaned from the relevant tables of the PIRLS 2011 Report (Mullis, Martin, Foy, and Drucker, 2012) for the 49 participating countries, including information of (1) student engagement, (2) instructional strategies, and (3) instructional resources. It stands to reason that, at the individual level, engagement, strategies, and resources will correlate with achievement as they are expected to contribute to student learning.

### Analysis

Correlations were estimated between country means for PIRLS Reading and the three sets of items for engagement, instructional strategies, and resources. As alluded to earlier, positive correlations may be expected since PIRLS has included them as possible positive contributors to reading performance consistent with individual level within-country studies.

## Results

### Student engagement

PIRLS deems student engagement as one of the critical conditions for the effective learning of Reading, stating that *"To help build a better bridge between curriculum and instruction, PIRLS 2011 collected information about the concept of student engagement in learning, which focuses on the cognitive interaction between the student and the instructional content"* (Mullis et al.: 21). This implies a positive correlation between student engagement and Reading achievement. However, as Table 1 shows, student engagement as reported by teachers has a non-significant *negative* correlation of r = −0.14 with Reading. However, student engagement as reported by students has a statistically significant *negative* correlation of r = −0.50 which indicates that there is a sizable shared variance of 25% with Reading. Such negative correlations seem to be the opposite of what would be expected of the relation between student engagement and reading achievement. Incidentally, a one-tailed test was applied to evaluate the significance of correlation because the expected correlation is directional.

### Instructional strategies

PIRLS places a premium on instructional strategies to enhance reading achievement as it states *"To become proficient readers, students should be introduced to increasingly complex reading skills and strategies as they advance through school. Also, if students are to be able to learn to read by the third grade,…, then introduction to reading skills and strategies should begin when students enter the first grade, if not before"* (Mullis et al.: 169).

Table 1. Country-level Correlations of Reading with Student Engagement.

|  | Correlation with Reading at Country Level |
|---|---|
| Engagement (reported by teachers) | −0.14 |
| Engagement (reported by students) | **−0.50** |

*Note*: Coefficient in bold is statistically significant (p < 0.05, d.f. 47, one-tailed).

**Table 2.** Country-level Correlations of Reading with Instructional Strategies.

| | Correlation with Reading at Country Level |
|---|---|
| Locate information within the text | 0.14 |
| Identify the main ideas of what they have read | −0.10 |
| Explain or support their understanding of what they have read | −0.15 |
| Compare what they have read with experience they have had | −0.04 |
| Compare what they have read with other things they have read | −0.13 |
| Make predictions about what will happen next in the text | −0.04 |
| Make generalization and draw inferences | 0.04 |
| Describe the style or structure of the text | −0.23 |
| Determine the author's intention | −0.15 |

Thus, positive relations between instructional strategies and reading achievement is implied. However, as shown in Table 2, the nine instructional strategies have non-significant correlations with Reading but they tend to be negative, excepting *"Locate information within text"* (which has a low positive correlation of r = 0.14), but the r = −0.23 for *"Describe the style of structure of the text"* just missed the mark for statistical significance (p = 0.06). Again, these are contrary to what could be expected of the strategies for enhancing learning, in this case, Reading.

## *Instructional resources*

Instructional resources are seen by PIRLS as important contributors to reading achievement as it states, *"Successful schools also are likely to have better working conditions and facilities as well as more instructional materials, such as books, computers, technological support, and supplies"* (Mullis *et al.*: 15). As can be seen in Table 3, Children's books and Class library as instructional resources have significant positive correlations (r = 0.32 and r = 0.54, respectively) with Reading; the shared variances are 10 percent for Children's books and 41 percent for Class library. These are consistent with the expectation that the availability of reading materials

**Table 3.** Country-level Correlations of Reading with Instructional Resources.

|  | **Correlation with Reading at Country Level** |
|---|---|
| Children's books | **0.32** |
| Textbooks | **−0.27** |
| Reading Series | −0.02 |
| Workbooks | −0.12 |
| Software | **−0.24** |
| Class library | **0.54** |

*Note*: Coefficients in bold are statistically significant ($p < 0.05$, d.f. 47, one-tailed).

contributes to reading achievement. However, Textbooks and Software have statistically *negative* correlations with Reading, $r = -0.27$ (six percent shared variance) and $r = -0.24$ (five percent shared variance) respectively. Moreover, Reading Series and Workbooks have negligible correlations with Reading, but tend to be negative. These later sets of correlations are, again, contrary to expectation.

By way of summary, while student engagement, instructional strategies, and instructional resources have been expected to contribute positively to learning (Reading, in this case), they nonetheless tend to be negatively correlating with learning at the *international* level where countries are the unit of analysis. Such inconsistent or contradicting relations could be puzzling at first sight and deserve attention and discussion.

## Discussion and Conclusion

The study seems to have come up with many surprises when the negative correlations are seen against commonly expected positive ones between reading performance and background factors (i.e., student engagement, instructional strategies, and instructional resources), based on within-country studies. The crux of the unexpected results is the *ecological fallacy*.

Using individual data, for example, a conclusion like the one below is likely to be valid:

*Students who are more actively engaged scored higher in achievement tests; there is a positive relation between student engagement and achievement.*

But the extrapolation below may or may not be valid:

*Therefore, countries where students are more actively engaged are more likely to score higher.*

In the second statement, the relation found for within-country studies, with individual students as the unit of analysis, is transferred to an international study, which uses countries as the unit of analysis. Such an automatic generalization is what causes the ecological fallacy.

The findings of the present study therefor have two important implications. First, like other international comparative studies of achievement (TIMSS and PISA), PIRLS reports student performance at the national level and tabulates the country means in the form of a league table. However, many within-country follow-up studies are conducted by re-analyzing data using students as the unit of analysis, and their findings may contradict the findings of a re-analysis using nations as the unit of analysis, as is done in the present study.

A question then arises as to which set of findings are valid and trustworthy — the within-country or the international? This is not a question specific to PIRLS but to other international comparative studies which report in the same style. It is therefore important to differentiate between international comparisons at the country or ecological level and, in contrast, with follow-ups comparing students within-country at the individual levels.

The point is that the ecological correlations and the individual correlations may or may not be contradictory; they may both be valid even if opposite in direction, i.e., positive in one context but negative or none in another context. The seeming contradiction is illustrated in Figure 1. As shown therein, within each of the four countries, the relations between the

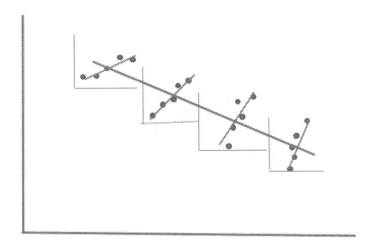

**Figure 1.** Individual and Ecological Correlations.

two variables (say, achievement and student engagement) are all positive, as indicated by the four southwest-to-northeast lines. However, when a correlation is estimated for the same two variables using the four country means, a negative correlation results, as indicated by the northwest-to-southeast line. Thus, the individual correlations and the ecological correlation are both truthful reflections of the relation between the two variables, in spite of the seeming contradiction.

Nevertheless, the negative ecological correlation indicates that students are less engaged in countries high in achievement, which goes against the grain that engagement is a positive contributor to achievement. How can the contradiction be reconciled?

As is well-known, correlation is bi-directional and does not indicate which of the two correlated variables is a cause and which an effect, if there is a cause-effect relation at all. With this in mind, it may be necessary to reverse the causal direction of the two variables by considering what used to be a cause an effect and vice versa. Thus, for instance, instead of seeing engagement as contributing to achievement, now achievement motivates engagement — that is, low achievement causes countries to engage their students more and, conversely, countries with high achievement find it unnecessary to engage students as much. For example, Soh's (2013) re-analysis of PISA data shows countries with poorer achievement assigning more curriculum time for learning. It is always assumed that more time for learning should always lead to better achievement, but the finding is just the opposite at the country level. Likewise, in the present study, things which should lead to better achievement have negative relations with them.

The puzzling negative correlations are meaningful if country means for PIRLS Reading are given an interpretation different from the usual meaning. Here, Reading performance may not be indexing the learning outcome *per se* but serves as a proxy measure of the felt need to enhance reading instruction by assigning more time as a coping strategy. In other words, countries doing well in reading do not see the need to increase instruction time but those doing not so well feel the urge for more time, hoping to rectify the situation of poorer reading performance of their students. The same interpretation applies to the other background conditions such as instructional strategies and resources.

This gives rise to yet another question: whether the usual strategies of more materials and engagement indeed help low-achieving countries as much as they do the high-achieving ones. In other words, it is not certain that the same approach works equally well and even in the same direction, irrespective of achievement level. Practically, does one size fit all? If not, as the findings show, countries with poorer performance may be well-advised not to follow what has been shown to work for countries with better performance. Then, it boils down to the aptitude-treatment interaction (ATI) propounded by Cronbach and Snow (1977) forty years ago, which suggests that for effective learning there needs be a good match between instructional strategy and learning ability, in this case, that of the countries.

Many of the strategies for raising student achievement originated from countries with more established education systems, especially the USA and UK. In view of the ATI effect referenced to above, a question can be asked whether it is wise to import wholesale such strategies to countries with less well-established systems like those in the low-achieving countries as the conditions and teaching-learning styles may differ. This, of course, is a question of cultural influence on teaching and learning which deserves a study in its own right.

Finally, it is necessary to look at how international comparative studies report their results. Compare the two extracts below from Mullis *et al.* (2012):

> Hong Kong SAR, the Russian Federation, Finland, and Singapore were the top-performing countries in PIRLS 2011. Looking at the results in Exhibit 1.1 and taking into account the information in Exhibit 1.3, it can be seen that these four countries performed similarly and had higher achievement than all of the other countries. The next tier of high-performing countries included Northern Ireland, the United States, Denmark, Croatia, and Chinese Taipei, followed closely by Ireland and England, who rounded out the top eleven high-achieving countries. (Chapter 1, 40)
>
> Most fourth grade students (71%) had teachers that used engaging instructional strategies, and nearly all the students reported being engaged (42%) or somewhat engaged (50%) in their reading lessons. Unfortunately, internationally, teachers reported limiting instruction because about one-quarter of the students were suffering from lack of basic nutrition and nearly half from not enough sleep (Chapter 8, Cover).

The first extract clearly is reporting on the reading performance of the nations and is distinctively an *ecological* study, since the nations' names are listed specifically. The context of the second extract is vague. It reads like reporting an *individual* study since it refers to the students and not nations. However, a quick check on the relevant table shows that the 71% (engagement reported by teachers) and 42% (engagement reported by students) are in fact average of the country means. In other words, although the impression of an individual study is created by the reporting, the fact is that it is an ecological study.

The relative merits of individual and ecological studies in medical research have been succinctly discussed by Oaks (2009, and also Subramanian *et al.*, 2009) and in educational research by Berninger and Abbot (1990) and Connolly, P. (2006). Although the data analyzed may be the same, individual and ecological studies have different conceptual frameworks and, more importantly, the outcomes often are not the same and even contradictory. It is therefore imperative that individual outcomes should be explicitly distinguished in reporting from ecological outcomes, lest the readers are misinformed and, when conflicting findings are reported, confused.

In view of this, the first sentence of the second extract from the PIRLS report could be preceded by a short phrase to indicate that it is reporting an ecological study, for example:

*The averages of national means shows that* most fourth grade students (71%) had teachers that used engaging instructional strategies, and nearly all the students reported being engaged (42%) or somewhat engaged (50%) in their reading lessons.

This slight amendment may look trivial, but it is needed to put the readers in the right perspective to avoid confusion and puzzlement when there is the risk of ecological fallacy. A spade needs be called a spade, and not anything else.

# References

Baer, J., Baldi, S., Ayotte, K., Green, P. J., and McGrath, D. (2007). *The Reading Literacy of U. S. Fourth-Grade Students in an International Context: Results from the 2001 and 2006 Progress in International Reading Literacy Study (PIRLS)*. Institute of Educational Science, National Centre for Educational Statistics.

Berninger, V. W. and Abbot, R. D. (1990). *Ecological Fallacy in Reading Acquisition Research: Masking Constructive Processes of the Learner.* Paper presented at the Annual Meeting of the American Psychological Association (98th, Boston, MA, August 10–14, 1990).

Connolly, P. (2006). Summary statistics, educational achievement gaps and the ecological fallacy. *Oxford Review of Education*, **32**(2), 235–252.

Cronbach, L. and Snow, R. (1977). *Aptitudes and Instructional Methods: A Handbook for Research on Interactions*. New York: Irvington.

EpiAnalysis (19 November 2012). *Chocolates consumption, Nobel laureates, and crappy statistics.* Available at http://epianalysis.wordpress.com/2012/11/19/chocolate/

Hamilton, D. (1996). *Fordism by fit.* Paper presented at the annual conference of the British Educational Research Association, Lancaster, September 1996.

Howie, S., Venter, E., van Staden, S., Zimmerman, L., Long, C., du Toit, C., Scherman, V., and Arher, E. (2008). *PIRLS 2006: South African Children's Reading Literacy Achievement*. Centre for Education & Assessment, University of Pretoria.

Kelly, D. (2003). Developing the PIRLS Background Questionnaires. In Martin, M.O., Mullis, I.V.S., & Kennedy, A.M. (Eds.) (2003). *PIRLS 2001 Technical Report*. Available at http://timssandpirls.bc.edu/pirls2001i/pdf/p1_tr_ch03.pdf

May, H., Boe, E. E., and Boruch, R. F. (2003). *The Ecological Fallacy in Comparative and International Education Research: Discovering More from TIMSS through Multilevel Modelling*. Philadelphia, PA: University of Pennsylvania, Center for Research and Evaluation in Social Policy.

Mullis, I.V.S., Martin, M.O., Foy, P., & Arora, A. (2012). *Trends in Mathematics and Science Study*. Chestnut Hill, MA: TIMSS & PIRLS International Study Center, Boston College. Available at http://timss.bc.edu/timss2011/international-results-mathematics.html

Mullis, I.V.S., Martin, M.O., Foy, P., and Drucker, K.T. (2012*). PIRLS 2011 International Results in Reading*. Chestnut Hill, MA: TIMSS & PIRLS International Study Center, Boston College. Available at http://timssandpirls.bc.edu/pirls2011/international-results-pirls.html

OECD (2013). *OECD Programme for International Student Assessment (PISA)* Available at http://www.oecd.org/pisa/aboutpisa/

Oaks, J. M. (2009). Commentary: individual, ecological and multilevel fallacies. *International Journal of Epidemiology*, **28**(2), 361–368.

Robinson, W.S. (1950). Ecological correlations and the behaviour of individuals. *American Sociological Research*. **15**, 351–357.

Scottish Government (29 November 2007). *Progression in International Reading Literacy Study (OIRLS): Highlights form Scotland's results*. Available at http://www.scotland.gov.uk/Publications/2007/11/23111011/1

Sjoberg, S. (April 2017). PISA as a challenge for science education: Inherent problems and problematic results from a global assessment. *Revista Brasileira de Pesquisa Educacao em Ciencias*, **17**(1), 327–363.

AUTHOR (2012). [Reference will be added later.]

AUTHOR (2013). [Reference will be added later.]

Subramanian, S. V., Jones, K., Kaddour, A., and Krieger, N. (2009). Revisiting Robinson: The perils of individualistic and ecologic fallacy. *International Journal of Epidemiology*, **38**(2), 342–360. Available at http://www.ncbi.nlm.nih.gov/pmc/articles/PMC2663721/ doi: 10.1093/ije/dyn359

Tainton, B. E. (1990). The unit of analysis problem in educational research. *Queensland Journal of Educational Research*, **6**(1), 4–19.

Tse, S. K. (2012). *Progress in International Reading Literacy Study (PIRLS) 2011 International Report: Hong Kong Section*. Faculty of Education, Hong Kong University. Available at http://www.hku.hk/press/news_detail_8975.html

## Chapter 13

# Mathematics Achievement and Interest *Negatively* Correlated!

*How can it be that mathematics ... is so admirably appropriate to the objects of reality?*

— Albert Einstein (1879–1955)

### Importance of Mathematics

When Einstein asked this question, he did not realized that it had been answered some 300 years ago by Galileo Galilei (1564–1642) who said, *"Mathematics is the language with which God wrote the universe."* These two great minds of the human history are saying the same thing: mathematics is anywhere and everywhere and everything can be expressed in mathematical terms. This is why mathematics is important.

In the U. S., the National Science Board is charged with advising the President and the Congress on national science policy. It urges a nationwide consensus on a core of knowledge and competency in mathematics and science, on the ground that in a culture dedicated to opportunity for all, nothing is more important than preparing our children for the future workplace (Gaillard, Mitchell-Kernan, Tapia, Rubin, and Suzuki, 1999). The Board further advocates what every student in a grade should know and be able to do in mathematics and science.

The same assertion is made by PISA when it argues that *"An understanding of mathematics is central to a young person's preparedness for life in modern society...Mathematics is a critical tool for young people as they confront issues and challenges in personal, occupational, societal, and scientific aspects of their lives"* (OECD, 2013a: 24).

Besides its existence in nature and function in life, mathematics has in the recent years been argued for an economic reason. Recently, Tosto, Asbury, Mazzocco, Petrill, and Kovas (2016: 1) argue from the perspective of economic development and human capital thus:

> Math matters. International surveys predict an increase of almost 1% in annual GDP growth per capita with half a standard deviation's increase in individual math and science performance (OECD, 2010). In addition to predicting national wealth, mathematical skills are associated with socio-economic well-being. For example, longitudinal research in the UK suggests that people with poor mathematical skills are more than twice as likely as those with better skills to be represented at the lowest level of employment, and are at increased risk of poor mental and physical health (Parsons and Bynner, 2006).

In short, from the various viewpoints, the importance of mathematics cannot be over-emphasized. This leads to the questions of how students can be motivated or interested to learn mathematics better.

## Interest and Achievement

Researchers have been conducting studies to investigate the relation between subject interest and achievement. There is therefore a plethora of such studies. Schiefele, Krapp, and Winteler (1992) conducted a meta-analysis of studies on the relation between interest and achievement published during the 25 years since 1965. Sixteen publications that fitted the criterion were located. These studies involved 121 independent samples of the size varying from 49 to 15,719 students in the Fifth to Twelfth Grades, covering nine different subjects. A total of 189 correlations were reported in these studies. The authors reported meta-analyzed correlations for the subjects in terms of correlations, 0.17 for Literature, 0.33 for Foreign Language, 0.34 for Social Science, 0.16 for Biology, 0.31 for Physics, 0.35 for Science, and 0.32 for Mathematics.

In the context of the present study, there are a number of studies on the relation between mathematics interest and achievement. These are summarized below to provide a backdrop for understanding the findings later.

In an early study, Koller and Baumert (2001) tested 602 students from academically selected schools in Germany three times, at the end of Seventh Grade, the end of Tenth Grade, and in the middle of Twelfth Grade. The authors also collected data of sex differences in achievement, interest, and course selection. These data show differences in favor of boys. Structural equation modeling shows that interest had no significant effect on learning from Seventh to Tenth Grades, but highly interested students were more likely to opt for an advanced mathematics course. However, interest at the end of Tenth Grade had both direct and indirect effects on achievement in upper secondary school. Moreover, from Seventh to Tenth Grades, high achievers expressed more interest.

In another early study, Singh, Granville, and Dika (2002) made use of data from the National Centre for Education Statistics for the U.S. Department of Education. A nationally representative random sample of 24,599 Eighth Grade students was selected. From this pool of students, 3,227 were further selected for analysis. Mathematics scores and grades were obtained and the students also completed a 45-miniute questionnaire with items on motivation, attitude/interest, and academic time. Data were analyzed through structural equation modeling. The results show that mathematics attitude/interest has a direct effect of 0.23 and an indirect effect (via academic time) of 0.11 on achievement, total effect being 0.34.

In a later study, Heinze, Reiss, and Franziska (June 2005) studied the relation between mathematics interest and achievement of 500 German students in Seventh and Eighth Grades. The results show that the development of a student's achievement was dependent on the achievement level of the specific classroom and therefore on the specific mathematics instruction. The authors concluded that interest in mathematics could be regarded as a predictor of mathematics achievement.

More recently, Lazarides and Ittel (2012) studied mathematics interest and achievement of 361 Eighth to Tenth Grade students from 10 public schools in Berlin. Mathematics interest was measured with an adapted nine-item Likert-type scale. Two example items are "*I value mathematics class particularly because of the interesting topics*" and "*I enjoy tasks and issues that are addressed in mathematics class.*" Achievement was indexed by six-point scale in the German tradition, ranging from 1 (Very Good) to 6 (Insufficient), reversed for the analysis. Data were collected twice, first in the middle of the school year (Time 1) and then three months later toward the end of school year (Time 2). For girls, the correlations are r = 0.399 at Time 1 and r = 0.501 at Time 2. For boys, the correlations are r = 0.330 at Time 1 and r = 0.293 at Time 2. On spite of the changes in magnitude, the correlations remain positive throughout.

Of late, Uysal (2015) conducted a within-country study re-analyzing Mathematics scores and related background measures of 4,848 Turkish students involved in PISA 2012. Using structural equation modeling, the author found a beta-coefficient of 0.30 from interest to achievement. At the same time, interest correlates positively with mathematic self-concept (r = 0.83) and negatively with mathematics anxiety (r = −0.51).

Most recently, Tosto, Asbury, Mazzocco, Petrill, and Kovas (2016) gathered data from 6,689 sixteen-year-olds who sat for a public examination (GCSE) and an online Math Web-test in the United Kingdom. The authors also gathered three intra-personal factors of mathematics self-efficacy, mathematics interest, and academic self-concept. They also administered a 17-item questionnaire measuring perceived classroom environment, with example items as *"The teacher shows an interest in every student's learning."* Analysis shows a positive r = 0.74 between the two mathematics, evidencing the concurrent validity of the two achievement measures. More relevant to the present study are correlations of r = 0.47 between interest and GCSE grades and r = 0.45 between interest and the Math Web-test. Incidentally, no correlation was found between achievement and perceived classroom environment.

Obviously, the studies summarized above all show a positive relation between mathematics interest and achievement, and the correlations are generally of a moderate magnitude. They tacitly assumed that mathematics interest is the cause of mathematics achievement, leading to an expectation that students more interested in mathematics will perform better in mathematics tests. Notably, these studies are within-country individual studies where the students are the unit of observation as well as unit of analysis. This gives rise to the question whether the same positive correlation will be obtain in the international arena when countries are the unit of analysis as is done in international comparative studies such as the PISA.

## Method

### Data

The data second-analyzed here are culled from PISA 2012 report (OECD, 2013b). PISA 2012 shifted its focus to Mathematics from Reading, which was the focus of PISA 2009. The shift of the focus from Reading to Mathematics was justified thus (OECD, 2013b: 17):

> Nearly all adults, not just those with technical or scientific careers, now need to have adequate proficiency in mathematics — as well as reading and science — for personal fulfilment, employment and full participation in society. With mathematics as its primary focus, the PISA 2012 assessment measured 15-year-olds' capacity to reason mathematically and use mathematical concepts, procedures, facts and tools to describe, explain and predict phenomena, and to make the well-founded judgements and decisions needed by constructive, engaged and reflective citizens. Literacy in mathematics defined this way is not an attribute that an individual has or does not have; rather, it is a skill that can be acquired and used, to a greater or lesser extent, throughout a lifetime.

As indicated above, participated in this international survey were samples of 15-year-old students in 64 economies, amongst which are 34 OECD Members and 30 OECD Partners, hereafter referred to as *countries*.

### Variables

Mathematics Achievement was measured by the PISA 2012 Mathematics Test which was said to be process-based assessing *mathematical literacy* and future-oriented, in contrast with the traditional knowledge-based and past–oriented tests. The Mathematics test was described thus (OECD, 2013c: 26):

> PISA assesses not only whether students can reproduce knowledge, but also whether they can extrapolate from what they have learned and apply their knowledge in new situations. It emphasizes the mastery of processes, the understanding of concepts, and the ability to function in various types of situations.

This achievement test was standardized across the 34 OECD countries, with a mean of 500 and a standard deviation of 100. This long scale enables PISA to spread out the participating countries according over a wide span. However, PISA tests have not been free from criticism (Mathews, 2009; Mortimore, 2009), especially on their verbosity making the Mathematics and Science tests highly dependent on reading ability (Sjoberg, 2007). Needless to say, this issue is beyond the scope of the present study and will not be discussed further.

PISA measures students' intrinsic motivation to learn mathematics by using four four-point Likert-type items with response categories from *Strongly Disagree, Disagree, Agree,* to *Strongly Agree,* with higher scores denoting stronger interest (OECD, 2013b: 73). The four mathematics attitude items are:

(1) *I enjoy reading about mathematics.*
(2) *I look forward to my mathematics lessons.*
(3) *I do mathematics because I enjoy it.*
(4) *I am interested in the things I learn in mathematics.*

## *Analysis*

Factor analysis was first run on the scores for the four interest items to derive an overall measure of mathematics interest. Factor score was then generated for further analysis. Note that the factor scores form a distribution with a mean of zero and a standard deviation of unity. The Pearson's correlation coefficient was estimated between this interest measure and Mathematic achievement to evaluate their relation. Regression analysis was then run to generate an equation for predicting achievement from interest.

## Results

### *Factor analysis*

Scores for the four mathematics interest items were submitted for a principal components analysis with Promax rotation. This rotation

Table 1. Factor Analysis of Interest Items.

|  | Factor Loading |
|---|---|
| (1) *I enjoy reading about mathematics.* | 0.954 |
| (2) *I look forward to my mathematics lessons.* | 0.936 |
| (3) *I do mathematics because I enjoy it.* | 0.952 |
| (4) *I am interested in the things I learn in mathematics.* | 0.904 |
| Total variance explained | 87.78% |

*Note*: Kaiser-Meyer-Olkin statistic 0.857.

method was chosen in case the four items form more than one factor which are correlated. However, as it turned out, the analysis returned with only one factor with very high factor loadings ($\lambda$'s > 0.9) for all items and it explained a very high proportion of the total variance, 88% at that. Moreover, the Kaiser-Meyer-Olkin statistic 0.857 which is far greater than the conventionally expected 0.5; this indicates that the factor analysis is adequate for the number of countries involved. The result is shown in Table 1. Factor scores were calculated for each of the 64 countries.

## *Correlation*

When the mathematics interest and achievement scores were processed, the Pearson's correlation coefficient obtained is r = −0.532. This is a medium-size correlation, indicating a coefficient of determination of $r^2$ = 0.28, or 28 percent shared variance between interest and achievement. The *negative* correlation is unexpected and contrary to what would be normally expected between interest and achievement measures.

## *Regression*

To establish an equation for predicting achievement from interest, simple regression was run, with interest as a predictor variable and achievement a criterion. Table 2 shows the results of regression analysis.

Table 2. Regression Analysis.

|  | b-coefficient | Beta | S. E. | t | p |
|---|---|---|---|---|---|
| Interest | −2.159 | −0.532 | 0.437 | −4.944 | 0.001 |
| Intercept | 569.515 | — | 20.243 | 28.134 | 0.001 |

Note: $R^2 = 0.283$; Adjusted $R^2 = 0.271$.

With the result as shown in Table 2, the regression equation in raw score form is as follows:

$$\text{Achievement} = -2.159 * \text{Interest} + 569.515$$

The equation indicates that for every single score of interest, there is a deduction of −2.2 score in achievement. This negative unstandardized regression coefficient, of course, reflect the negative correlation reported earlier.

In standardized form, the equation is as follows:

$$\text{Achievement} = -0.532 * \text{Interest}$$

The equation indicates that if both the interest and achievement scores are standardized (with a mean of zero and a standard deviation of unity), an increase of one standardized interest score will lead to a decrease of half a standardized achievement score. In other words, a *country* moving up by one standard deviation on the interest scale will move *down* half a standard deviation on the achievement scale.

## Discussion and Conclusion

This study set out to find the relation between mathematics interest and achievement. Although many studies reviewed reported positive correlations between the two measures, a surprising negative correlation of medium magnitude was found when the participating countries in PISA 2012 were used as the unit of analysis. On appearance, this finding is counter-intuitive and is contradictory to those review studies.

To understand the paradoxical *negative* correlation between country means for Mathematics interest and achievement, it is necessary first to differentiate between an *individual* correlation (calculated for individual scores of the students) and an ecological correlation (calculated for aggregated score, the mean of country). As depicted in Figure 1 below, within each of the four countries (represented by the short slanting lines), the correlations are all positive (as shown by the dots distributing around the slanting lines) though varying in magnitude. When a correlation is calculated using countries means (represented by the points where the long slanting line and the shorter ones intersect), the result is a negative one. Thus, it is obvious that both positive and negative correlations co-exist (and each is a valid representation of the specific situation) but at different levels, thus creating the initially puzzling paradox. Therefore, when the results obtained for within-country individual studies are applied to, or expected of, a between-country ecological study, *ecological fallacy* is committed.

Then, there remains the question of which is the cause and which the effect. The within-countries individual studies summarized above lead to the expectation of a positive correlation between mathematics interest and achievement — interest being the cause and achievement the effect.

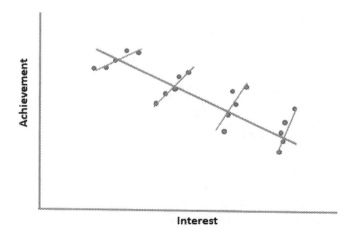

**Figure 1.** Ecological Fallacy.

However, the data do not support the expectation of a positive relation when calculated at the between-country level (where the data are country means and not individual scores).

The reversal of the direction of correlation (from positive to negative) calls for a different interpretation by reversing the status of interest and achievement. For the negative correlation to be meaningful, achievement should be seen as the cause and interest the effect. That is to say, high achievement countries have students who, on average, score low in PISA Mathematics interest and, conversely, low achievement countries have students who, on average, score high in Mathematics interest as measured in PISA. Note the qualifier "on average", because ecological fallacy is basically a group phenomenon.

One implication of this secondary analysis is that when reading the results of international comparative studies, such as PISA, TIMSS, and PIRLS, care needs be taken to avoid ecological fallacy, as the reporting does not always make this interpretative problem explicit and the readers might thus be misinformed or, really, unguided.

## References

Gaillard, M. L., Mitchell-Kernan, C., I., Tapia, R. A., Rubin, V. C., and Suzuki, B. H. (1999). *Preparing Our Children: Math and Science Education in the National Interest.* National Science Board, U. S. A.

Heinze, A., Reiss, K., and Franziska, R. (June 2005). Mathematics achievement and interest in mathematics from a differential perspective. *Zentralblatt füur Didaktik der Mathematik (ZDM Mathematics Education),* **37**(3), 212–220.

Koller, O. and Baumert, J. (2001). Does interest matter? The relationship between academic interest and achievement in mathematics. *Journal of Research in Mathematics Education,* **32**(5), 448–470.

Lazarides, Rebecca and Ittel Angela (2012). Mathematics interest and achievement: What role do perceived parent and teacher support play? A longitudinal analysis. *International Journal of Gender, Science and Technology,* **5**(3), 207–231.

Mathews, J. (October, 2009). *Test that makes U.S. look bad may not be so good.* Available at http://voices.washingtonpost.com/class-struggle/2009/10/politicians_ and_pundits_are_ us.html

Mortimore, P. (2009). *Alternative Models for Analysing and Representing Countries' Performance in PISA*. Brussels: Education International Research Institute.

OECD (2010). *The High Cost of Low Educational Performance: The Long-Run Economic Impact of Improving Educational Outcomes*. Programme for International Student Assessment.

OECD (2013a). PISA 2012 Assessment and Analytical Framework Mathematics, Reading, Science, Problem Solving and Financial Literacy. http://dx.doi.org/10.1787/9789264190511-en

OECD (2013b). *PISA 2012 Results: What Students Know and Can Do — Student Performance in Mathematics, Reading and Science (Volume I)*, PISA, OECD Publishing. http://dx.doi.org/10.1787/9789264201118-en

OECD (2013c), *PISA 2012 Results: Ready to Learn: Students' Engagement, Drive and Self-Beliefs (Volume III)*,PISA, OECD Publishing. http://dx.doi.org/10.1787/9789264201170-en

Parsons, S. and Bynner, J. (2005). *Does Numeracy Matter More?* National Research and Development Centre for Adult Literacy and Numeracy, Institute of Education, University of London.

Schiefele, U., Krapp, A., and Winteler, A. (1992). Interest as a predictor of academic achievement: A meta-analysis of research. In Renninger, K. A., Hidi, S., and Krapp, A., Editors (1992). The role of Interest in Learning and Development. Lawrence Erlbaum Associates, Inc.

Singh, K. Granville, M., and Dika, S. (2002). Mathematics and science achievement: Effects of motivation, interest, and academic engagement. *The Journal of Educational Research*, **95**(6), 323–332.

Sjoberg, S. (October 8, 2007). PISA and "Real Life Challenges": Mission Impossible? Contribution to Hopman (Ed): *PISA according to PISA Revised Version*. Available at folk.uio.no/sveinsj/Sjoberg-**PISA**-book-2007.pdf

Tosto, M. G., Asbury, K., Mazzocco, M. M. M., Petrill, S., and Kovas, Y. (August 2016). From classroom environment to mathematics achievement: The mediating role of self-perceived ability and subject interest. *Learning and Individual Differences*, **50**, 260–269.

Uysal, S. (2015). Factors affecting the mathematics achievement of Turkish students in PISA 2012. *Educational Research and Reviews*, **10**(12), 1670–1678.

## Chapter 14

# Does Ranking Tell the Truth in International Academic Comparisons? An Example from PISA 2012 and 2015

The world is obsessed with ranking in international educational comparative surveys. Immediately after the release of such ranking results, many national commentaries popped up on the Internet. A glaring common feature of these commentaries is the almost exclusive mention of rankings to the exclusion of the scores used as the basis of ranking. Tacitly, the assumption is that a better ranking indicates an improvement in performance; countries which have improved rankings are assumed to have improved performance and *vice versa*. This assumption is in fact flawed. By focusing exclusively on changes in ranking and neglecting changes in score, there is a risk of misinforming, for the simple fact that rankings and scores are not perfectly consistent. In short, an improved ranking in a particular year is not always a bona fide indicator of an improvement over the previous year's performance.

Before looking at the inconsistency between changes in ranking and changes in score, it is interesting to see how commentaries appear on the Internet. Of historical and practical significance, quoted below are typical responses to PISA surveys from countries over the world. The exclusive over-emphasis on ranking is too obvious to miss.

From Finland, the country which has attracted a lot of attention for her PISA 2009 performance (so much so that an 'educational tourism' emerged), Sahlberg (2013: 2) is emphatic that an appropriate use of PISA data is not to create global league tables that praise or shame countries for their performances, although it is the most common way to report PISA results, especially in the media. He laments that, in Finland, media bluntly concluded that Finnish school system has collapsed, pointing to the country's dropping from sixth best in the world in Math in 2009 to 12th three years later in 2012. Also from Finland, Yle (2013: 1) points out that Finnish pupils' PISA results decline in PISA 2012, thus,

> Finland's position has slipped in the OECD's comparison of test results from teenagers in 65 countries and regions, the Programme for International Student Assessment (or PISA). The figures were released at noon Finnish time on Tuesday. Finland dropped to 12th in Maths, which was the focus of this year's tests. The last time this was the theme was a decade ago.

Writing in the American context, Walker (2012: 1, 7) highlights that in PISA 2012 in comparison to PISA 2009, the United States ranked 26th in Math, 21st in Science, and 17th in Reading. He then cites a study, which takes into account social class and sampling, showing that the United States placed fourth in Reading and 10th in Math, up from 14th and 25th in the PISA ranking, respectively.

Again, from the United States, Zhao (2012), in an illuminating writing (*Numbers Can Lie: What TIMSS and PISA Truly Tell Us, If Anything?*) about the United States, cites a long list of ranking such as,

> PISA Reading Literacy: 15$^{th}$ out of 30 countries in 2000, 17$^{th}$ out of 77 countries in 2009
> PISA Math: 24$^{th}$ out of 29 countries in 2003, 31$^{st}$ out of 74 countries in 2009
> PISA Sciences: 21$^{st}$ out of 30 countries in 2003, 23$^{rd}$ out of 74 countries in 2009

*The Economist* (2013: 4) draws attention to changes in PISA 2011 ranking with such a statement as "*Britain gained sixth place, whereas in the PISA 2011 report England (without Scotland and Wales) came 25th in Reading and 28th in Maths.*" Also about the United Kingdom, Webster (2012) highlights that in the PISA 2009, the UK was ranked 28th for Math, 25th for Reading, and 16th for Science. This is a drop of four, eight, and two places, respectively, from the 2006 tests. It was further cited for comparison that the USA came in at 5th for Math, 14th for Reading, and 17th for Science. Moreover, according to Adams (2013), the United Kingdom slipped back four places in Science, to rank 20th out of 65 countries and regions taking part in exams administered by the OECD; in Math and Reading the UK gained two places to reach 26th and 23rd, with results comparable to France's.

The exclusive emphasis on ranking is common in other countries, too. Alphonso (2013: 1) makes comparisons with previous PISA surveys and laments that Canada has dropped out of the top 10 in international Math education standings, a decline that is raising alarms about the country's future prosperity, and highlights that Canada placed 13th overall in Math, down three places from 2009 and six from 2006, in the latest results from the PISA.

From New Zealand, Davison (2013) reports, "*It showed that New Zealand's ranking had fallen from seventh to 18th in Science, 12th to 23rd in Maths, and seventh to 13th in Reading.*" As for Australia, the competitiveness is clearly reflected in the national report (Thomson, De Bortoli, and Buckley, 2013: ix) thus:

> In Mathematics literacy, Australia was outperformed by 16 countries in Mathematical literacy... Australia's performance was not significantly different from seven countries... All other countries performed at a level significantly lower than Australia (p. ix).
>
> In Science literacy, Australia was outperformed by seven countries in scientific literacy... Australia's performance was not significantly different from 11 countries... Australia performed significantly higher than all other countries (p. xii).
>
> In Reading literacy, Australia was outperformed by nine countries in Reading literacy... Australia's performance was not significantly different from 11 countries... All other countries performed significantly lower than Australia (p. xii).

Asian commentators on PISA are not free from the exclusive preference for ranking to the neglect of score. Panday (2012) laments that PISA results shame India, putting the country at the second from the bottom out of 73 participating countries. Ziri (2013) comments on the performance of Israeli students, *"For the printed test, Israel ranks 40th in Math, 33rd in Reading and 40th in Science. For the computerized test, the country ranks 27th in Math and 26th in Reading."* In Singapore, a country which has been doing very well in international studies ever since 1995, Tan (2013: 3) comments that *"Singapore ranked among the top five in all three subject areas of Mathematics, Reading, and Science. It took second place in Mathematics, and third in both Reading and Science."* On Singapore's closest neighbor, The Malay Mail Online.com (2013: 5) reports, *"Malaysia was now ranked 55th for Science, down two spots from the previous assessment. The combined results meant Malaysia was 52nd overall out of the 65 countries, and firmly entrenched in the bottom third of the survey."*

While the exclusive emphasis on ranking cannot escape attention, a few commentators also cite, in addition to focusing on rankings, the relevant scores which make comparison more meaningful. For example, Price (2013) comments on the performance of American students, thus, *"The United States dropped in rankings for every PISA test in 2012, compared to 2009. Among OECD nations, the US now ranks $17^{th}$ in Reading, $21^{st}$ in Science, and $26^{th}$ in Math. These rankings are all lower than in 2009.* **US scores have remained stagnant while other nations improved, causing the change in rankings**" (Emphasis added). He draws attention to the scores which remain *unchanged* although the rankings drop! This is a good example of the score-rank inconsistency where a country maintains her performance but suffers a loss in ranking, creating an erroneous impression of retrogression.

From Hong Kong, Tam and Zhao (2013: 3), comparing the three top-ranking East Asian countries (Hong Kong, Singapore, and Shanghai-China), refer to changes not only in ranking but also in scores:

> But compared with their counterparts in Singapore… Hong Kong pupils improved less, gaining only 11 points more in Reading and six in Maths and in Science from the 2009 assessment. The Singaporeans gained 16 points in Reading, 11 in Maths and nine in Science. Shanghai students also showed more improvement, gaining 14 points in Reading and 13 in Maths compared with 2009.

Similarly, Oh (2013: 2–3), writing about Korea, cites both rankings and scores to make comparisons:

> According to the report, Korea received the highest average score of 554 in Mathematics among the 34 OECD countries, followed by that of Japan with 536 and Switzerland with 531. Korea also ranked second in Reading table with 536, only two points behind top-placed Japan with 538. Japan also topped in Science proficiency with 547 points, followed by Finland and Estonia with 545 and 541 respectively. Korea came fourth in Science with 538 points, still well above the OECD average score of 501.

As is abundantly clear from the above, there is an overwhelming emphasis on ranking to the exclusion of score. However, the world, being attracted by ranking perhaps because of the prevalent global competition (almost in anything and everything), seems to be generally oblivious to the importance and usefulness of score, not only as a basis of ranking but also providing the information the countries really need if their education systems are to be improved, even if just to avoid being misinformed.

This is the issue addressed in the present article with illustrative cases from PISA 2012 (OECD, 2014) and 2015 (OECD, 2016). Although PISA shifts its focus cyclically on Reading, Mathematics, and Science in turn over the years, the present study has its focus on Reading so as to enable inter-year comparison. The data re-analyzed here are for the 54 countries participated in both PISA 2012 and 2015. For the purpose of the present study, these countries were re-ranked using their respective country means for Reading. Of the countries, there are 19 (35%) with rank-score consistency of positive gain, 26 (48%) with rank-score of negative gain, and nine (17%) with rank-score inconsistency.

## Countries with Positive Gain

Table 1 lists the 19 countries with positive gains from PISA 2012 to 2015 in descending order of gains. For these, the average score gain is 10.79 and the average rank gain is 6.11, suggesting that a score gain of 1.8 leads to a rank gain of one. The score gains vary from one to 26 and the rank gains span from one to 16.5.

**Table 1.** Countries with Positive Gains in Score and Rank.

| Country | PISA 2015 Reading | Rank | PISA 2012 Reading | Rank | Gain Score | Rank |
|---|---|---|---|---|---|---|
| Uruguay | 437 | 41 | 411 | 48 | 26 | 7 |
| Slovenia | 505 | 14 | 481 | 35 | 24 | 21 |
| Colombia | 425 | 47 | 403 | 51 | 22 | 4 |
| Russian Fed | 495 | 26 | 475 | 38.5 | 20 | 12.5 |
| Sweden | 500 | 17.5 | 483 | 34 | 17 | 16.5 |
| Peru | 398 | 54 | 384 | 56 | 14 | 2 |
| Qatar | 402 | 53 | 388 | 55 | 14 | 2 |
| Albania | 405 | 52 | 394 | 54 | 11 | 2 |
| Portugal | 498 | 21.5 | 488 | 29.5 | 10 | 8 |
| Jordan | 408 | 50 | 399 | 52 | 9 | 2 |
| Norway | 513 | 9 | 504 | 19 | 9 | 10 |
| Spain | 496 | 25 | 488 | 29.5 | 8 | 4.5 |
| Montenegro | 427 | 46 | 422 | 47 | 5 | 1 |
| Canada | 527 | 2.5 | 523 | 7 | 4 | 4.5 |
| Denmark | 500 | 17.5 | 496 | 22 | 4 | 4.5 |
| Estonia | 519 | 6 | 516 | 10 | 3 | 4 |
| Croatia | 487 | 29.5 | 485 | 33 | 2 | 3.5 |
| Finland | 526 | 4 | 524 | 5 | 2 | 1 |
| Germany | 509 | 11 | 508 | 17 | 1 | 6 |
| Mena | 472.47 | 27.71 | 461.68 | 33.82 | 10.79 | 6.11 |
| SD | 47.30 | 18.33 | 50.66 | 16.95 | 7.91 | 5.44 |

However, as is always said, the average hides important information. For instance, Uruguay gains 26 in score and seven in rank and Germany gains one in score and six in rank, almost as much as Uruguay. At the same time, Sweden gains 17 in score but 16.5 in rank; thus, when compared with Uruguay, less score gain leads to higher rank gain. It is also interesting that Peru, Qatar, Albania, and Jordan all have gained two positions, but their gains in score vary from nine

**Table 2.** Countries with Negative Gains in Score and Rank.

| Country | PISA 2015 Reading | Rank | PISA 2012 Reading | Rank | Gain Score | Rank |
|---|---|---|---|---|---|---|
| Latvia | 488 | 28 | 489 | 26 | −1 | −2 |
| Mexico | 423 | 48 | 424 | 46 | −1 | −2 |
| U. Kingdom | 498 | 21.5 | 499 | 20 | −1 | −1.5 |
| U. States | 497 | 23.5 | 498 | 21 | −1 | −2.5 |
| Brazil | 407 | 51 | 410 | 49 | −3 | −2 |
| Austria | 485 | 31.5 | 490 | 24.5 | −5 | −7 |
| Italy | 485 | 31.5 | 490 | 24.5 | −5 | −7 |
| Czech Rep | 487 | 29.5 | 493 | 23 | −6 | −6.5 |
| France | 499 | 19.5 | 505 | 18 | −6 | −1.5 |
| Israel | 479 | 34 | 486 | 32 | −7 | −2 |
| Luxembourg | 481 | 33 | 488 | 29.5 | −7 | −3.5 |
| UAE | 434 | 42.5 | 442 | 42 | −8 | −0.5 |
| Netherlands | 503 | 15.5 | 511 | 13 | −8 | −2.5 |
| Australia | 503 | 15.5 | 512 | 11.5 | −9 | −4 |
| Belgium | 499 | 19.5 | 509 | 15 | −10 | −4.5 |
| Greece | 467 | 39 | 477 | 36.5 | −10 | −2.5 |
| Poland | 506 | 13 | 518 | 9 | −12 | −4 |
| Switzerland | 492 | 27 | 509 | 15 | −17 | −12 |
| Hong Kong | 527 | 2.5 | 545 | 1 | −18 | −1.5 |
| Hungary | 470 | 38 | 488 | 29.5 | −18 | −8.5 |
| Korea | 517 | 7 | 536 | 4 | −19 | −3 |
| Japan | 516 | 8 | 538 | 3 | −22 | −5 |
| Taipei | 497 | 23.5 | 523 | 7 | −26 | −16.5 |
| Thailand | 409 | 49 | 441 | 43 | −32 | −6 |
| Tunisia | 361 | 56 | 404 | 50 | −43 | −6 |
| Turkey | 428 | 45 | 475 | 38.5 | −47 | −6.5 |
| Mean | 475.31 | 28.92 | 488.46 | 24.29 | −13.15 | −4.63 |
| SD | 40.42 | 14.42 | 37.18 | 14.63 | 12.37 | 3.60 |

to 14. The correlation between the two sets of gain is only a moderate r = 0.55 (df 17, p < 0.05, two-tailed).

Thus, even among countries which gain both in score and rank, there are inconsistencies which cannot be ignored.

## Countries with Negative Gain

The 26 countries with negative gains in both score and rank are listed in Table 2. The average loss in score is −13.15 and that in rank −4.63, indicating that a score loss of 2.8 contributes to a rank loss of one position. The score losses vary from −1 to −47 and the rank losses −2 to −16.5. The correlation between the two sets of gain is only a moderate r = 0.45 (df 17, p < 0.05, two-tailed).

It is of note that both France and Turkey lose −6.5 in rank but they lose −6 and −47 in score, respectively. At the same time, Czech Republic and France both have −6 score loss but −6.5 and −1.5 rank loss, respectively. Moreover, Hong Kong and Hungary both lose −18 in score but they lose −1.5 and −8.5, respectively, in rank.

Table 3. Countries with Opposite Signs for Score and Rank Gains.

| Country | PISA 2015 Reading | Rank | PISA 2012 Reading | Rank | Gain Score | Rank |
|---|---|---|---|---|---|---|
| Indonesia | 397 | 55 | 396 | 53 | 1 | −2 |
| Macao-China | 509 | 11 | 509 | 15 | 0 | 4 |
| Ireland | 521 | 5 | 523 | 7 | −2 | 2 |
| New Zealand | 509 | 11 | 512 | 11.5 | −3 | 0.5 |
| Bulgaria | 432 | 44 | 436 | 45 | −4 | 1 |
| Romania | 434 | 42.5 | 438 | 44 | −4 | 1.5 |
| Lithuania | 472 | 37 | 477 | 36.5 | −5 | −0.5 |
| Singapore | 535 | 1 | 542 | 2 | −7 | 1 |
| Slovak Rep | 453 | 40 | 463 | 40 | −10 | 0 |
| Mean | 458.06 | 26.47 | 466.67 | 24.19 | −7.76 | −2.05 |
| SD | 100.51 | 15.43 | 101.45 | 14.94 | 12.02 | 4.63 |

Such cases are sufficient to show that in spite of losses both in score and rank, there are conspicuous inconsistency between score and rank.

## Countries with Opposite Signs for Score and Rank Gains

Shown in Table 3 are nine countries with score and rank gains which have opposite signs (treating Macao-China's zero gain as negative). Thus, Indonesia has a positive score gain of one but a negative rank gain of −2. In contrast, Slovak Republic has a negative score gain of −10 but no change in rank. Looking down the score gain column, five countries (from Ireland to Singapore, except Lithuania) have *negative* gains in scores (varying from −2 to −7) but *positive* gains in rank of varying magnitude, indicating that the performance retrograded but they were ranked better than previously. In short, poorer performance resulted in better ranking — a contradiction that is hard to reconcile.

The average score gain is −7.7 and the average rank gain −2.05, giving an average of 3.8 score loss for each rank loss. The correlation is $r = 0.14$ (df 7, $p > 0.05$, two-tailed), indicating the gross lack of consistency.

## Quo Vadis?

Although the countries are grouped as having positive gain consistency, negative gain consistency, and inconsistency between score and rank gains, these are broad classifications with consideration only for the signs. Detailed comparisons show the problem of score-rank inconsistency is much more severe than it appears. In short, an improved rank cannot be trusted as indicating a better performance, especially when the magnitudes of score and rank changes are taken into account.

Improved ranking may be an *indirect indicator* of a country's advancement *in relation to the advancement of all other countries in the same ranking exercise*. In other words, ranking may but does not always indicate how well a country has improved; it acquires meaning if and only if interpreted with reference to the performance of other countries. When a country gets a better ranking in a year, there is no guarantee that it has performed better over the previous year; it only means its score is better than the other countries' scores *in the same year*, but *not necessarily better than its own performance in the previous year.* In short, improved ranking is not necessary a valid indicator of improvement in performance.

In contrast with ranking, increased score is the *bona fide* indicator of improved performance, *unconditioned by the performance of other countries in the same exercise.* Inter-year comparison on two years' scores of a country is not affected by how the other countries have performed. This, of course, assumes that the test used for the two exercises is the same (or at least, parallel) and that the students samples for the two years are equivalent, allowing for sampling error.

## Conclusion

By way of summary, the present study shows that improved ranking between two years in an international comparative achievement study does not necessarily indicate improved performance and, in fact, may even indicate the opposite. This is confusing and unfair to all parties concerned. To avoid these untrustworthy and unpleasant consequences, countries should not look exclusively at ranking but need to look at their own inter-year score changes which are independent of the other countries' performances. It cannot be over-emphasized that inter-year score change, or the lack thereof, is the true indicator of improvement, not the rank change which is currently widely used.

As gathered from the quotes this article begins with, some commentators are aware of the problem of misinformation arising from the exclusive use of ranking, but many others are not. This article may look like it is making a mountain out of an ant mole but in continuing to use ranking in the way it has hitherto been used, countries are simply barking up the wrong tree.

## References

Adams, R. (December 3, 2013). *UK students stuck in educational doldrums, OECD study finds.* The Guardian. Available at http://www.theguardian.com/education/2013/dec/03/uk-students-education-oecd-pisa-report

Alphonso C. (December 3, 2013). Canada's fall in Math-education ranking sets off alarm bells. *The Globe and Mail.* Available at http://www.theglobeandmail.com/news/national/education/canadas-fall-in-Math-education-ranking-sets-off-red-flags/article15730663/

Davison, I. (December 3, 2013). *Significant drops in NZ educational achievement — OECD report.* The New Zealand Herald. Available at http://www.nzherald.co.nz/education/news/article.cfm?c_id=35&objectid=11166346

OECD (2014). *PISA 2012 Results: What Students Know and Can Do — Student Performance in Mathematic, Reading and Science (Volume 1, Revised Version, February 2014),* PISA, OECD Publishing. http://dx.doi.org/10.1787/9789264208-en

OECD (2016). PISA 2015 Results (Volume 1): Excellence and Equity in Education, PISA, OECD Publishing, Paris. http://dx/doi/org/10.1787/978956426490-en

Oh, K-W. (December 3, 2013). Korea tops OECD in Math proficiency. *The Korean Herald.* http://www.koreaherald.com/view.php?ud=20131203000925

Panday, P. (January 15, 2012). PISA results shame India....but is anyone surprised really???? *The Times of India|Blogs.* Available at http://blogs.timesofindia.indiatimes.com/the-real-truth/entry/pisa-results-shame-india-but-is-anyone-surprised-really

Price, E. (December 2013). Topline: PISA 2012 Results. *Whiteboard Advisors.*

Tam, J. and Zhao, S (December 3, 2013). *Shanghai teens still world's best at Reading, Maths, and Science in Pisa survey.* South China Morning Post. Available at http://www.scmp.com/news/hong-kong/article/1372060/shanghai-teens-still-worlds-best-Reading-Maths-Science-pisa-survey

Tan, Q. (December 3, 2013*). S'pore edges up in PISA rankings as weaker students improve.* Channel NewsAsia. Available at http://www.channelnewsasia.com/news/singapore/s-pore-edges-up-in-pisa/908160.html

The Economist (January 19, 2013). *Testing Education: PISA Envy.* The Economist. Available at http://www.economist.com/news/international/21569689-research-comparing-educational-achievement-between-countries-growing-drawing

The Malay Mail Online.com (December 4, 2013). *PISA: Malaysia up in Maths, down in Science and Reading.* The Malay Mail Online.com. Available at http://www.themalaymailonline.com/malaysia/article/pisa-malaysia-up-in-Maths-down-in-Science-and-Reading

Thomson, S., De Bortoli, L., and Buckley, S. (2013). *PISA 2012: How Australia Measures Up.* Australian Council for Educational Research.

Walker, T. (December 3, 2012). What do the 2012 PISA Scores Tell Us about U.S. Schools? *NeaToday.* Available at http://neatoday.org/2013/12/03/what-do-the-2012-pisa-scores-tell-us-about-u-s-schools/

Webster, A. (August 30, 2012). How PISA Rankings Could Make or Break a Country's Education System. *Eudumic: Connecting Education and Technology.* Available at http://www.edudemic.com/the-importance-of-pisa-rankings-for-countries/

Yle (December 3, 2013). Finnish pupils' PISA results decline. *YLE UUTISET.* Available at http://yle.fi/uutiset/finnish_pupils_pisa_results_decline/6966136

*Zhao, Y. (December 2012). Numbers Can Lie: What TIMSS and PISA Truly Tell Us, if Anything? Yong Zhao: Creative. Entrepreneurial, and Global 21$^{st}$ Century Education.*

Ziri, D. (March 12, 2013). PISA test results: Israeli pupils' scores remain behind those of OECD countries. *The Jerusalem Post.* Available at http://www.jpost.com/National-News/PISA-test-results-Israeli-pupils-scores-remain-behind-those-of-OECD-countries-333863

# Epilogue

It has to be honestly acknowledged that, although the 14 articles put together here seem to have been systematic, they are in fact a result of being wiser after the event. In other words, the themes that organize the articles into Parts are *post hoc*; the result of reading the original reports combined with some random thoughts.

Nevertheless, they are the fruits of integrating research beyond education and applying statistical concepts. Hopefully, in doing so, the outcomes of international comparative studies such as PISA and PIRLS can be seen with a broader perspective and deeper sophistication beyond the simplistic concern with ranking which seems to have dominated the education scene.

As is true of things educational, nothing is perfect. This volume has its strengths and weaknesses and, therefore, readers will both agree and disagree with the articles. That is simply a fact of human nature and our inevitable preferences. For this reason, any conceptual errors and technical flaws, to be tolerated, only reveal my limitations and lack of perfectionism.

Soh Kaycheng

Printed in the United States
By Bookmasters